"Sharp and never satisfied with the obvious, Kees Bolle handles key subjects like secularization, fundamentalism, and the religious structure of modern man. Listening to him when he is speaking in-depth about politics and religion that are inevitably intertwined, whether in Islam, Hinduism, Buddhism or Christianity, opens our eyes to all those easy statements of today that commonly spring from what the author aptly calls 'knowledge-cum-ignorance.' This book will last, and encourage us for a long time."

—Karel R. van Kooij, Professor Emeritus,
University of Leiden, The Netherlands

"This book, like Kees' other ones, compels us to confront the role of religion in the lives of both individual and social bodies. By exploring the religion of ancient cities (Egyptian and Greek), Near Eastern high god traditions (Judaism, Christianity, and Islam), and Indian and Buddhist traditions, he is actually inviting us to better understand ourselves."

—Jennifer Reid, from the foreword

Religion among People

Religion among People

ESSAYS ON RELIGIONS AND POLITICS

Kees W. Bolle

CASCADE *Books* • Eugene, Oregon

RELIGION AMONG PEOPLE
Essays on Religions and Politics

Copyright © 2017 Kees W. Bolle. All rights reserved. Except for brief quotations in critical publications or reviews, no part of this book may be reproduced in any manner without prior written permission from the publisher. Write: Permissions, Wipf and Stock Publishers, 199 W. 8th Ave., Suite 3, Eugene, OR 97401.

Cascade Books
An Imprint of Wipf and Stock Publishers
199 W. 8th Ave., Suite 3
Eugene, OR 97401

www.wipfandstock.com

PAPERBACK ISBN: 978-1-5326-0450-8
HARDCOVER ISBN: 978-1-5326-0452-2
EBOOK ISBN: 978-1-5326-0451-5

Cataloging-in-Publication data:

Names: Bolle, Kees W., author.

Title: Religion among people : essays on religions and politics / Kees W. Bolle.

Description: Eugene, OR: Cascade Books. | Includes bibliographical references.

Identifiers: ISBN: 978-1-5326-0450-8 (paperback). | ISBN: 978-1-5326-0452-2 (hardcover). | ISBN: 978-1-5326-0451-5 (ebook)

Subjects: LCSC: Religions. | Religions and politics.

Classification: BL48 B5851 2017 | BL48 (ebook).

Manufactured in the U.S.A.

Scripture quotations marked (NIV) are taken from the Holy Bible, NEW INTERNATIONAL VERSION®, NIV® Copyright © 1973, 1978, 1984, 2011 by Biblica, Inc.® Used by permission. All rights reserved worldwide.

Scripture quotations marked (RSV) are taken from the Revised Standard Version of the Bible, copyright © 1946, 1952, and 1971 National Council of the Churches of Christ in the United States of America. Used by permission. All rights reserved worldwide.

Contents

Apologia ix
Foreword xiii
Preface xix
Acknowledgments xxiii

PART ONE: Change in Religion

1. Religion: The Troubling Subject | 3
    The Confusion Concerning Religion
    Piety and Psychology and the "Inner" Life
    Shortcomings of Our Terminology
    Religion as an Institution
    Being Aware of Real Differences

2. Interpretation | 18
    Pseudo-religion
    Persistence of Religion
    Interpretation
    The Significance of the Particular
    Traditions

3. Secularization and Sanctification: Euhemerism | 35
    Secularizations
    Euhemerism
    The Euhemerizing Mentality
    Euhemerismus Inversus
    Euhemerism's Power of Preservation
    Popular Secularizations as Religious Structures
    Euhemerism Later
    "Secularization"

4. Secularization in Modern History | 57
    The Problem of Losing the Sacred
    "The Sacred" and "The Profane"
    "Secularization" and "Sanctification" at the Present Moment
    Secularization as a Concealed Process
    The Choice of Words
    Fundamentalism
    Secularization is Inevitable
    Secularization and Mythification
    The Surpassing of Authority
    A Role for the History of Religions

PART TWO: Religion and Politics

5. Early Kingship | 87
    Spirit and Power
    The Ancient City
    The Hittite Kings; Alexander the Great; Egypt

6. Israel, Early Christianity, Greece | 100
    Biblical Kingship
    David and Nathan
    Religious Imagery of Israel
    Sophocles' *Antigone*
    Categorical Imagery

7. Brahmanism: The Balance of All and Everything | 115
    The Brahmanic Texts
    A Case from Ancient India: the *Rājasūya*
    The Ritual Events
    Spiritual Certainty
    Ananda Coomaraswamy: Politics as Part of a Total Unity
    Coomaraswamy: Remarks of Caution

8. Buddhism | 134
    Buddhism and Kingship
    Aśoka
    Caṇḍāśoka
    The Sense in Other Structures

Structure of Buddhism
   Tokugawa Ieyasu's Edict
   Buddhism within a Worldwide Discourse

9. The Monotheism of Islam | 164
   The "Threat" of Islam
   Discrimination
   Monotheism and Prophecy
   Authority
   Absolute Power and Consensus: "Ruler over the Faithful"
   Power and Consensus Enacted
   Fear of Theocracy

10. The Religious Structure of Modern Man | 193
    Religious Types
    Ourselves
    Modern Religious Man
    The Modern State
    Recent Times
    A Religious Symbolism of Modern Man
    Immediacy of Religion

Bibliography | 221
Name Index | 233
Subject Index | 239

Apologia

Religion among People ("RELAMP" as Kees abbreviated it in his computer) is a volume that was virtually completed by its author. Unfortunately, Kees was unable to participate in its final editing and he passed away before the manuscript was submitted for publication. As we move toward publication, I find that several caveats are in order, an *apologia* in its original sense of "defense."

Kees was renowned for his passionate involvement in his work and was rarely shy about expressing an opinion. Consequently, he could excite a great deal of consternation in an audience and, often, ungovernable disgruntlement. He belonged to an age in scholarship where personal opinions were accepted as part of scholarly writing. Kees applied the linguistic dictum "to know one language is to know none" to the field of the history of religions, declaring that "to know one religion is to know none." He also believed that, in order to be an effective student of religion, one needed to be fully and consciously rooted in a particular religious culture, without apologies.

The tone in these pages is vintage Kees: full of fire, humor, and an inimitable sense of irony, all the while fighting against "solemnity" in favor of the truly "serious." His is a style no longer easily acceptable in academic circles. For all these reasons, there are numerous details in this volume that are not "fixable" in order to make it more palatable to modern scholastic tastes. No effort has been made to tone down the decidedly personal stance Kees often assumes. To do so would be to betray him. I am infinitely grateful to Dr. K. C. Hanson, editor-in-chief at Cascade Books, that he has been willing to let Kees be, well, Kees.

I think it fair to say that this book would not have existed without the work of Ellen Kaplan, who has edited Kees' writing since she was his student at Brown University in the early 1960s. Her enduring zeal for this particular manuscript and her concern for the presentation of its themes have been crucial to the volume's form and expression. No matter how obstinate Kees could be at times, the one person he inevitably deferred to when it came to written expression, was Ellen.

Tim Copeland, my former Maine neighbor, has been indispensable in pulling this manuscript together in its final form. His electronic wizardry and, like Ellen, his sense of detail, have made a computerized manuscript possible. When Kees started his teaching career, it was not unheard of for a scholar to hand over his handwritten pages to the publisher—a far cry from current requirements! Thanks to Tim's artistry, this volume assumed the digital form that was needed. He and Ellen conferred by telephone and mail (not e-mail!) to produce this final form.

Two dear friends have helped out with specific linguistic details. Professor John Hayes of the University of California at Berkeley read through all the Islamic material to ensure that Arabic terms and names are rendered in up-to-date transcriptions. Professor Karel R. van Kooij, Professor emeritus, Leiden University, The Netherlands, with whom Kees and I lived during our first year in Holland in 1980 and himself an Indologist, was kind enough to check all the diacritical marks on Sanskrit words and phrases, as well as reading through the entire manuscript. In 2014, he and his wife visited me in our home in Maine, and he spent several days organizing the Indological books in Kees' library. As a result, he also unearthed a number of much-sought-after books that Kees used and which I was in dire need of locating to confirm numerous footnotes; for his help I'm deeply appreciative.

Finally, I'm endlessly indebted to Professor Jennifer Reid of the University of Maine at Farmington, who composed the foreword to this volume. Kees and I met her our first year in Maine when she invited Kees to participate in an annual conference she assembled, that also included Professors David Carrasco and Charles Long. Over the years, she invited Kees to present lectures to the Farmington students. She knows and understands Kees' work better than most anyone I know, and I think she's captured the essence of Kees' thought and purpose most succinctly. I am grateful beyond words for her friendship and the innumerable nocturnal discussions that the three of us shared for many years, and which she and I continue to have. Kees would have been proud to find her name on the foreword.

Again, my warm thanks to Dr. K. C. Hanson for being a friend to me and admirer of Kees' work. Without him, the impetus to publish this manuscript with Wipf and Stock Publishers could not have happened.

It's most unfortunate that Kees is unable to address criticisms that may arise after the publication of "RELAMP." He would have wholeheartedly welcomed them, eager, as always, to initiate new rounds of discussions on topics he felt were at the essence of human experience. He was fond of quoting an old Frisian expression, itself filled with the sort of irony he lived by, here slightly modified, that I know he'd agree with once again: *het had nog erger kunnen zijn* ("it could have been worse").

Sara J. Denning-Bolle, PhD, DO
Biddeford, Maine

Foreword

I met Kees Bolle for the first time in the spring of 2001. I was living in Maine, and Kees and his wife, Sara (and their Maine Coon cat Ragatz—named for a nineteenth-century Swiss theologian), had moved to Biddeford from Portland, Oregon, the previous year. Sara was making a dramatic career shift from teaching ancient New Eastern Studies to studying medicine at the University of New England. While I had met neither of them prior to this, I knew them well through my mentor, Charles H. Long. Both Charles Long and Kees Bolle had studied the history of religions at the University of Chicago in a department and program that had been defined by Joachim Wach in the 1940s and 1950s. That tradition was continued by the two of them alongside Mircea Eliade, Joe Kitagawa, and others. Chicago was a formative time and space for all of them (as well as for the field itself), and when I mentioned to Charles Long that I was planning on hosting a conference at my campus in April of 2001, he insisted that I reach out to Kees and invite him to participate in it.

When we met, Kees was a diminutive seventy-four-year-old man with intense, animated (almost mischievous) eyes. My first glimpse of him was actually only of his eyes and the top of his head—all that was visible above the dashboard of their massive, heavy-duty royal blue truck as they pulled into my driveway the day the conference began.

My second introduction to Kees occurred a few minutes later. It was a short exchange of words as he and Sara walked into the house.

"I'm Jennifer," I said, as I reached my hand out to take his.

"Ah," he replied. "So good to meet you. You look very different in person than you do over e-mail."

I didn't ask him what he meant. Come to think of it, I don't think I ever did at any point later on either. Kees was so full of pregnant one-liners that one rarely had the opportunity or inclination to go back. Now that he's gone, my friend Randal Cummings (Kees was his doctoral advisor) and I often pass e-mails back and forth across the continent reminding ourselves of some of those one-liners: things like "Equality is a great idea. There are just no examples of it." Or, "That's an interesting theory I'd like you to pursue, but of course to do so you would actually have to read the text."

My third first-impression followed in short order. I discovered that Kees could savor a glass of single malt scotch with more esprit than most anyone I knew, and in quick turn he sidled up to the piano in my living room and played Debussy flawlessly. Sara and I were already talking like old cronies as he began to play.

A venerable historian of religions who could hardly see over the dashboard of the truck he was driving, who spoke in riddles, who had a soft spot for scotch, who was an accomplished musician, and whose wife instantly seemed like someone I had met years before—it wasn't hard for me to see that the three of us were going to become fast friends.

After that first meeting, Kees and Sara and I would share many long wonderful evenings over food and wine (well, technically Sara and I drank wine; Kees always drank single malt) and disputation. Kees also spoke at my school many times. Even as his health began to fail, somehow his fifty years of intellectual life overrode the illness, and he was easily able to maintain the rapt attention of an audience of colleagues and students for as long as he wanted (often an hour or more, no mean feat for even the sturdiest and most engaging of scholars). For all these reasons and more, it is a distinct honor for me to have been asked to write a few words of introduction to this posthumous book. And to situate the book within Kees' big life, of which I was blessed to share a small part.

Intending to study theology and to become an ordained minister, Kees traveled from his home in Holland to the University of Chicago in the early 1950s as part of the University's World Church Fellowship program. Through the Fellowship, young scholars were given an opportunity to study for a year at the University. It would turn out to be a decisive year for Kees, as he was introduced to the work of Joachim Wach. He returned home to Holland when his Fellowship expired, but it wasn't long before he decided to apply to the University of Chicago for admission as a regular graduate student to study under Wach. Unfortunately Wach passed away just before Kees returned. As he considered his options (returning to Holland was not among them, since he didn't have the money for the fare), it was suggested to him that the newly hired Mircea Eliade could serve as his doctoral advisor. He completed his PhD, thus making himself

Eliade's first doctoral student. While his primary area of specialization was, and remained, the religious traditions of India (he spent two years in India while writing his dissertation), he was trained as a general historian of religions and so he never shied away from asking tough theoretical questions. His approach to the study of religion was firmly hermeneutical, something that had been of critical significance to Joachim Wach as he drew a community of young scholars to him in the 1950s and 1960s.

In some ways this book could be regarded as a kind of apogee of Kees' publishing career. In its pages we find numerous themes that were present in his earlier work, many reappearing in a more developed and thorough way. Because he was unable to fully prepare the manuscript for publication before his passing, it fell upon his longtime editor, Ellen Kaplan, and his computer-savvy friend Tim Copeland to do so. It was a time-intensive task, and Ellen and Tim threw themselves into it out of their deep regard for Kees and his work—a true labor of love.

And that work was substantial. His first book, *The Persistence of Religion* (1965), was a study of the role of tantrism in the development of Indian religion from Vedic ritualism to the rise of Brahmanism. This was followed by *The Freedom of Man in Myth* (1968), in which he explored the relationship between mysticism and the creation of myth. His translation of *Perspectives in the History of Religions* was his next project (1977), Jan De Vries' survey of writing about religion ranging from antiquity to the twentieth century. Kees followed this with significant translations of the *Bhagavad-Gita* (1979) and Jean Bottéro's *The Birth of God: The Bible and the Historian* (2000), a classic text on the cultural, social, historical and religious construction of the Tanach, as well as the impact of ancient Israel on modern Western culture. Kees' next book seemed like a bit of a departure in some ways. *Ben's Story* (2001) was based on his translations of both the letters of a young man, Ben Wessels, who died at Bergen-Belsen and other pieces that appeared in the Dutch underground press during the same period. Kees' last completed book was *The Enticement of Religion* (2002), a book-length hermeneutical essay on the nature of the study of religion that grounded the field in a long tradition of hermeneutics and steered well clear of contemporary trends (i.e. postmodernism) in interpretation.

In a sense, *Religion among People* is a complement to *The Enticement of Religion*, picking up on methodological and historical threads that were left loose in the earlier book. In fact, one could go so far as to say that here we find, in one book, a kind of aggregate of the concerns that drove his earlier work: concerns with methodology, hermeneutics, the terror of history (Eliade's phrase), modern alienation, and the role and responsibility of scholarship on religion.

In all his work Kees confronts the mixed legacy not only of religion but also of the study of religion, which he believed bears a level of culpability in adversely affecting modern events. He reminds us here, for example, that academic discussions helped to precipitate modern racism. Thus, he argues that given the nature of their subject matter, historians of religion bear a good deal of moral responsibility in doing their research and scholarship. Ultimately, we must never lose sight of the fact that "human lives are at stake."

Religion among People is divided into two parts. The first is methodological and the second explores specific situations of interplay between religion and political power. The book ends in a way that is somehow reminiscent of Eliade's *The Myth of the Eternal Return* where Eliade set "modern man" in his desire for autonomy against "archaic man," who lives in continual symbolic reconnection with a collective primordium. Kees, too, concludes his discussion with modern humans. Unlike Eliade, however, he finds no disconnect between us and the people of the ancient and premodern societies he has explored throughout part 2 of the book. In fact, by subjecting ourselves (and himself, more on this presently) to the same critical perspectives used previously in the text, Kees discerns a very religious character to Western modernity.

Harkening back to his long-term interest in mysticism, he concludes here that "concern for the inner life" is the defining property of religion in modernity, and that a desire to preserve and nurture the inner life has been fueled by the rise of rationality and bureaucracy. By bureaucracy he doesn't mean the relatively benign—but annoying—systems that tie us up for hours on the phone struggling to get something done. (Anyone who attempted to sign on for 'Obamacare' in its first months knows this frustration all too well.) What Kees means by bureaucracy is "racial categorizing, deportations, concentration camps, saturation bombings"—all of which, he notes, are "reasoned" acts intended to "break the spirit."

We hear echoes not only of Eliade in this book, but also of Wach and even F. Max Müller (the nineteenth-century founder of the comparative study of religion). Kees spent his career grappling with the meaning of religion as both otherness and intimacy—the ambiguity of religious experience versus the lived reality of religious expression. In this we see the legacy of Wach, whose work bridged the divide between experience and expression without ever giving primacy to either. Like his colleagues from Chicago, Kees inherited this antireductionist tendency from Wach that has marked out a modest but powerful space in the field. Like his fellow Chicago-ites, Kees also remained true throughout his career to Wach's deep concern for hermeneutics. As he writes in these pages, "I care more for the honesty of our mutual approach to the problem of ourselves than for the technical accuracy of our religiohistorical vocabulary."[1]

Another focus throughout his career was Kees' concern with the role of the study of religion as an academic discipline. In this respect he has channeled the best contributions of Max Müller to our discipline (that's not to say that Müller didn't also saddle us with some rather unsavory baggage). But Müller's best basic question was also Kees': how can, and why should, we study religious data that are substantially removed from us in terms of time and place? Müller's answer was to set out a trifold method whereby religion should be studied comparatively, cross-culturally, and historically. *Religion among People* does just that and, further, demonstrates why this must be our best approach. Studying others' traditions, writes Kees, is the mode by which we can arrive at some understanding of both religion as a universal phenomenon and religion as situationally specific. And that, he shows us, is a fruitful way of coming to understand ourselves.

This book, like Kees' other ones, compels us to confront the role of religion in the lives of both individual and social bodies. By exploring the religion of ancient cities (Egyptian and Greek), Near Eastern high god traditions (Judaism, Christianity, and Islam), and Indian and Buddhist traditions, he is actually inviting us to better understand ourselves. But this book (and the others, I believe) also helps us to understand the man behind the curtain. *Ben's Story*, for example, was a moment of turning an expatriate's critical skills inward and grappling with the meaning of home—in this case the Dutch coastal village of Oostvoorne (where Kees did much of his growing up) and his high school friendship with Ben Wessels. Insinuated in this were the German occupation of Oostvoorne from 1940 until the end of the war, Ben's death in a concentration camp, and the broader place of Holland in the German project. For a scholar trained to scrutinize tangled human actions, allegiances, alliances, and turmoil, it made sense that Kees would ultimately cast a critical eye on his own ambiguous story.

1. See p. 217 below.

But even a text like *Religion among People*, ostensibly a purely academic work, provides a glimpse into the man himself. As I noted above, he writes at length about modernity and the modern concern for the inner life. This, he tells us, is a response to state brutality and the sterility of pure reason; and it can often generate a kind of pacifism. Perhaps this is a more personal statement that it might seem at first glance. Perhaps this was why Quakerism held a special place in Kees' heart, and why he became a practicing Quaker for the last decade of his life, essentially from the time he wrote *Ben's Story*.

Kees once said that becoming a scholar and teacher was his second choice for a career. What he really wanted to be was a clown. I'd like to think that those mischievous trickster eyes that I first saw peering over the dashboard of his truck in 2001 are also peeking through this text at us, affably inviting us all to sit back, sip a little single malt, and try to cultivate something strong and peaceable and joyous within ourselves that will counter the sterility and brutality that too often defines our modern world.

Jennifer Reid
University of Maine Farmington

Preface

The essays in this book attempt to show that religion is more than the stirrings in an individual's heart, and that at the deepest level religious traditions determine what goes on between one human being and another, between one community and another, and between human beings and whoever holds power over them.

We begin with the assumption that religion in general is a dimension of all human existence—an assumption that can be made without undue speculation, given the significance of religion in all human societies. At the same time, we will keep in mind that only the specific religious traditions give us the documentation we need for our study.

Our topic is religion *among people*, for the function of religion is not and has never been limited to the inner reflections of the individual. And it is among people that the traditions have been handed down, kept alive, and given constantly changing forms. A special focus of this discussion will be the many ways in which, in various ages and traditions, the dictates of sacred authority were reflected, followed, or contradicted in the ordinary world of power and conflict. Yes, occasionally they were also contradicted, or even fought. But what we, "moderns," need to be told is that they were never ignored.

Religion is poorly understood among those of us who like to consider ourselves *readers*. We know of "the religious right" and we speak of "liberals" in religion. There are many such terms we hear and use, yet could not adequately explain. We know of problems concerning "church and state," yet as a rule have no understanding about how religion and state relate to each other elsewhere in the world. And even with the best intentions, by what method do we hope to arrive at a fair understanding of religious orientations in cultures distant from us in place or time? An inadequate understanding of religion and religions is rampant among the journalists who inform us, among educators in grade schools and high schools, and among college professors in the humanities and social studies.

Experts on religion are often reticent about the fact that religions have something to do with *truth*. And yet everyone else knows it! I hope that my book is welcome and useful for people with open minds, with ordinary interests in others as they think and behave, like and dislike each other, in social life and in our struggles for power. I have been told that sometimes I appear rude when I discuss my topic. Nevertheless, I am convinced calling things by their name is not resented so much by normal inquisitive readers as it is by academic experts who wrap themselves in blankets of thick prose. Not only "evil scientists" hide behind the irrefutability of their formulations when concocting poisons; the study of human beings has its parallels here. Therefore very simple questions are worth asking again.

I am grateful to the Academic Senate of the University of California, Los Angeles for grants that helped me in my work. I am grateful also to the UCLA Center for Medieval and Renaissance Studies for providing a research assistant, Rhona Zaid, who rendered invaluable bibliographical help, especially in matters concerning Islam. I owe many thanks to her, as well as to the UCLA graduate students who helped me in this project.

This book reflects the fruit of conversations that took place over a good many years. Next to my students in graduate seminars, I wish to remember here with warmth the names of some UCLA colleagues who have passed on: Gerhart Ladner, the remarkable medievalist, art historian, and historian of ideas; Lynn White, best known as historian of medieval technology, but most vivid in my memory as a man sparkling in discussion, always positive and encouraging; Truesdell Brown, the classical historian, whose work first alerted me to the entwining of religion and secularization, even in antiquity.

The chapter on Hinduism is for me inseparable from hospitable colleagues in the Triangle South Asia Consortium in North Carolina: Joanne Punzo Waghorne, Carl W. Ernst, John F. Richards, Satti Khanna, and many others. I express my thanks no less for questions raised by audiences in many places, including Franklin and Marshall College, Penn State University, and campuses of the University of California system. Casual discussions often turned out to be of the highest value, as was so with Hans Rogger and Amos Funkenstein—now too no longer among us. Many, many thanks go to Peter Loewenberg; Annette Aronowicz; Fr. John Hilary Martin, OP; Noel Q. King; Gary Lease; and my old friend and colleague Jerome Long of Wesleyan University, who continues to keep me alert.

At the end of this list of helpful friends, I gladly follow the standard pattern of accepting all blame for remaining errors. At the same time, however, how many more there would have been if not for the attentiveness of my marvelous wife, Sara!

Whatever has been expressed here is well expressed thanks to Ellen Kaplan, who went over the book many times to clarify its themes. Finally, without the generous work of Tim Copeland, who would deny that he knows more about computers than just about anybody, nothing on all these pages would have materialized.

A most unexpected blessing was bestowed on me when I settled in Biddeford, Maine—a place far away from the major libraries I had gotten used to, beginning with those of the University of Chicago and the Research Library at UCLA. In Biddeford I found the splendid bibliographical services of the McArthur Public Library. I owe an enormous debt of gratitude to Lynn Bivens, Assistant Director, to Peter Howell, Reference/Technical Coordinator, and to Sally Leahey—all of whom located and provided much information I needed, including some of the most "farfetched" writings.

Kees W. Bolle

Acknowledgments

In some of the essays in this book I have made use of my earlier writings. Even though in virtually all cases that earlier work is so completely rewritten as to be unrecognizable, I want to thank my publishers for permission to use the following materials:

"In Defense of Euhemerus." In *Myth and Law among the Indo-Europeans: Studies in Indo-European Comparative Mythology*, edited by Jaan Puhvel, 19–38. Publications of the UCLA Center for the Study of Comparative Folklore and Mythology 1. Berkeley: University of California Press, 1970.

"Secularization as a Problem for the History of Religions." *Comparative Studies in Society and History* 12 (1970) 242–59.

"The Idea of Mankind in Indian Thought." In *History and the Idea of Mankind*, edited by W. Warren Wagar, 2–26. Albuquerque: University of New Mexico Press, 1971.

"Views of Class, Caste, and Mankind." *Studia Missionalia*: "Man, Culture and Religion" 20 (1980) 165–76.

"Reflections on the History of Religions and History." *History of Religions* 20 (1980) 62–80.

Only reality can call to life another reality.
(Osip Mandelstam)

Part One

CHANGE IN RELIGION

1

Religion: The Troubling Subject

The Confusion Concerning Religion

The trouble about religion is that everyone has an opinion on it. Moreover, almost everyone presents his or her opinion without knowledge, without reflection, and without inhibition. The result is a cacophony, a Babylonian confusion. In view of this confusion, what is one to think? The first order is to recognize that a confusion exists, and to examine its scope and nature.

There are of course many subjects that most of us are ignorant about, whether mathematics, astronomy, Russian history, or Tamil literature. However, unlike the subject of religion, none of these other subjects gives people the feeling that they are *expected* to know and *obliged* to volunteer their view.

This self-styled expertise of so many is a phenomenon that demands further thought. Among the voices raised, some dismiss religious impulses, while others defend or extol them. They seem to be in flagrant opposition, and yet the remarkable thing is that in a historical perspective, the voices of our time begin with two assumptions in common. The first is that religion is somehow the same wherever we find it in the world; in the general verbal skirmishing and sparring on the subject, the *essential homogeneity* of all religion is presupposed. The second assumption is that religion is an inner matter by definition; even though our evaluations of its significance vary wildly, religion itself is assumed to be somehow a matter of the emotional or "inner" life. By recognizing these two assumptions, these items of unanimity in an ocean of confusion and indiscrimination, we may gain the critical faculty we need to approach our subject.

We do not often realize that we are at the beck and call of prevailing ideas. Yet this simple fact largely accounts for our unexamined assumption that all religions are in some unexplained manner the same. More than anywhere else, in our dependence on fashionable thoughts, which often come to us from ill-digested or outdated textbooks, or the mere drone and hubbub of daily conversation, we show ourselves to be, as anthropologists have taught us to say, "culture-centric." One can also say, more bluntly, that human beings are mentally and spiritually provincial. Confronted by things religious, whether we laugh derisively, grope for terms, or react with enthusiasm, we are not likely to be original. We rely on tradition.

The religions of mankind are not the only matters of tradition. Likewise, our *opinions* concerning religion and religions are handed down, often unexamined. This fact should be obvious to everyone who gives the subject some thought. However, the general eagerness to present our views on religion, the very urge to know what religion amounts to, makes us rather conveniently oblivious to the reliance of our opinions upon tradition. One such tradition goes back to the protests in eighteenth-century France against the *ancien régime*. That long-standing rule comprised not only the king's authority, but also the power of the Church. In their opposition, French thinkers articulated certain opinions against religion, but obviously, all this newly expressed criticism addressed itself to the particular features of the Catholic Church. Prominent among these was dogma. In popular usage, "dogma" became synonymous with enforced doctrine, a restraint on the human mind. Disapproval of such restraint is a constant part of the critical assessment of religion among Westerners to this day.

But what about other traditions? At a certain period in Indian history, practice of the many and very precisely regulated rituals prescribed by the ancient Vedic tradition began to wane, and for almost two thousand years now, mainstream Hinduism has not been characterized by such Vedic rituals and sacrifices. In the centuries when this change came about, critical voices were occasionally raised against the earlier tradition. This criticism, however, was unlike the eighteenth-century Western protest against religion. It was not antidogmatic, and had no reason to be, because in the Indian case there was no equivalent for what the West generally calls "dogma." Instead, critique of religion in India, ever since the waning of the Vedic tradition, has been directed against ritualists,[1] (or, to put it more circumspectly: among the voices raised against traditional elements, the antiritual tone has been quite noticeable). We can safely say that in general, *the sort of tradition they object to* determines antireligious ideas. No wonder, then, that negative views of religion have their own traditions.

Indeed, every society has its own traditional way of discussing the subject of religion, and no bona fide study of religion can go very far if it does not critically perceive that same state of affairs in our own culture. If we wish to be serious, we cannot be uncritical with respect to our own predilections.

Piety and Psychology and the "Inner" Life

The assumption that religious facts are governed by emotion demands special attention, for it has sent many well-intended discussions into a conceptual fog. In the United States, two very special mental streams came together and gave an unusual force to the idea that religion is a matter of inner life. The first, and by far the more powerful, was Protestant pietism. Originating in various communities in Europe, it developed independently in the New World,[2] and in the nineteenth and twentieth centuries took on forms that Europe could not have imagined.[3] The second movement, which had its impact not in religious circles per se but primarily on intellectuals and members of the middle class who had lost their ties with organized religion, is summed up in the words *psychology* and *psychoanalysis* and is symbolized by the name of Freud. In the United States, Freud's influence increased by leaps and bounds in the years following the Second World War. He was translated and interpreted, and applied in the study of literature, history, and anthropology.

Pietism and psychology may seem strange bedfellows, and yet it is precisely these two, the one looking from within religion, the other picturing itself as looking at religion from without, that agreed on the "heart," the emotion, the feelings of conversion, the inwardly attested

---

1. For some details of this antiritualism, see my "Remarks on Bhakti."

2. Ahlstrom, *A Religious History of the American People*, especially chapters 17–30, 48, 61, 62.

3. See especially Marsden, *Fundamentalism and American Culture*.

signs of being saved. Pietism (although its origins lie in particular historical attitudes) interprets the relationship to God virtually without reference to the surrounding world. In the past, as a rule, it shied away from political involvement.[4] It is immersed in the "inner" life. Psychology, on the other hand, arose from (biological and medical) science and presents an "objective" view of religion and religions. Hence a conflict and confusion at the center of most of our discussions of religion is found between the groping for an inner certainty and the urge to judge rationally, scientifically.

Thinking about a religious orientation in a very different time and place can shed unexpected light on the "provincial" views we hold. Few religious and cultural traditions have an equivalent for our term "religion."[5] This fact cannot be regarded as an ordinary linguistic matter, for when we look at particular cultural contexts, the issue becomes more and more complex. Egypt in antiquity lacked an equivalent for "religion," but it did have more than twenty very specific expressions with very specific connotations for which we have nothing better than the blanket term "ritual." It is useful to reflect that any Egyptian of the ancient world could have noted our poverty of understanding, attested by our scarcity of precise words for religious acts. We cannot imagine what this person, accustomed to the *practice* or *performance* of religion, might have made of our obsession with the inner life and the question of whether there is any reality to it.

Hindus are thoroughly familiar with the "inner life." Still, only *praxis*, a consciously executed, purposeful routine, is the center. For that reason alone, Hinduism is far removed from the reliability of "feeling" that makes most discussions among us so confusing. In fact, it is closer to the ancient Egyptian insistence on acts performed. The Indian texts dealing with yoga, from the Upaniṣads and medieval tantras to modern philosophical and popular treatises, use ritual and sacrificial terms. Such terms (for instance, "sacrifice of breath" in describing yoga techniques) really have little relation to our sense of religion or explanations of religion as an inner emotion.

---

4. A most illuminating study on this subject is Mead, *The Old Religion in the Brave New World*.

5. Wilfred Cantwell Smith discussed this elaborately in *The Meaning and End of Religion*.

The conclusion must be that our discussions, though perfectly comprehensible as our cultural product, are not adequate to deal with the general subject of religion.

Shortcomings of Our Terminology

Misconceptions regarding religion appear frequently in our vocabulary. Although we know in general that certain terms we use in our discussions are not really appropriate in all cases, we do not often take the time to replace or delete them. Nevertheless, when we want to make correct statements about "the religions of mankind," or "the religious nature of man," then for reasons of decency that form a minimal basis of any science we have to eliminate certain terms or see to it that we use them only when they truly make sense. Sometimes these terms, bequeathed to us by our culture, are quite ingrained. Among such terms are "scripture" and "faith." Both words can really only be used within certain limits. Very few religions have anything that can be called a canon, and most have nothing resembling scriptures at all. And contrary to all common use of language in the West, "faith" is not universal, and in the plural ("faiths") the term is dubious most of the time. In formal, general terms, religion is not characterized by "faith" or "scripture" any more than the universe is sufficiently defined by "planets" or "black holes."

The peculiar alliance of pietism in "believing" circles and psychologism in "intellectual" circles has a great deal to do with these widespread misconceptions. For these misconceptions are born from the very assumption both pietism and psychologism as a rule have made: that religion is a matter of feeling. In spite of their enmity on most issues, both agree in their insistence that the locus of religion is a special inner abode. On the extremes of the disputation, one side considers that abode invulnerable and sacred, while the other side makes the claim that it is sick or illusory. However, the difference in point of view on this central assumption looks superficial on the world scene of religious phenomena.

In Buddhism we find a religion that is structurally very different from the religions rooted in the biblical texts. It is a religion in which such keywords as "convenant," "rightousness," or "kingship of God" are not found—in fact, there are no significant religious terms in Buddhism with a juridical or political overtone, no key terms from the world of man. Instead, we have a "Buddha," an enlightened being; *nirvāṇa*, "liberation";

"meditation," the inner discipline practiced to gain the ultimate end. When we look up from Buddhist texts, biblical passages seem unduly "mixed up." And compared to the biblical religions, Buddhism seems altogether nonworldly, completely "spiritual." Nevertheless, Buddhism has existed in the world for about as long as Judaism. The oldest Buddhist texts tell us how the religion of the Buddha acquired royal patronage, and how under this patronage the first monasteries were established. Among the duties of those early monks was the duty to overcome cravings. Of course, it did not escape their attention that the nature of kings consisted in cravings: for power, for land, for money, for dominion. But this phenomenal world of possessions and cravings became the central theme of the monk's discipline (in the theory of the *skandhas*) and the platform for his release. The distinction between the reality that supercedes the world of appearances and the ongoing passing existences of phenomena in the world was the focal point in the activity of meditating from the beginning. In the basic teachings, there was no place for thoughts of any prophet to oppose the king on a worldly level. (Although inevitably, of course, in the history of Buddhism as in all history, we find power politics and war.)

It is a fundamental fact that the key terms of Buddhism are "nonworldly" when compared to the central biblical terms, and decidedly nonpolitical. Revolutionary political movements have been rare phenomena in the history of Buddhism (notwithstanding notable exceptions); most certainly, the cases where Buddhism can be said to have instigated them in any manner are even rarer. By contrast, such movements are virtually the rule in traditions affected by the religions rooted in the biblical texts. Whatever one's "feelings" about religion are, the structures of religions are open to investigation, and we can see to what a remarkable extent events and institutions are given their shape as a result of basic patterns in religious symbolisms and teachings.

Our inquiry into religion demands that we try to dispel the confusion of tongues on the subject. Let us briefly return to some of the terminology that is symptomatic of the general confusion, the shortcomings in our customary speech about religion and religions.

As we said, one confusing and inadequate term in most discussions is "faith." The term has a venerable history in Christianity, also in Judaism, and certainly in Islam, and its basis in the religion of Israel, that is to say in the Hebrew texts, is undeniable. One could not describe any of these religions without giving proper attention to "faith," although one would find that differences among the three show themselves almost at once. Christians have argued about faith throughout their history, and the issue of salvation "by faith alone" is inseparable from the Reformation. In comparison to Christians, Jews have not normally given a lot of attention to the topic of faith, and have instead been more preoccupied with cultic observances. More than in Judaism and Christianity, the structure of Islam is characterized by legal and political institutional concerns, and as a result the act of instituting faith, of establishing its correct expression, became a central issue in its own right, but invariably in an immediate relationship to the community's life rather than to the hairsplitting of theologians.

More than the differing aspects of faith in these three religions, the insignificance or absence of notions of faith in other traditions must catch our eye in the present context. The ancient Egyptian religion and the ancient Indian religions of the Vedas and Brāhmaṇas are joined by the religion of ancient Rome, Shinto, the Confucian tradition, and many others in their central concern for things *done* rather than "*believed*."

The principal rule for the study of religion is that we must listen to what people express in their documents. It seems almost superfluous to say something as obvious as this, because evidence is of course the principal concern for all science. In spite of that, we must repeat again that in the study of religions, evidence counts. If there is no concern in the documents for what many of us within our province of the world have come to regard as central to religion, then our task must be to discover what *is* central in the documents. We cannot superimpose our own notion of what ought to be the central concern.

Why is it so difficult to see this obvious point with respect to religions? Even in superb scholarly circles, the error of superimposition is sometimes committed.[6] The persistent use of "religion" and "faith" as synonyms is not sufficiently explained as a weakening of the meaning or understanding of the term "faith" among Christians. The real explanation, I think, is to be found once more in the accidents of history that brought about the intellectual habit of associating religion with inner emotion. The inner stirrings of the heart in revival movements and worship and the endeavor to understand religion in terms of psychological mechanisms have coalesced here once more. The inner emotions that "made up" religion, as it was recognized by the pious and by the psychologically

---

6. One of the best one-volume works on the world's religions, edited by Zaehner, is titled *The Concise Encyclopedia of Living Faiths*.

inclined, had their own convincing power, and it was but a small step from these feelings to "ideas." And nothing seemed awry in defining these "ideas" in the hearts of religious adherents as "faiths." (Also, it is not impossible that for some, speaking of "faiths" may have been a way to show their willingness to view other religions as on a par with their own.)

But don't all people have ideas? Of course. Don't all religious people have ideas too? No doubt. Don't they have special ideas? Probably, yes. Aren't those ideas their beliefs? And don't they form their *faith*? The answer is and must be no—and there is no other answer until you have established on the basis of the documents of the religion you are speaking of whether "faith" is important within it. In the vast majority of religions it is insignificant or absent.

Religion as an Institution

Religion should be viewed as an *institution*, in whatever specific tradition we find it. As an institution, religion cannot be overlooked any more than the kinship structure or the language of a civilization.[7] At almost every point religion is as vital to the expression of historical, human facts as language is. Not by chance, but for purposes of its own a religious system has bearing on a conception of the whole. Religions are diverse in structure, but everywhere they link the "fragmentary" groups of data that we are inclined to examine separately: political power, economics, and the rest.

The philosopher Henry Duméry, who introduced the term "institution" into the discussion of religion, has rendered us a great service with a small survey of the philosophy of religion from classical Greece to the present.[8] Duméry draws attention to a shift that took place in the early Christian world in the manner of thinking about religion. Throughout the classical age, before Christianity became an intellectual power, the subject of religion had been part of the given reality philosophers tried to deal with. No matter what arguments Plato, Aristotle, and others made with respect to its nature and function, or to the popular and lower versus the educated and higher understanding of religion, religion as such was,

---

7. I do not believe I do injustice to Henry Duméry's notion of "institution," developed in his *Phenomenology and Religion*, although I am using the term in a wider sense.

8. Duméry, *Phenomenology and Religion*, 84–110.

without question, part of the world. Religion becomes a different kind of problem when Christianity extends its hold over the minds of Europe. Then, religion can be looked at only from the Christian point of view; religion can no longer be seen as the self-evident element of reality-to-be-thought-about that it once had been.[9]

It became natural to make a distinction between true and false religion. Saint Augustine was one of those who stressed this distinction again and again. A typical statement, in a letter from Augustine to a pagan dignitary who apparently was reluctant to forbid non-Christian festivals, runs as follows:

> ... it is in the churches, the sacred lecture-rooms, one might say, of the nations, that . . . the piety [is being taught] with which worship is paid to the true and truthful God, who not only commands men to undertake, but also gives them the power to perform, all those things by which the human spirit is trained and fitted for fellowship with God and for dwelling in the everlasting heavenly country. It is for that reason that He predicted the future overthrow of the images of the many false gods and enjoined that that overthrow should begin now. For there is nothing that makes men so unsuited for fellowship by reason of their depraved lives as does the imitation of those gods, such as they are described and commended by literature.[10]

The reasoning of Augustine and, more generally, the ways of arguing in the Latin Church concerning religion and history are well known. In fact, scholars can be rather glib in pointing out the negative judgment passed on paganism by the early church.[11] It is important to realize that the Greek Church recognized a different relationship between Christianity and paganism. It did not relinquish the contrast of true and false, Christian and pagan, but the image of an organic relation occurred in the Eastern Church. Comparisons were made to soul and body rather than to truth and falsehood. Saint Basil points out that Moses and Daniel were trained in pagan wisdom before they applied themselves to divine

---

9. Ibid., 100.

10. I slightly revised the translation of James Houston Baxter in Augustine, *Select Letters*, 155–57. Baxter adds a footnote to Augustine's words concerning God's prediction of a future overthrow of the images of false gods, referring to Lev 26:30; Ezek 6:4; 30:13; Hos 10:2; 1 Kgs 15:11–13; 2 Chr 23:17, 31:1, 33:15, 34:3–4.

11. See, for instance, de Vries, *Perspectives in the History of Religions*, chapter 2.

teachings, and this sets the tone for his exhortation to young men to make a proper use of Greek literature.[12]

Thus "East" and "West" in European Christianity are variations of importance to Church historians and to all historians of Europe; but for historians of religions (who, professionally, cannot permit themselves to ban the world as a whole from their mind) what is essential is that the prevailing attitudes of the Eastern and Western churches are variations on one and the same theme. Whether they denounce paganism or see it as prefiguring Christianity, both hold that only one religion has an authentic metaphysical vantage point. This familial insistence makes Eastern and Western Christianity conspicuous within the vast array of the world's religions. This is not to say that other religions do not have ways of expressing their ultimate truthfulness; but Christianity East and West has distinctive mannerisms in proclaiming its uniqueness, and precisely in these the one family structure shows itself. One would never mistake them for the expressions of Inuit or Mbutu or even Islamic traditions.

Whether the relation or the contrast between Christianity and paganism was stressed, both churches were characterized by a structural necessity to reason fervently about the distinction.[13] Christianity as a whole had brought about something new, a certain "artificiality"—artificiality from the point of view of classical thought—that had come to stay. This artificiality was literally part of the *institution* of Christianity. From now on, religion was no longer in general a self-evident part of "all there is." The first genuine endeavor to overcome this "artificiality" was made in the nineteenth century by Hegel. He was the first to reflect purely rationally on the meaning of Christianity, and he quite consistently tried to grasp the meaning of Christianity as an *institution*,[14] without such artificiality.

I shall not try to discuss the value or the effects of Hegel's work. It is enough to remark on the sanity, the orderliness of his return to an almost classical view. Religions always and everywhere are *institutions*. Historians are well aware of the importance of institutions; they never ignore states, corporations, judicial systems, alliances of nations; they

---

12. Basil, *Saint Basil, Letters*, 363–435.

13. Let it be noted that in serious Christian theological writings wholesale condemnations of paganism are rare. Liberal American theologians, who as a rule on closer inspection have not read him, often attribute such condemnations to Karl Barth, the great twentieth-century Swiss theologian.

14. See Duméry, *Phenomenology and Religion*, 100–105.

never refuse to consider them. For that reason as well, the word "institution" applied to religion seems useful.

Being Aware of Real Differences

The Muslim Ibn Khaldūn (1332–1406) was a pioneer in historical scholarship. His work is of immediate relevance to the genesis and structure of social and socioreligious studies. It clearly demonstrates that the differentiation between falsity and truth, as well as reason and revelation, was not present only in Christianity. We also can say of Ibn Khaldūn that his work is strikingly modern in its main ideas. Most practicing historians striving for the highest degree of objectivity would recognize him as a member of their guild.

Ibn Khaldūn conceived his *Introduction to History*[15] as a "new science." Written in the fourteenth century, the work impresses scholars today because of its remarkable insights. The author observes social organization in detail and articulates the function of political power. He discusses the way religion generates power in politics.[16]

"Religious propaganda cannot materialize without group feeling"[17] says Ibn Khaldūn. It seems an obvious fact, and Ibn Khaldūn demonstrates its truth with clear examples. Every one of our contemporary general historians would probably agree, and would ascribe a general validity to this rule, which helps them greatly in establishing certain series of historical occurrences. Even Western contemporary historians who through training or habit learned to ignore religion in establishing "what really happened" are not likely to find fault with the statement. It applies surely to European and American and all other histories, does it not?

At this point it is not a professional conceit but a concern for the proper understanding of general history that must make the historian of religions call for a moment of reflection. The statement by Ibn Khaldūn, no matter how obvious it appears to us, is anchored in his religion. And the fact that most Western intellectuals would accept it at face value is principally a matter of their own religious conditioning.

Let us suppose that we are asked to translate this statement into another religious ambience. Christianity, whether of the Latin or Greek

---

15. Ibn Khaldūn, *The Muqaddimah*, 1:78.
16. Ibid., 319ff.
17. Ibid., 322.

tradition, presents no problem for the simple reason that Christianity in its crucial, symbolic forms is akin to Islam. "Religious propaganda" is a *sine qua non*; missionary activity is part of history; the prophetic word constitutes a community; people are responsible for acting upon that word; the community, established in a uniquely sacred manner, is expected to address the surrounding world in conformance to its calling. Crucial terms in the biblical vocabulary are legal and political: "justice," "righteousness," "mercy," "covenant," "kingdom of God," and the *ekklesia*, the church itself, are some of these. Christianity and Islam, both offshoots of the Hebrew, biblical tradition, are vibrant with concern for the community—its well-being, growth, and laws, its just governance. Legitimate authority and the right of succession have been overwhelming objects of religious zeal in Islam since the days of the Prophet. Christianity has had its own distinct share of the same vintage in the struggles between pope and emperor, church and state. All this is familiar for a Westerner who has taken history courses, although it is not often pointed out to him that the worlds of Christianity and Islam are so similar in their events and problems because of their similar religious structures. "Religious propaganda cannot materialize without group feeling." Of course; even the most consciously secularized intellectual knows it.

But suppose we try to translate that statement into, say, the world of India. Its significance would no longer be assured. In India there are proselytizing movements. Buddhism at one time expanded enormously; Jainism expanded and had its martyrs; and no doubt factors of power politics and economic change have not been sufficiently studied in their effects on the various Indian religious communities. But looking at periods of such events makes it evident that there is nothing resembling a law relating community feeling to *propaganda*. The notions of *varṇa*, "class," *āśrama*, "stage of life," and of course, *jāti*, "caste" or "stage of life," belong to the core of Hindu ideas and practices. These have a lot to do with "group feelings"; they are social realities, and various studies have traced their changes and effects in history.[18] But one would have to redefine the term "propaganda" so extensively as to deprive it of all its original meaning to make it fit the Indian situation.

Even if we substitute the word "instruction" for "propaganda" and thereby bend toward Indian traditions, Ibn Khaldūn's words do not

---

18. See especially Dumont, *Une sous-caste*; see also Conlon, *A Caste in a Changing World*; and Leonard, *Social History of an Indian Caste*.

become more applicable or more significant. "Group feeling" in India is simply not the same as in the Islamic or Christian world.

Śaṅkara, the most famous of all Hindu spiritual preceptors, wrote a classic guidebook of teachings leading to liberation. One passage is particularly illuminating for our discussion. Śaṅkara takes it as obvious that proper teachers and proper students are brahmins—a social fact of the first order. However, the significant statement, occurring at the very beginning of the treatise, asserts that the pupil, in order to grasp reality (*ātman*), must realize that such things as birth and lineage are irrelevant and not real.[19] This is the beginning of instruction. And this is also part of an intellectual, religious tradition that has affected India for many centuries. The hierarchy of Indian society would have been an altogether different thing if it had not been accompanied and interpreted throughout its history by teachings such as these. *We misinterpret historical "facts" if we strip them of the religious forms that make up their actual existence.*

Notions like "propagation of the faith" are an inextricable part of Christianity and Islam and have strongly influenced the way Muslim and Christian adherents and their (secular?) successors have grasped history. Although in our time historical inquiry and issues such as "subjective" versus "objective" take on a scientific exterior, structurally the distinction true/false that we find in Saint Augustine and Saint Basil continues to preside as a model in the discussion. Hence "group feelings" (always conjuring up some contrast to those outside the group) remains for us a vital topic in assessing historical evidence. Yet often this topic is superimposed by our efforts, and does not arise from the people and human documents being studied.

Albeit unintentionally, an Indian scholar, N. K. Devaraja, sheds still more light on our discussion here. He provides us with a learned, or, perhaps more correctly, a secular academic treatise, in which he addresses the question of whether a meeting of religions is possible, and therefore handles the distinction insiders/outsiders, subjectivity/objectivity.[20] His conclusion is a plea for objectivity—but how different is this objectivity from that conceived by most Western historians! The author advocates that everyone learn to see the relative and complementary character of all authoritative scriptures and traditions. At the same time, and almost in the same breath, he singles out certain Hindu texts as expressing the

---

19. *Upadeśasāhasrī* 1.12–15.
20. Devaraja, "Is the Meeting of Religions Possible?"

ultimate value of the unity of religions, a unity underlying his laudable historical and intellectual attitude. This ultimate unity calls forth phrases like "spiritual discipline," "self-control," and "truthfulness"—all thinly veiled fundamental Hindu terms: *yoga, saṃyama,* and *tapas, satya,* and *sattva.* In a comparative study we cannot help but register that none of these terms, crucial as they are in pan-Indian religious tradition, are reminiscent of the legal/political terminology of Christianity. The author assures us, nevertheless, that "new schemes of thought lending support to religious attitudes and values must be evolved by thinkers who do not owe exclusive allegiance to any particular set of scriptures or a particular religious tradition."[21]

It would be inadequate to suggest that since religious traditions in our background will cast their shadow in our choice of words, what we are seeing here is a matter of survivals and fossils in our language. We must realize that we are not dealing with tendencies of our vocabulary but with fundamental assumptions concerning the world and its people. It is essential that we look quite thoughtfully at the obvious: the Indian scholar, in spite of his suggestion that he has gone beyond allegiance to one tradition, is thoroughly wrapped up in a religious institution that is not universal in nature. It differs considerably from the ideas of Ibn Khaldūn that we "Westerners" can concur with so easily.

Some might downplay this one Indian fragment as a mere instance of popularized *advaita,* but let us take notice most especially of the strength of the scholar's proposal. It is at least as substantial as the urge for "objectivity" that we are more familiar with and that seemingly bypasses religious factors. Instead of repressing religion, the Indian scholar assumes that behind the various historical forms some core, as yet invisible, is the same. What underlies his argument—and a historian of religions would wish that he had spelled it out and added even more force to the argument—is not the Augustinian or Basilian distinction true/false, but the thoroughly Indian distinction unmanifest/manifest (*avyakta/ vyakta*); what is ultimately and absolutely true, supreme reality, remains hidden, even though part of it appears to us. That part that is visible, in our empirical world, in our "history," is quite literally only relative, and could not be anything else. One could not do justice to history except by assuming its relativity in the sense of its relatedness to that "other" that is unmanifest. The Indian scholar's reasonings are clearly related to

---

21. Ibid., 39.

Śaṅkara's philosophical structures, in which, as we saw, social divisions recede. They recede precisely because something quite different from the distinction true/false, or inside/outside, or even our usual understanding of objective/subjective, became *instituted* in India.

The inclinations of so many of our own historians have their origin not in a straightforward urge for a real, intellectually defensible, or even merely neutral objectivity, but in a religious heritage that has become misleading because it is concealed, inarticulate, unconscious. Self-consciously "secular" scholars have their problems relating religion and history, and when they try to solve the problem by ignoring religious facts as secondary by-products, epiphenomenal to what was "really" going on, we have reason to be concerned. All of history, all our endeavors to understand human beings are victimized when the history of religions is neglected.

Most concisely, the lesson must be drawn that religion is part of history. Is that too obvious to mention? It certainly needs to be said at the present time. In the history of religions, we may draw our conclusion as follows: a historian of religions can do his job only if he copes with the roots of his own religion as he is expected to delve into the ground of others'. This is a position that has been formulated most cuttingly by the poet Osip Mandelstam: "Metaphysics has nothing to do with it. Only reality can call to life another reality."[22]

---

22. Mandelstam, *Selected Essays*, 64.

2

Interpretation

A most comprehensive and least controversial formulation concerning religion came from Edvard Lehmann (1862–1930): the content of religion is available to us in sacred words, sacred acts, and sacred places. In terms that Mircea Eliade and other scholars have made familiar, the same is expressed with "myths," "rituals," and "symbols."[1]

In America, and looking no further than what we have come to regard as "civil religion,"[2] we may observe the symbol of the Statue of Liberty; no one would dare laugh at its monstrosity, for it is a primordial, unassailable veracity, not in need of proof or justification. Similarly, with solemn regularity pilgrimages assemble in front of the Supreme Court building, the nation's central shrine of Righteousness. In these simple examples the "structure" of sacred places, words, and rites is clearly visible. Should one object and argue that the *transcendent* referent of the Statue of Liberty is hazy, the answer is not difficult: the transcendent referent

---

1. See Lehmann, "Erscheinungswelt der Religion," in *Die Religion in Geschichte und Gegenwart* (hereafter referred to as *RGG*) 2nd ed. and his opening chapter in Chantepie de la Saussaye, *Textbuch zur Religionsgeschichte*, 4th ed. On the same subject, see van der Leeuw, "Phänomenologie der Religion," in *RGG* 2nd ed. The significance of Lehmann's elementary enumeration can hardly be overestimated. Eliade's attention certainly covers the same three, yet his work pertains almost wholly to only two: symbols and myths. See Eliade, "Methodological Remarks on the Study of Symbolism." Rituals receive short shrift here; to quite an extent, this omission has to do with Eliade's lack of interest in social life. See Bolle, *The Enticement of Religion*, 303–5.

2. Robert N. Bellah coined the term "civil religion." For a discussion of the national, ritual coherency it signifies, see Bellah, *The Broken Covenant*; Mead, *The Nation with the Soul of a Church*; Mead, *The Old Religion in the Brave New World*; Albanese, *Sons of the Fathers*; and chapter 11 of Albanese, *America: Religions and Religion*.

can be equally hard to find in a Buddhist stupa or a Hindu temple. And moreover, the objection commits the mistake of trespassing into a metaphysical argument if it insists on the nature of what should be sacred. Here we recall that we have no empirical evidence anywhere of a human tradition without religion.[3]

There is a compelling idea about the *essence* of religion in the book *Das Heilige* (*The Idea of the Holy*) written by Rudolf Otto and first published in 1917. The experience of the holy, according to Otto, is something irreducible to other areas or faculties, whether of knowledge, perception, or experience. It is terrifying (*horrendum*) and appealing (*fascinans*) at the same time. The holy is by definition "das ganz Andere," the altogether different. Otto's book has an element of what we might call safeguarding religion from attack. Or perhaps it would be more fair to say that others sought out this element in Otto's work. Even if this was not Otto's intent, it caused his popularity to grow among the many who felt apologetic about religion and now saw a weapon of defense to be used against the onslaught of "secular" or anticlerical philosophers and scientists.

We must notice that Otto's great attempt does not bring us closer to identifying the nature of persistence in religion; we cease to deal with the specifics, the multiform varieties through which the inner force of a religion *persists*. "The Holy" is posited in splendid isolation, far beyond all perceivable and accessible human expressions. Precisely because of

---

3. A book that once became quite popular—written by John Nance, *The Gentle Tasaday: A Stone Age People in the Philippine Rain Forest*—gave out the impression that a pristine absence of religion was found at last. A hitherto unknown tribe in the Philippines, a tribe that had no previous contact with the outside world: the gentleness of the newly discovered ones, their natural nobility, apparently was so great as to make the actual *practice* of religion superfluous. The book was later revealed to be a hoax. The fact that it was ever believed at all is instructive, for Nance's presentation of the "Tasaday" had all the telltale signs of uneducated journalism addressing itself to uninformed readers.

Lack of knowledge and discernment with regard to religion is common among us; it results from a peculiar lopsidedness in our education. The modern child's religious education in America and much of Europe is normally completed around the age of twelve, if instruction is given at all. From then on, in astoundingly many cases, the subject of religion receives no more attention. At about the same time, education in high school begins. This means dealing with the "real" things, things that matter. When the child has grown up, the ostensibly mature person has no framework in which to consider or even recognize religious phenomena. One would not expect a mathematician on the level of an average twelve-year-old to present authoritative calculations for a life insurance company, and yet childish assessments of religion are still commonplace in circles regarded as the territory of adults.

this problem with which Otto's work leaves us, it seems more than happenstance that *The Idea of the Holy* appeared in 1917. From its contents one would not guess that the author's country was then involved in one of the most horrible wars in the history of mankind. Where do "the holy" and human existence meet? Must the academic teachers of a nation each do their special job while keeping at a safe distance from the horrors to which defenseless people fall victim? The problem becomes a *horrendum* more than a *fascinans*.

Pseudo-religion

We must pause and take note of the fact that the route of serious scholarship is not the only way to assert continuity. Another, more convenient road is commonly followed; along it, stately remnants of the past are turned into abstractions that appeal to our thirst for perfection and power, power of the group, above all power of the state. Forms are born that are not really continuations of religions but rather pseudoreligious self-assurances. On this road of naïve pseudoscholarship, we are led to bypass what people and traditions actually lived or expressed. Instead, there is a reaching out for forms that give easy comfort. The mind has its spells of fatigue; it wants certainty *now*. These forms fill the need for unending power.

The distinction between religion and pseudo-religion must always be made. The eagle, since oldest days the king of birds soaring over all, becomes the symbol of America and many a modern nation; it presents very well the desired absoluteness. The pillar and lions built by Emperor Aśoka, who ruled over much of India in the third century B.C., were rediscovered, cleaned up, and became the seal of the Indian republic. Ominously, such rebirths may turn into instruments that feed false hopes for a millennium brought to fruition by a particular nation possessed of perfect righteousness—and of course a preordained right to invade the others. Nazi Germany, embracing the reinstatement of a reputedly original Germanic mythology, is perhaps the most glaring example of these terrible uses to which scholarly findings can be put. (Pre-Christian Germanic religion, after all, was a virtually unknown ancient heritage when learned scholars unearthed it in the nineteenth century, deciphering runes, interpreting Norse and Icelandic texts, reinvestigating proverbs, riddles, and children's games for traces of ancient paganism, and searching every inch of the foundations of every church that might have been built on the place of an old temple.) National Socialist Germany, fascist Italy, and imperialistic Japan yield powerful examples of pseudo-religious, "fabricated" revivals of the past, but they are not alone. Little of modern nationalism is devoid of comparable, cruel self-delusions. One thinks of President Ronald Reagan conjuring up the "Evil Empire." (Perhaps we should be very grateful that Reagan's counterpart in Moscow, Chairman Gorbachev, was someone without immature pseudoreligious delusions. For if he too had been like that . . .)

Anyway, the professional historian of religions cannot resist noting that allegories of the "good" Christian world versus the "evil" world of some others are the very sort of tangible opposition between "the good" and "the evil" that would have been condemned when the Church reigned supreme, as such stuff was the *heresy* of the Manichaeans. Furthermore, on the subject of heresy, the historian of religions or for that matter anyone familiar with the Bible might have noticed that the vow of President George W. Bush to eliminate all "the evildoers" marked a turning away from what the first book of the Bible tells us; the book of Genesis makes clear that it is *Man*, the human being, who has fallen.

The absolutes of pseudo-religion were very much in use in the war which devastated oil-rich Iraq. Now the bogus delineation "Islamofacism" has entered our minds and shapes policies of the present day. Scholarship can take a strange part in the propagandistic and self-deluding proceedings. Indeed, to speak of the worst of it: how many scholars, how many "pundits," have worked secretly, and work secretly, for secret portions of the state whose offices are filled with individuals having no grownup understanding of human traditions, no grownup understanding of their own tradition?

Now we are speaking about the morality of scholarship. We owe it to the love for our subject of study to speak up. I know very well that in the history of religions serious and moral scholarship exists. Such scholarship requires continuous watchfulness, in the first place because of the nature of our *living* object. Our morality should not escape scrutiny any more than the morality of modern physics. In the study of religions also, human lives are at stake.

This problem, of morality in scholarship, is closer than we like to think. Merely academic discussions in the nineteenth century helped generate modern racism. One would not like to make an equally outright statement about the responsibility of the invention of the "social sciences" for reducing human beings into countable and analyzable entities ... and subsequent mass deportations, mass bombings, and mass murders—but can it not be discussed? Whatever in the study of man belittles in any way the lives of individuals requires a critical review.

Persistence of Religion

When I first became aware of the extraordinary force of continuity in religion, I turned to Indian materials to look more closely at the evidence. My professors, Mircea Eliade and the Sanskritist Hans van Buitenen, guided me. Eliade also gently chided me for having chosen the most complex continent of religion, India, as the scene for my inquiry, and, to make matters worse, within this continent the most complex tradition of philosophy and cultic practices, known as Tantrism. But India, I thought, should be one of the few regions enabling one to trace symbolic and mythological themes over a long period of time. India, in spite of its many vicissitudes and abundance of religious creations, did not undergo radical events similar to the triumph of Christianity in the West, the breakup of a classical world, or the Reformation.[4]

In thinking that India would reveal continuity without change, did I not know that change is essential to human life? All I can say is that it takes time to grow up, and the history of religions conspicuously demands maturity. One has to learn about the meaning of changes in history somewhere, and for me, India was the place. Indeed, I found in the Indian materials that religion does persist, and persistence can be traced—even in cases where breaks seem most in evidence, such as those between the ancient Vedic and the medieval Tantric traditions—*for religion persists by changing*; every appropriation of the existing tradition means *change*; not only each generation, but each individual child asking questions implies it and brings it about. An additional discovery, of no less importance, is this: the changes themselves provide a perspective; they give us clues and help us detect the meaning of each moment in the continuity.

We are able to speak of meanings only because we see changes in time. The difficulty we have with the Vedic hymns—and the same thing holds true for all earliest texts in any civilization—is that they are indeed

---

4. This effort resulted first in a doctoral dissertation, Chicago, 1961, and eventually in the book *The Persistence of Religion: An Essay on Tantrism and Sri Aurobindo's Philosophy*, with a preface by Mircea Eliade.

earliest; we cannot refer back to earlier literature to shed light on the meaning of words and idioms and metaphors. Here the principal dimension needed to speak of meaning at all is missing. The line of changes in time, which we use intuitively, is incomplete. This particular discovery is of enormous importance; we see that meanings, understanding, interpreting, are not narrow technical problems, solvable by structuralism, functionalism, postmodernism, or any current and fashionable "-ism."

After all, religion does things for which none of our most widely invoked theories and ideologies, none of our -isms, provide sufficient explanation. The persistence of religion is not primarily a puzzle to be solved but a fact to be registered. A Christian priest has no reason to discuss the resurrection, theologically or otherwise, with the parishioner to whom he is administering the sacrament; an explanation in, say, Freudian or Durkheimian terms has its own value in theological discussion, but the *effect* of the sacrament does not have that as a prerequisite. On the contrary, the effect precedes it; the persistence of religion is a fact to be registered, and only then, when it has been duly noted, can we begin to discuss matters sensibly. Or, to return to the image, the Christian priest may well discuss the resurrection rationally with his fellow priests, the Hindu pandit will discuss the order and sense of the ritual in detail, but even under the weight of the most skeptical arguments the religious efficaciousness is what is given: it remains the starting point. In precise analogy, the discussions of historians of religions, anthropologists, and sociologists must recognize the persistence of their subject. This recognition is the principal warranty that the ensuing discussion will make sense.

Interpretation

We see and study each religion in its continuity, the totality of its phenomena—yet we are not part of each whole of time, with its inevitable and absolute demands; we stand elsewhere, in another specific place and time, with its own demands, equally absolute and inevitable, but different.

At this point, the traditional terminology and the religious imagery of *time* offer an illuminating distinction. We can study the *chronos*, the duration of lives and events, the general space of time. It is a rather scientific kind of time; it is the time of the clock and the calendar. That time, however, is ultimately the same time that was depicted with hair-raising exactness in Mithraism, the early rival of Christianity, and, still earlier, in the ancient Zervanite religion: a winged monster, with the head of a lion, insatiable, forever devouring, dressed in coiling snakes and spewing a breath of flames.[5] Time in our actual existence is not only a matter of the "measurability" of duration. The inner and the outer of persistence in religion—the external, observable continuity and the inner force—touch each other here.

"Time" in religious traditions is not ever expressed only as a measurable and quantifiable something. It is always also more than that. Our religious existence is never a continuum under a neutral clock or calendar, but a matter of *kairoi* (as New Testament students express it) or *samayāḥ* (in Hindu texts), specific moments in time, times agreed upon, favorable and auspicious moments, or periods of mourning or celebration.

The old Greek notion of *kairos* is one that is easily ignored as an archaism, an oddity of "primitive minds." The habit of looking down on such a notion (when it still occurs, for instance, in Christian theological discussions) is unwise, as it only helps to reinforce the uncritical reliance on an abstract conception of time—attractive under the prevailing fashions merely because it is calculable. But the abstraction of time, as all of us realize at one time or another, is useless in its divergence from our immediate experience—as distant as the little lines on a thermometer are distant from our sensation of cold and heat. The sheer habit of relying on "scientific" abstractions is certainly a common cause of our blindness for religion of whatever kind. The last two or three centuries in the West have simply made the vast majority of us, urban Westerners, far more distant from immediate sensations than our ancestors were. By contrast, most classical religious texts are immediate, not abstract, in the sensations they describe. This is the case also with the traditions that are meditative by nature, such as Buddhism.

One of numerous stories may be illustrative. A brahmin who had been studying with the Buddha for quite a while felt a particular need to go and see the Blessed One, because something worried him. He had realized the profundity of the Buddha's teachings, but there was a question that remained: if one has accepted the Buddha's teachings and followed his teachings and disciplined way of life, fully aware of the lasting importance of those teachings—but leaves the Buddha's presence, returns to one's self, and faces fear and dread, what then?

---

5. See Pettazzoni, "The Monstrous Figure of Time in Mithraism."

Many a modern city dweller might miss the immediacy of the question the brahmin asks, for many of us have barely had the experience of utter fear and dread. Nevertheless, that is precisely what the ensuing discussion between the Buddha and the brahmin pupil is about. "Master Gotama," says the brahmin, "remote jungle-thicket resting places are hard to endure, seclusion is hard to practise, and it is hard to enjoy solitude. One would think the jungles must rob a bhikkhu [monk] of his mind, if he has no concentration."

As with most religious teachings the world over, what follows is a story, a story moreover that is repetitious—like many truly worthwhile stories. The Buddha does not respond with an explicit, logical answer, thereby setting the questioner's mind at ease. The argumentations of a good modern counselor would be useless here. The man has no "problems." He just knows from experience what it is to be scared. There is no problem to be *solved*. There is a life to be *lived*.

And with truly absorbing repetitiousness, the Buddha responds by narrating his own experience.

> Before my enlightenment, while I was still an unenlightened Bodhisatta, I too considered thus: "Remote jungle-thicket resting places in the forest are hard to endure . . . the jungles must rob a bhikkhu of his mind, if he has no concentration."
>
> I considered thus: "Whenever recluses or Brahmins unpurified in bodily conduct resort to remote jungle-thicket resting places in the forest, then owing to the defect of their unpurified bodily conduct these good recluses and brahmins evoke unwholesome fear and dread. But I do not resort to remote jungle-thicket resting places in the forest unpurified in bodily conduct. I am purified in bodily conduct in the forest as one of the noble ones with bodily conduct purified." Seeing in myself this purity of bodily conduct, I found great solace in dwelling in the forest.[6]

The Buddha continues at great length as the text spells out in detail how he overcame fear and dread to arrive at proper meditation. When he caught himself plagued by dread while walking, he would walk until the dread left him. Likewise while sitting, lying down, and on and on it goes—until we, modern "enlightened" and dreadfully hasty people, become impatient to "get to the point." I do not think we need to feel ashamed of catching ourselves in our impatience. On the contrary, in our

---

6. For the entire story (with all its necessary repetitions), see Nanamoli and Bodhi, *The Middle Length Discourses*, 102–24.

rush to "get to the point" it is useful to glimpse our own hastiness as an obstacle to understanding other people and, in fact, our stepping over the religious realities of other human beings.

The notion of *kairos* can help us. *Kairos* is a much simpler matter than might appear from its sometimes heavy use in theological writing. It is an ordinary Greek word, and not restricted to the Greek of the early Christians. The occasional suggestion that it is an exclusive Christian theological possession is a needless obstacle that can be explained only by ignorance in Christian theological circles. I have already set it side by side with a near equivalent in Sanskrit: *samaya*. The fact of a division between the general stream of time and the specific times of observance, celebration, or other enactments is a normal part of human existence. As such, this division is not bound to one culture or one religion, not dependent on one revelation. Wherever we live and move as human beings, we apparently *must* make the differentiation in order to have any hold on our experience of time.

The time of the clock, *chronos* (*kāla* in Sanskrit), is in the first place a matter of our *observation*—no matter what else it is, and in spite of the fact that it may be ultimately revealed as an omnivorous monster. *Kairoi*, *samayāḥ*, specific times with all their variance in different traditions, are principally matters of our *experience*. We can approximate the life spans of ancient Egyptian or Hittite religion by ordinary (sometimes ancient, for us extraordinary) calendars—for in such cases, within certain limits, we are allowed to generalize. When we come to the specific times and celebrations in these religions, our customary manner of dealing with time is of little avail. And yet, here we touch on the very fiber of religion's existence. Religions do not merely *last*, but they have their *moments*. The latter fact must be understood if we want to gain insight into the inner force that carries a religion on and on in the general space of time. How else could we ever begin to imagine, say, the sensation of joy at an Easter celebration in the ancient Church?

To speak of the life spans, births, and deaths of ancient civilizations and their religions is part of scholarship and is based on evidence. And yet, even in such "external" accounts, each date assigned has its uncertain fringes. When did the religion of ancient Egypt "die"? How much of the ancient religion lived on with the Copts, the Coptic Church, and the Egyptians' Islam? How much is not most of the world in debt to the "dead" Neolithic cultures and their religions? Did not the Buddha make use in his teachings of the rich heritage preserved in the ancient language of Hinduism? How could Christianity have existed if Israel had not known of the "Messiah"? Even in our "external" accounts we observe continuity. We can prove its reality by its effects, and serious scholarship does this. We owe to Mircea Eliade a magnificent endeavor to show such persistence in all its complexity, for that is what his *The History of Religious Ideas* is about.[7]

The Significance of the Particular

The problem of persistence in religious traditions demands that we turn to the inner force of a religion, and this means our problem cannot be settled under the heading *chronos*, but we must pay serious attention to *kairos*. And *kairos*, or *samaya*, cannot be qualified in general terms, even though we can understand them as real powers that make persistence possible. The peculiar thing is that for us, human beings, time as duration, as time of the clock and the calendar, is not our experience of time, but a pure abstraction. It is only the specific moments we undergo or celebrate that mark time concretely as *ours*.

One cannot say of *kairos* that it is a "hierophany," for indeed, it hardly ever is something that can be said to manifest the sacred. Consider, for instance, my or some other average Christian's *samaya* on the first day of the week. It is not the crucifixion, and it is not the resurrection of Christ. It is merely a reminder of his death by sacrifice on a cross, and of an empty grave, and I partake of the bread and wine in memory of him. And nevertheless this mere thing in time, this mere experience on my part allows me to understand the Hindu Holi festival or the Tamil New Year, and to comprehend the sense of the procession at a Brahmotsava (a communal celebration in an Indian village) together with the slicing of the coconut when the parade halts before my door. I fully realize that none of these and innumerable other celebrations the world over could take the place of another. Each is *particular*.

Each moment, each feast, each *samaya* or *kairos* is too common an affair, too specific, and too close at hand in its ordinariness to warrant so formal a label as "hierophany," which after all is no less than "manifestation of the sacred"; the intense emotion of some of them does not alter this observation.[8] The time of Easter, or of the *akitu* festival in ancient

---

7. Eliade, *The History of Religious Ideas*.

8. In the wake of Rudolf Otto, and indebted to Paul Tillich, Joachim Wach lists four

Mesopotamia, or of the Holi festival in India, or of our trip to the Statue of Liberty, is part of our human orientation, by which we puzzle each other and recognize each other at the same time. It is a little like our facial features, which have something, but only something to do with the existence of faces in general. We may also think of the unmistakability of our fingerprints or the immediacy of our tone of voice. We can take note of each other's "times," but we cannot trade or equate them.

Some Shiʿite wise man, some Śrīvaiṣṇava pandit, some rabbi, some Christian priest—many a person will recognize the practical rule that must be observed here, and they will each have their own examples. After all, the actuality of confronting and interpreting is not a possession of one tradition. It is an ordinary part of life.

Even the true general statement that every tradition has its *kairoi* bypasses the uniqueness proper to each moment or act in a religion. It is only a beginning, and everyone must use his own word for his "time," and I—as a scholar—must take the freedom to leave my method for interpretation nameless. On the level of scholarly generalizations, it should remain nameless. On the level of religious traditions, *it is each one's particular experience*.

Each *kairos*, each moment of significance commemorated and celebrated anywhere in the world of religions belongs wholly where it is alive. It is the living rootedness of such moments that helps us recognize the drive, the power, the persistence of other traditions. Here is the ultimate reason why crucial terms in a religion's vocabulary cannot be rendered in a neutral jargon, and from there equated with those of another tradition. Unlike noncommittal intellectual equations, this fact about our documents should really enable us to head toward interreligious understanding.

The particulars, the "moments" in religious traditions are not to be confused with "strictly individual experiences," for such an interpretation would put us back in that intellectual provincialism we discussed in the first essay. A sacrament, a *saṃskāra*, each of the deeds done in preparation and celebration of the Sabbath, a Dayak funeral procession, owes its significance exactly to the fact that it is not merely an individual affair; nor does it increase in power or veracity by some investigator's

---

characteristics of religious experience. Among them is "the most intense experience of which man is capable." See Wach, *Types of Religious Experience,* 32–33. Without denying the importance of intensity, I cannot help separate it in our discussion from the particulars that matter within a tradition.

pointing to it as one more example of a general human habit. It is not only more than personal, but also *true*. And precisely for this reason, the moment that gives a religion the power to persist provides also the window through which another tradition can be seen in its actual existence. Understanding cannot proceed without generalizations, of course, but the most important thing to realize is that *understanding cannot go on at all if it does not proceed from the particular*.

Traditions

All this is not unrelated to an insight we should have gained in the aftermath of the Nüremberg trials; it is murderous to generalize about human beings, for when we "block off" human beings into groups as if they formed separate entities, we do not merely misunderstand: we end up by killing. Arriving at a "final solution" mentally is the first step to arriving at it *actually*. In precise analogy, there is no final explanation regarding Confucianism, Shinto, or any of the other ways of the human race. This insight has much in common with the old and well-worn *epoché* ("patience in passing judgment"), an ancient but lasting practical stance, not a difficult philosophical concept so much as an "attitude," of immediate use, owing its existence to its long tradition and its spontaneous occurrence in ordinary circumstances.

Gerardus van der Leeuw suggested that it is not easier to understand our next-door neighbor than some ancient pharaoh. Indeed that is true, and yet we have the windows of our own tradition's *kairoi* for both distant and nearby views. If this still sounds strange, let us conclude with some thoughts that touch on the basics in our discussion.

How can we know we have a tradition? We in fact do not *have* one. It has us. But this is not something to which "educated" people give much thought. Let me remind you that the reason why it is so unnatural for many of us to see our tradition at all is that we associate our intellectual basis of understanding *everything* in the world with whatever science we have learned in high school. And it hardly dawns on us that this basis of understanding everything is very small. It is precisely here that we have to look for the reason why many trained historians have difficulty dealing adequately with religion.

We know that religious symbols have rarely functioned in total isolation. Sooner or later there were contacts with other people, for our existence as human beings and our social nature made our orientation depend on others. Traditions are handed down. Our religious traditions and assumptions are never our inventions. Only when the idea of individualism is born (very recently, not earlier than a few centuries ago), gradually a world of tradition and religion that seemed as natural as vegetation turns into a puzzle for the individual mind.

In most human exchanges the test of religion, of symbols, of myths, is not antagonistic or cruel. In general, people do not draw on religion in order to argue, and they do not talk about truth in order to exclude others. A nice example is found in a tribe in central Flores, in Indonesia; it may well typify a sort of thing that happened to humankind for most of its existence on earth. In the last century, a scientific expedition found to its surprise that in this tribe's mythology the names of the first people were Adang and Ewang.[9] The names were too close to Adam and Eve to be accidental. The incorporation of these first people may have occurred through nothing more than a chance contact with Portuguese traders centuries earlier. For whatever is presented as real, people of course tend to accept and to assign a place in their own tradition. And here we are dealing with *persistence*—which is not just a continuing sameness.

The problem of religious tradition shows a particularly haunting face in our modern existence. Many of us know a feeling of being uninvolved in any religious tradition, and perhaps being embarrassed by religion in general. I do not want to attempt an explanation of the historical causes of this common feeling, beyond pointing out that such "subjectivism" has been with us for a long time, and has in fact shaped philosophical and theological propositions in the West for centuries.[10] The distaste for religious traditions so prevalent among our intellectual contemporaries is one fruit of this subjectivism: something must be *real for me*. That has become part of an uncritically accepted heritage, functioning as an assumption in discussion rather than a topic to be examined.

Let us look more closely at the "embarrassment" about religious traditions, the difficulty in "being involved." The remarkable French thinker

---

9. Arndt, *Mythologie, Religion und Magie im Sikagebiet*, 16, 19, 24, 67.

10. The work by Pannenberg, *Anthropology in Theological Perspective*, though written and translated in rather careless fashion, presents a useful survey of this problem in the introduction. See also essay 1 in this book. Vattimo, *After Christianity* is a very stimulating study for this subject. Far from dismissing religious influences, Vattimo understands the enormous influence of Christianity in history for European consciousness today.

and activist Simone Weil engaged in a struggle that is in some ways a clear presentation of the fix we are in. She grew up in a secularized Jewish family in France, earned a degree in philosophy, participated passionately in the struggles of labor unions, and attempted, in spite of her weak health, to engage in the civil war against Franco in Spain. We see the irruption of the Second World War into her life; she escapes to England, where she refuses to eat more than what her fellow Frenchmen receive with their rations; her health deteriorates, and she dies before Germany is defeated.

Throughout Simone Weil's life, a religious struggle unfolds. And, it seems to me, her life fascinates many a modern despiser of religion because her personal involvement in struggles shows us a person like ourselves, or a person we would like to be compared to. She is a human being of our age, acting, searching without cease, truly engaged in all she does.

She fascinates us because of her hesitations with respect to "established religion." She refused to be baptized—though most of her religious reflections circle around Christianity. What she did seem to meditate on day and night was the human calling to row against the stream of power and greed, and against all ordinary human desires and needs. What shall we call this? Any student of Hinduism recognizes the main features of yoga, and she herself saw the resemblance. She also recognized the model of her quest in the mystery religions, in ancient Egyptian texts, in her beloved Plato, and in Buddhism. She saw continuity, in spite of the jumble of historical facts, and in spite of the disjointedness of present-day existence. The most important thing for the present discussion seems to me this: at the moment she recognizes that peculiar, nearly impossible continuity, which strikes us moderns as not really capable of belonging to reality, she does not repress it, but takes notice of her surprise at *grasping the persistence that is in oneself and still remains something transcendental*. It is something real and truthful, not *merely* her experience.

Our own feelings may be less profound, but from one point of view, Simone Weil seems to sum up the existence of all of us as modern people, educated in ever so advanced and ever so diffuse ways, exposed constantly to innumerable claims to truth. Suspicious as we are of any proposal of unity in human understanding or sense in a given religion, we keep suffering from our thirst for it.

We may add the question, is Simone Weil's objection to baptism all that remote from the attitude of many modern, educated people? I do not think so. If one would care to express it in pop psychologese, Weil might be called a "role model." Her lifelong, conscious occupation with the issue of religion still makes her different, but it is a difference only in degree of intensity; something is genuine in our recognition of her as an emblem.

The aloofness to any religion in particular, the hesitancy to "commit" oneself is worth considering. Simone Weil had a certain disregard for Judaism (the tradition of her birth); she could not bring herself to embrace Christianity (which was closest to her); and she reached out toward Buddhism, Platonism, and elsewhere. Today we have journals in the Western countries that focus on esoteric customs of Tibetans, or the wisdom of Taoism, but avoid Christianity and Judaism. (Let it be noted that those journals would not touch on religion in its relationship to politics with a ten-foot pole, and this fact points to a more than superficial difference from Weil.)

In our time, alienation from one's own tradition seems firmly established among some as a standard feature of growing up and reaching adulthood. Teaching historians of religions cannot fail to notice it, because their students bring it to their attention so frequently; it is not unusual to meet college students with common Anglo-Saxon or European names who have nothing come into their minds with terms such as "Eucharist" or "Holy Communion." Moreover, slightly more technical, but even more surprising, it is common to meet colleagues who lecture on Western civilization for whom Calvin's "predestination" is an equivalent of philosophical determinism. At the same time, these students and intellectuals may be steeped in the *Tibetan Book of the Dead*, or give you details on the practices of whirling dervishes. Such knowledge-cum-ignorance typifies the modern alienation from religious roots.

I am not mocking anyone's knowledge of esoteric religious phenomena, but surely there is room to interrogate the aloofness from our own heritage. Some of us, who know our aloofness, can have helpful moments of irony; perhaps a realization of the comical with respect to vast cultural distances between ourselves and what we think we know and the inner kinships we fancy. Might some of us even conclude, if only between these pages and ourselves, that aloofness from our own religion cannot be the last word?

As a method of understanding, denial fails. The reality of persistence is there before us in the evidence we have and does not allow some private denial. In the end, the persistence of religion is a stream that moves on, no matter what we think we are doing.

Superficial contemporary despisers of religion who nevertheless flaunt their "knowledge" on the subject are tangentially related to serious opponents of established religion. The prime example, Nietzsche, has been omitted from the present discussion. His attacks are aimed at the heart of Christian theology, and are certainly not repetitions of majority or fashionable opinion. Also, he would require a metaphysical discussion rather than a merely "methodological" one. Perhaps it is not altogether right even to bring in Simone Weil, for no one who has gone through danger and hardship should easily be connected to popular intellectualisms. (Yet one cannot resist speaking of Weil, and looking to her as an exemplar of our "alienated" intellectuals.)

I am not suggesting that our common contemporary experience of distance is devoid of sense, in spite of its deficiencies. Somehow, it is still tied to the great models of the past. We can briefly look at some very different, and seemingly faraway, examples of "alienation"; but conscious, well-considered, and instructive ones, available to us in indubitably religious documents.

We can examine a statement from Saint Augustine (even Wittgenstein took the trouble at times to reflect on some statement from Saint Augustine,[11] and surely every intellectual, alienated or not, can refer unblushingly to Wittgenstein). In *De vera religione* (vi.11), Augustine writes about the need for a possible distance from the church, a willful alienation that may be called for: "Often, too, divine providence permits even good men to be driven from the congregation of Christ by the turbulent seditions of carnal men. When for the sake of the peace of the Church they patiently endure that insult or injury, and attempt no novelties in the way of heresy or schism, they will teach men how God is to be served with a true disposition and with great and sincere charity."[12]

Distancing oneself varies with traditions and circumstances, of course, but let us bear in mind that Augustine stresses "true disposition." Likewise, whether successfully or not, our modern habits do not intend deceit, but honesty.

We can surmise that Nāgārjuna, the Indian monk who revolutionized Buddhist philosophy, did not seal his acceptance in the Buddhist community squarely and instantaneously by writing his *Mūlamādhyamikakārikā*. Over the centuries, his little treatise has never

---

11. See Wittgenstein, *Philosophical Investigations*, 3.
12. Augustine, *Of True Religion*, 12.

ceased to stir the mind, because of the force of his meditations. As a result, he has been given the honorific title of "the second one who set the wheel of dharma in motion." The second one after the Buddha is certainly not a negligible place! We are ignorant about Nāgārjuna's life, but—even if he was not an obscure figure in his own time—it is indeed difficult to imagine that his immediate surroundings had a full appreciation of him. One of his surprising, indeed revolutionary, teachings concerns the identical nature of *saṃsāra* and *nirvāṇa*, which is the ultimate state of liberation—hence freedom from *saṃsāra*. Yet, for Nāgārjuna, proper meditation would reveal the sameness of the two. Nāgājuna's meditative discoveries must surely have "put some distance" between him and his surroundings. Exactly how this "distance" manifested itself, how it presented itself—to him, to the others—we cannot really imagine anymore. But if some aloofness or acceptance of aloofness can be deemed necessary in "phenomena" like Augustine and Nāgārjuna, then the present distance between some of us and our own traditions can hardly be considered unbearable.

We should always refrain from hasty pronouncements about the condition religion is in. There is no hard evidence for any final judgment on the "mood" of our time, which has witnessed lives such as that of Simone Weil. Who is to say that her aloofness itself was not religious? And who can offer proof that the general mood of aloofness with respect to organized, established religious tradition is nonreligious? Distaste for traditional forms is nothing new in the history of persistence in religions.

Although the history of religions is not the history of intellectual ideas, one of its tasks is to see ideas in perspective, and that means subjecting to critical review the ideas that our time swallows whole. Common biases such as disdain for "the religious establishment" should not be mistaken for signs of a destructive process of secularization. Secularization processes do occur, but they look different, and will occupy us later.

3

Secularization and Sanctification: Euhemerism

Secularizations

The very first statement to be made about "secularization" is that it is not all one thing. We cannot restrict ourselves to the singular "secularization"; we must use the plural "secularizations" as well, just as in the case of the singular "religion," which leads the discussion almost at once to the plural of "religions." We know that we must distinguish between our general concept for the process of symbolizing that we call religion, and the many existing traditions themselves. Likewise, "secularization" is an abstract denotation that covers a multitude of different phenomena.

What we think of when we say "secularization" might as well be called "desymbolization," exactly because it is the reverse of symbolization. "Secularization" could be considered the general process of loss in religious meanings, just as "religion" is the general process of singling out and imbuing with meaning certain things. We can recognize traditions by the fact that they hold certain acts, words, or places as totally distinct from others. Analogously, we speak of "secularization" because we are familiar with the loss of such distinctions.

We can hardly overemphasize that "secularization" is an abstract concept. It does not constitute a law that helps us explain anything. At most, it introduces a subject that—like religion—requires inquiry. It refers to a wide variety of changes that occur in history.

The loss of sacredness is as specifically tradition-bound as religion itself. Things that were at one time singled out as "real reality" (Eliade's term) lose their extraordinary quality. "Secularization" is spoken of as a thing-in-general in our popular discussions, but it does not take on meaning until we focus on specific traditions and compare them. As in all religiohistorical research, comparison is required for understanding.

In what follows, we will try to show a continuous intertwining of symbolizing and secularizing tendencies in various times and places. Surprises abound, for religious traditions at their core are not dogmatic and not unchanging.

First, there is a "surprise" that should not surprise us at this point in our essays. Secularization is not a recent, not a modern process at all. Precisely to the extent all sorts of things can be made sacred in the course of history—to that same extent do things lose their sacredness as well. Religions are always changing; this is, as we have seen, the nature of tradition. *Tradere*, the word basic to the term "tradition," is an active verb, meaning "to pass on," "to hand down." It is always an activity of communication between people, and in each instance, of a human being appropriating what is given to him or her. Furthermore, the act of appropriating is not mere copying, but an event that is as open toward reinterpretation as the minds of human individuals themselves.

Thus secularization, if properly understood, is attestable much earlier than the assumptions of our present culture would imply. An early and certainly most illuminating example is the phenomenon known as euhemerism.

Euhemerism

"Euhemerism" is the term that is used for a certain way of reading and explaining myths. The name of the procedure is taken from the name of Euhemerus (ca. 340–260 B.C.), a Greek writer of rather fanciful tales. The method that became attached to his name—suggesting perhaps a bit too easily that he invented it—can be summed up in two words: historization and humanization. Myths are understood as if the narrated events really happened, and as if the actors were originally really human beings.

Our knowledge of Euhemerus himself is scanty. A complete scholarly collection amounts to barely more than three pages and all of it is indirect.[1] The most important fragment of his work, or rather, the most unmistakable rendition, we owe to the early Church historian Eusebius (ca. A.D. 300), who in turn owed his information to the historian Diodorus (first century B.C.), who quoted Euhemerus. Although we have much of Diodorus' great compilation of history, book 6, where he begins to speak explicitly about Euhemerus, is among the lost books, and hence we cannot get any closer to Euhemerus than by way of this incomplete chain of references.

What we can gather from our meager sources is nevertheless quite interesting. Euhemerus created a romance, and we can sense the flavor of its popularity. The protagonist, presumably himself, traveled once to some islands in the East, where he visited a people named the Panchaeans. Euhemerus would have us believe—assuming, as is generally done, that this information given elsewhere by Diodorus also comes from Euhemerus—that from one of these islands, at least from a promontory on it, India could be seen, "misty, because of its great distance."[2] On the principal island stood a temple of Zeus: Zeus Triphylios, to be exact. And, climactically, Zeus himself caused inscriptions to be made on a golden pillar in this temple. The inscriptions recorded his own deeds, those of his father Kronos, and of his grandfather Ouranos. Zeus, like his father and grandfather before him, was king of the inhabited earth. And like his forebears, the narration tells us, he had divinity bestowed upon him because of the great tasks he undertook for mankind. Panchaea, the island itself, is described as sublime in all respects, and we are told particularly that a city on the island, Panara by name, enjoyed remarkable felicity. This wonderful felicity should be noted, for it is a regular feature in traditional euhemeristic accounts.

The nucleus of the "interpretation" of Euhemerus is simply that the gods at one time were human beings, and that they came to be worshiped because of their acts on behalf of men. Admittedly, as a scholarly theory on the origin of myth Euhemerus' romance is hardly worth considering, but the reason why a specific method of interpretation associated with his name became persistent and still has much to show us was perhaps precisely that he wrote not a learned treatise but something with wide appeal.

---

1. See the texts of ancient authors concerning Euhemerus in Jacoby, *Die Fragmente der griechischen Historiker,* 300–313.

2. Diodorus, *Diodorus of Sicily* 5.42 (p. 215).

From the point of view of a historian of religions there are several reasons why euhemerism deserves serious attention. The most conspicuous point of interest is its tenacity in intellectual circles in the West; unabated, it flourished throughout the rise and spread of Christianity, the Middle Ages, and the Renaissance, still survived in eighteenth-century scholarship, and lingered even in the nineteenth century. Furthermore, a number of documents that inform us on Indo-European mythology are euhemeristic; our fragments concerning Euhemerus are part of this group. It is necessary to understand euhemerism itself to make proper use of such documents. Finally, most important for our present inquiry is the very particular secularizing tendency of the tenacious theory to which Euhemerus' name is attached.

The Euhemerizing Mentality

We have every reason to believe that the ideas Euhemerus promoted in his romance were not original, even if he gave them their most popular expression. Two centuries before Euhemerus, another Greek, the philosopher Xenophanes of Colophon, spoke words that testify to the occurrence of more or less "euhemeristic" tendencies even then. What Xenophanes said has been quoted many times since:

> But the mortals think that the gods are born and dress, speak, and look just like they themselves do . . .[3]

> The Ethiopians imagine that their gods are black and have snub noses, but the Tracians think of their gods as blue-eyed and having red hair . . .[4]

> If cows, horses and lions had hands and could use them to paint and make artifacts, as people do, then the horses would paint divine images like horses, the cows like cows; they would create images appearing like themselves.[5]

Xenophanes does not speak with the irony of a modern demythologizer. Another of his fragments asserts: "[There is] only one single God,

---

3. Diels, *Die Fragmente der Vorsokratiker*, frag. 14 (my trans.).
4. Ibid., frag. 16 (my trans.).
5. Ibid., frag. 15 (my trans.).

SECULARIZATION AND SANCTIFICATION: EUHEMERISM

the supreme one among gods and people, unlike the mortals both in appearance and in thought."[6]

In this context, we may think of Aristotle (384–322 B.C.), an older contemporary of Euhemerus. Aristotle would hardly pass as an adherent of traditional religion. There are parts of his work that compare with some of the fragments of Xenophanes. For instance, he observes, "[people] say that the gods have a king, because they themselves either are or were in ancient times under the rule of a king. For they imagine not only the forms of the gods, but their ways of life to be like their own"(*Politics*, 1252b, 24–25).[7]

Nevertheless, this same Aristotle is explicit with respect to his concern for *real* religion, as when he speaks of the paramount importance of perpetual, regular motion. This he finds in the cyclical course of the heavenly bodies, as he tells in *De Caelo* (e.g., 285a29, 292a20, 292b1). He makes corresponding statements in his *Metaphysics* (see 1074a30). According to Aristotle, we must make a distinction between popular conceptions and the true nature of the heavens. Aristotle speaks of the celestial bodies as "divine" (*theios*) [*Metaphysics* 1074a30]. This passage expresses his conviction:

> A tradition has been handed down by the ancient thinkers of very early times, and bequeathed to posterity in the form of a myth, to the effect that these heavenly bodies are gods, and that the Divine pervades the whole of nature. The rest of their tradition has been added later in a mythological form to influence the vulgar and as a constitutional and utilitarian expedient; they say that these gods are human in shape or are like certain other animals, and make other statements consequent upon and similar to those we have mentioned. Now if we separate these statements and if we accept only the first, that they supposed the primary substance to be gods, we must regard it as an inspired saying; and reflect that whereas every art and philosophy has probably been repeatedly developed to the utmost and has perished again, these beliefs of theirs have been preserved as a relic of former knowledge. To this extent only, then, are the views of our forefathers and of the earliest thinkers intelligible to us. (*Metaphysics* 1074b1–14)[8]

---

6. Ibid., frag. 23 (my trans.).
7. Aristotle, *Politics*, 555.
8. Aristotle, *Metaphysics: Books X–XIV*, 163.

The outlook Aristotle defines here had become widespread in Greece. In the context in which Diodorus quoted Euhemerus a distinction is made that is almost identical to Aristotle's. Certain of the gods are said to be eternal and imperishable. It is interesting to note that Diodorus expressly mentions that the ancients have always known this. Such gods, he says, are for instance, "the sun and the moon and the other stars of the heavens."[9] And he adds that "for each of these the genesis and duration are from everlasting to everlasting."[10]

The argument that the ancient tradition supported the greater divinity of one type of deity over the other, and that the divinity of the celestial bodies was the most ancient and everlasting would not stand up to any modern historical or anthropological inquiry into ancient Greek thought. For Diodorus, however, as for Aristotle, this evaluation was beyond dispute. Distinctions of the sort Diodorus and Aristotle made must have been an ordinary part of Euhemerus' world of ideas, accepted without question in intellectual circles.[11] They formed part of the world in which Euhemerus was alive and to which he reacted.

We learn from Diodorus that Euhemerus' theory deals only with the sort of deity accepted by the multitude, and it is worth mentioning too that Diodorus, and presumably also Euhemerus, makes reference to a commonly held tradition: "But the other gods, *we are told*, were terrestrial beings who attained to immortal honor and fame because of their benefactions to mankind."[12] This is the group to which Zeus belongs, and the other deities who play a role in Euhemerus' story.

Yet the critique by Xenophanes and Aristotle on vulgar notions concerning the gods is somehow not shared by Euhemerus. Whatever moved him in writing his story was conservative of the deities of the multitude. His distinction between gods and divinized human beings, as recorded in the text of Diodorus, is not radical at all, and is in harmony with one indubitable certainty we have concerning Euhemerus: he attributes the divinization of some special people in a particularly positive way to the value of their exploits for mankind.

Finally, let us note that Euhemerus' treatment of the gods could not have been offensive, for the simple reason that the Greek gods are unlike

---

9. Diodorus, *Diodorus of Sicily*, "Fragmenta Libri VI," 1.2. (p. 331).
10. Ibid.
11. As shown by Schippers, *Euhemeristische godencritiek*, esp. 22–23.
12. Diodorus, *Diodorus of Sicily*, 331 (italics added).

the God of the Old and New Testaments in that the sacred traditions of the Greeks were given in the form of stories in which the gods consorted with people and in many ways behaved like them.[13]

Euhemerismus Inversus

The model attributed to Euhemerus changed considerably under the impact of Christianity. While Christianity was growing in strength, many quarters of imperial Rome also saw the spread of new multiform religious cults and ideas, and not in the last place demonologies.[14] More and more the pagan gods were seen and explained as humans elevated not because of their benefactions and virtue but through their tremendous immorality. Indeed they were demonic. Furthermore, according to biblically oriented lines of thought, their divinization was in and of itself a sinful affair.

Consequently, a type of theorizing became customary that at first sight appears hardly worthy to be called euhemerism. We shall have no difficulty identifying it, although we lack an exact term for it. We may call it a *euhemerismus inversus*, an upside-down or improper euhemerism.

Our word *inversus* implies that this euhemerism with a new twist is directed toward the opposite sense from before. Yet, as we shall see, it is perhaps even more ambivalent than it is inverted; the ambivalence, touching superhuman divinity and base humanity at the same time, shows a feature that we know so well from mythology: *les extrêmes se touchent*. Nicholas of Cusa's expression *coincidentia oppositorum*, the coincidence of opposites, was brought into the scholarly discussion by Eliade as a technical term for this characteristic feature in religious symbolism. (An understanding of improper euhemerism should be embarked upon by first recalling the difficulty we have in assessing Euhemerus' own intentions. We do not know enough about him or the spirit of his time to know, for instance, whether irony played a role in his romance.)[15]

---

13. Rightly, this point has been stressed by Brown, "Euhemerus and the Historians," 263.

14. Bayet, *Histoire politique*, 255–66. For a very different account, though equally revelatory of Roman religious complexity, see Dumézil, "Ideological Innovations."

15. The diversity in scholarly interpretations of Euhemerus' intentions is rather baffling. An elaborate discussion is given in Susemihl, *Geschichte der griechischen Literatur*, 316–22. Susemihl sees Euhemerus as one depicting to some extent his own ideals (318), but he also reproaches Euhemerus for *Plattheit* (vulgarity) (319), follows

We find in the Wisdom of Solomon (ca. 80 B.C.), an apocryphal book written in Greek that formed part of the Septuagint, a passage that clearly condemns the divinization of human beings and contemptuously attributes it to human need for consolation:

> For a father afflicted by untimely grief made a likeness of his child that had been quickly taken from him, and presently honored as a god him who was once a dead man, and handed down to his subjects mysteries and rites. Then the ungodly practice, strengthened by time, came to be observed as law, and by the order of monarchs carved images were worshipped. And when men could not honor them in their presence because they lived far away, they imagined how they looked, far away, and made a visible image of the king they honored, so as by their zeal to flatter the absent one as though he were present.[16]

Ideas like these, nourished by the biblical tradition spreading in the process of European Christianization, helped form a matrix for improper euhemerism. The oracular writings known as the Sibylline Books,

---

in the scholarly tradition of classifying Euhemerus in more or less the same category as Lucian and Voltaire (320), and concludes by saying: *thatsächlich war er ohne Zweifel ein unbedingter Atheist und ward dann auch vielfach als ein solcher angesehen* (the person was without a doubt an atheist, and was seen as such) (322). To add to the riddle of Euhemerus' intentions, cf. Pohlmann, *Geschichte der sozialen Frage*, 293–305. For Dörrie, *Der Königskult*, 218–24, Euhemerus' romance supports an ideology enabling kings to enhance their political prestige. In fact, Euhemerus becomes much like a blueprint for apotheosis. Granted that "divine kingship" in late antiquity, beginning with Alexander, is a problem for scholars, Dörrie—like those who summarily see in Euhemerus some modern blasphemer or atheist—ignores the subject of existing traditions that made the very process of divinization possible and acceptable. Vallauri, *Evemero di Messena* and *Origine e diffusione*, is very important in this context, because she addresses herself in the first essay precisely to the question of what Euhemerus himself might have had in mind. Her writings are also noteworthy because of the scrupulous textual references. But this author, too, is mesmerized by sociopolitical views. There is little consideration for the fact that Euhemerus *told a story*. Euhemerus' text becomes the crystallization of a sociopolitical ideology, accelerating a process of religious decay (see especially *Evemero di Messena*, 23). All these diverse explanations of Euhemerus—personal crudeness, atheism, antireligious irony, utopianism, commitment to one political ideology—have in common that they intend to take away the strangeness of the data by substituting something familiar to the modern author. In Eliade, *The Encyclopedia of Religion*, Euhemerus and euhemerism do not have their own entry but receive brief treatments under "Animism and Animatism" and under "Manism"; some other articles that touch on the subject perpetuate the misconceptions and inadequacies mentioned.

16. Wis 14:15–17, in Smith and Goodspeed, trans., *The Complete Bible*.

important in late antiquity,[17] show us in the third book a euhemeristic narration of a motif in Greek religion whereby euhemerism is used to show the inferiority of paganism.[18] Euhemerizations fostered by the biblical tradition occur frequently in the church fathers and the medieval bishops.[19]

By the fourth century A.D., biblically inspired euhemerism had become so widespread that Saint Augustine devoted some lengthy expositions to it. The general acceptance of euhemeristic ideas in intellectual circles of the time, whether inside or outside the church, compelled him to discuss the honor paid to Christian martyrs in order to differentiate such worship from paganism. Augustine assumes the validity of euhemeristic derivations applied to pagan customs and to Greek and Roman deities. (In some passages he shows himself familiar with the name of Euhemerus.) In *The City of God* (8.26) he writes:

> ... with such blindness do impious men, as it were, stumble over mountains, and will not see the things which strike their own eyes, that they do not attend to the fact that in all the literature of the pagan there are not found any, or scarcely any gods, who have not been men to whom, when dead, divine honours have been paid.[20]

Augustine concludes the same section with a passage that clearly shows the amalgamation with the demonic to which original euhemerism had become subject:

> It was the grief of the demons which was expressing itself though his [Hermes Trismegistus'] mouth, who were sorrowing on account of the punishments which were about to fall upon them at the tombs of the martyrs. For in many such places they were tortured and compelled to confess, and were cast out of the bodies of men, of which they had taken possession.[21]

Considering the gathering strength of Christianity and of its intellectual protagonists (soon joined by political rulers), it is astonishing that euhemerizations could continue to flourish that were not totally

---

17. For a convenient historical survey, see Momigliano, "Sibylline Oracles," 305–8.
18. Nilsson, *Geschichte der griechischen Religion*, 2:112.
19. Schippers, *De ontwikkeling der Euhemeristische godencritiek* on Cyprian, 84, 85, and passim.
20. Augustine, *The City of God*, 348.
21. Ibid., 350.

improper and that could serve as real vehicles for mythical motifs—for example, as we will see, in Saxo Grammaticus. It would seem as if this use of the negative potential of euhemerism provided a framework within which a "proper" euhemeristic construction could go on, preserving the mythological material rather than divesting it of its inner power.

Euhemerism's Power of Preservation

The Christian apologist Lactantius (fourth century A.D.) is one of our sources for Euhemerus; he does not quote Euhemerus but provides a little treatise on him,[22] and even this eloquent and militant Christian avows that Jupiter, in the way he went about constituting his own worship, was very clever indeed.[23] J. W. Schippers, in discussing this passage, adds a footnote to the effect that actually Euhemerus rather than Jupiter should have been called the clever one.[24] It is revealing that Lactantius did not look at it that way and apparently saw in Euhemerus an authoritative interpreter. Lactantius finds no reason at all to label the very figure of Jupiter a figment of the imagination. Precisely here, in an unexpected corner of Christian apologetics, we catch a glimpse of euhemerism's power to preserve.

Even though it is difficult to establish Euhemerus' full psychological attitude, we realize he did not sneer at the gods. It is interesting to notice the way in which Diodorus (in book 5) speaks of the gods in the fabulous land of Panchaea (in all likelihood drawing on Euhemerus). In 5.45 he renders the local tradition concerning Ouranos. The relationship of Ouranos to the sky, of course well established in traditional lore, is perfectly preserved under the new euhemeristic garb. There is a mountain, says Diodorus, made sacred to the gods and called "throne of Ouranos" (*Ouranou diphros*): "For the myth relates that in ancient times, when Ouranos was king of the inhabited earth, he took pleasure in tarrying in that place and in surveying from its lofty top both the heavens and the stars therein."[25]

---

22. Schippers, *De ontwikkeling der Euhemeristische godencritiek*, 19–25.

23. "Quod ille astutissime excogitavit, ut et sibi honorem divinum et hospitibus suis perpetuum nomen adquireret cum religione coniunctum" (Jacoby, *Die Fragmente der griechischen Historiker*, 312).

24. Schippers, *De ontwikkeling der Euhemeristische godencritiek* 22, frag. 2.

25. Diodorus, *Diodorus of Sicily* 5.44.6 (p. 221).

Apparently the narrative traditions were simply too strong to allow either Diodorus or his sources to transfer Ouranos into the realm of everlasting deities—in spite of the fact that the very name of Ouranos, meaning "heaven," and the fashionable fascination among intellectuals for the heavens might have seemed conducive to exactly that. Rather, Ouranos is presented humanly—although not *just* humanly but as some ancient king-astronomer. Thus a theme constitutive of the Ouranos myth is preserved. The fragments of book 6 complete the image of Ouranos, with explicit reference to Euhemerus, by recounting "that Ouranos was the first to be king, that he was an honorable [*epieikes*] man and beneficent [*euergetikos*], who was versed in the movements of the stars, and that he was also the first to honour the gods of the heavens with sacrifices, whence he was called Ouranos or Heaven."[26]

Clearly the words "historization" and "humanization," which we used to define the euhemeristic procedure, must be employed with care, keeping in mind that the euhemeristic documents and language do not express a reduction to *mere* human aspect, even though the temper of our own time has its inclination to think of man as *mere* man. Ouranos' primary kingship, his knowledge of the stars, and his institution of sacrificial ceremonies for the gods of the heavens give Euhemerus' account itself the flavor of a *myth of origins*.

Comparable traits of a positive rendering of ancient mythological tradition can be pointed out in later Western texts. Not only were certain themes of myths preserved, but we can see evidence of this positive attitude itself, in spite of the increased concern with demons of pagan genesis, and in spite of changes brought about by Saint Augustine, Lactantius, and other members of the Christian intellectual elite.

Eloquent examples of the positive evaluation and preservation of paganism are given with an inner contradiction we come upon in Saxo Grammaticus (ca. 1200) and his younger contemporary Snorri Sturluson (1179-1241). On the one hand, the traditional gods are not gods according to these Christian historians. But on the other hand these very same authors simply cannot be silent about their divinity. The result is wonderful euhemeristic narration.

In the first book of Saxo's *Danish History* a curious passage occurs about the Norse god Odin, much like an interlude in the historical account. It begins: "At this time there was one Odin, who was credited all

---

26. Ibid., 6.1.8. (p. 335).

over Europe with the honour, *which was false*, of godhead [*falso divinitatis titulo censeretur*]."²⁷ This introduction would hardly seem to set the tone for a sympathetic exposition, and the next couple of pages strengthen that impression. But one soon begins to wonder about the astonishing abilities of this "false" godhead. The kings of the North are eager to worship Odin, and, much to his pleasure, they make a golden image in his likeness. Then Frigga, Odin's wife, enters the story. She has the image stripped by smiths, to use the gold herself. Odin hangs the smiths, and then Saxo tells us that he "mounted the statue upon a pedestal, which by the marvelous skill of his art he made to speak when a mortal touched it."²⁸ This fabulous magic of Odin as reported does not appear in conflict with Saxo's personal misgivings. (Perhaps more accurately we might speak of Saxo's official Christian misgivings.) Saxo elaborates on Frigga's low morals and greed; Frigga goes so far as to submit herself to "the embrace of one of her servants," and she breaks the image of her husband. And Saxo sighs, ". . . but what should I here add, save that such a godhead was worthy of such a wife?"²⁹ Nonetheless, Odin is not depicted as without a sense of honor. Filled with shame, he goes into exile. In his absence, another person, Mit-Othin, "famous for his juggling tricks . . . was likewise quickened, as though by inspiration from on high, to seize the opportunity of feigning to be a god."³⁰ The period of Mit-Othin's reign is portrayed as catastrophic. He upsets the cultic practices and must finally flee to Finland, where he is slain. So uncanny is his evil power that even his death does not put an end to the misery he brought over the land: ". . . he spread such pestilence that he seemed almost to leave a filthier record in his death than in his life."³¹

After this episode of Mit-Othin, Saxo exhibits a curious change of tone as he concludes the story, narrating the return of Odin, which becomes possible after Frigga's death:

> The death of Odin's wife revived the ancient splendor of his name, and seemed to wipe out the disgrace upon *his deity* [*coniugis fato pristinae claritatis opinione recuperata ac veluti expiata divinitatis infamia*], so, returning from exile, he forced

27. Text in Olrik and Raeder, *Saxonis Gesta Danorum* (1.7.1). Translation in Elton, *Nine Books of the Danish History*, 110 (italics added).

28. Ibid.

29. Ibid.

30. Ibid., 1.7.2. (p. 111).

31. Ibid.

all those who had used his absence to assume the honors of divine rank to resign them as usurped; and the gangs of sorcerers that had arisen he scattered like darkness before the advancing glory of *his godhead* [*superveniente numinis sui fulgore*]. And he forced them by his power not only to lay down their divinity, but further he made them quit the country, deeming that they, who tried to foist themselves so iniquitously into the skies, ought to be outcasts from the earth.[32]

One wonders about this ending. It suggests that after all Odin was not "foisting" himself "into the skies" like the others. And certainly in the Latin in which Saxo so solemnly wrought his history the references to Odin's divinity could not be a slip of the pen.

The only sensible conclusion we can reach is that the inner contradiction that strikes us did not disturb Saxo. And why should this surprise us? What we observe as ambivalence had not yet appeared in Saxo's twelfth and thirteenth centuries. His "sense of history" was different from ours. It allowed him to include a story like this one in his historical narrative. The Christian teachings would still need centuries to filter into the lives of communities and would go through their own transformations. The idea that Odin and other pre-Christian deities were "nonexistent" would not become possible in a general conversation until the nineteenth century.

It may be useful here to remember that the telling of history is always typified by *change*. With respect to our own sense of history, it may be pointed out that we must wait for a nineteenth-century German scholar, Leopold von Ranke (1795–1886), to be told that the work of a historian is to find *wie es eigentlich gewesen*, "what really happened," and even then Ranke did not mean this in that neutral or pallid sense in which we generally hear it repeated; in the century and a half since Ranke, considerable further changes have occurred in our thought. Still, Ranke has been called "the incarnation of historical sense,"[33] and probably typifies us collectively as modern people. It is essential for our understanding of medieval writers to remind ourselves how recent our own consciousness of history is. Glib pronouncement about "primitive ideas" would have been inconceivable in earlier centuries of our civilization.

The euhemerizations of Saxo Grammaticus must not be taken as cut-and-dried explanations of myths. That systematic notion is of much

32. Ibid., 1.7.3 and 1.7.4 (p. 112; italics added).
33. Wach, *Das Verstehen*, 89.

later date. When we speak of Saxo's euhemerism we should understand it in a disconcertingly less didactic way: as a broad popular and intellectual movement in which storytelling *meant* something. It was not a matter of elaborating on one sweeping causal explanation, but a matter of recording what had already been experienced in previous narrations.

The works of Snorri Sturluson have greater artistic balance than Saxo's and show the function of traditional euhemerism as an agent of preservation quite clearly. Snorri's narratives are also much more widely known. The "inner contradictions" of his euhemerizations form a window through which we can view the sense of a world very different from our own in its dealing with ancient religious materials.

The prologue of Snorri Sturluson's work, the *Prose Edda*, has the god Thor traveling north from ancient Troy, making a deep impression wherever he passes. The narration gradually fills with the Norse pantheon, and it is as if Snorri applies a most "orthodox" euhemerism, making use—like Euhemerus in the case of Ouranos—of striking etymologies. Thor, of course, is of royal descent. He is the son of a king in the area of Troy. His mother was a daughter of the Trojan king Priam himself. Priam, we are told, was called Tróán, and Thor's original name was Trór. Thor's character is in no way changed in the euhemerizing process. At the age of twelve he has attained his brutal strength, kills the foster parents to whom he was entrusted, and afterwards on his journeys through the world kills berserkers, giants, and wild beasts left and right. Among his descendants is Odin, who with his wife Frigga likewise travels north and finally settles in Sweden. Odin and his companions bring blessings wherever they go. People call them Aesir, which, Snorri assures us, meant "men of Asia."

> Their travels were attended by such prosperity that wherever they stayed in a country, that region enjoyed good harvests and peace, and everyone believed that they caused this, since the native inhabitants had never seen any other people like them for good looks and intelligence.[34]

(This state of felicity, as we mentioned earlier, is often found in euhemeristic accounts.)

Was Odin, were the gods, really human or were they really divine? The text does not raise such a question. It is *our* question, and perhaps not a very good one. If we ask Snorri's text and insist on an answer, the

---

34. Young, trans., *The Prose Edda of Snorri Sturluson*, 27.

cumulative thematic evidence points to mythical structures and not to a theory of historical facts:

> Odin, and also his wife, had the gift of prophecy, and by means of this magic art he discovered that his name would be famous in the northern part of the world and honoured above that of all kings. For this reason he set out on a journey from Turkey.[35]

The very beginning of this particular passage is revealing, for Snorri underlines that the place where Troy is situated, "where what we call Turkey lies," is "near the center of the world."[36] It could not be put more mythologically.

In Snorri's time, great changes had taken place with the Christianization of the world. Yet there is no explaining away of the ancient gods. The actuality of life that must be dealt with by the writer is first and foremost the confluence of fundamental orientations that are each too powerful to be pushed aside. As a result we find a great concern for relating the traditions in the midst of which Snorri as a man of his time had to orient himself. This implies a mythological integration, and the means for it was the narrative. Snorri's way continues what Euhemerus did almost a thousand years earlier. Something strange to our "modern" historical consciousness is that such narrative integration did not merely have a popular appeal but was a major intellectual understanding. And not a single abstraction or intellectual conceptualization as to what constitutes "divinity" passes Snorri's lips.

It is well known that the history of Troy was a constant inspiration for medieval poetic historians, not least in the time of Snorri (e.g., the poet Jacob van Maerlant in the Low Countries). And as if linking up Norse and classical traditions were not enough, Snorri's endeavors at integration are prefaced by a summary account of the biblical creation story and the story of Adam and Eve.

The euhemerism of a Snorri is a powerful mythological tool. The "ambiguity" that first struck us is our misapprehension of a crucial mythologic characteristic that makes it possible to *relate* where later generations would insist on a dogmatic choice, and where still later generations of philological and social science scholarship saw only decay of sacred traditions.

---

35. Ibid., 26.
36. Ibid., 25.

Thus there is indeed reason for not being hasty in separating a "proper" from an "improper" euhemerism. Rather, we should speak of a double edge to euhemerizing narratives. This double edge is built into euhemerism from the beginning, even though it was brought to the fore in Western history only through the spread of Christianity. Thus we are always dealing with the same power to preserve old themes in a new encounter of traditions, each of which is irrefutably valid, thereby providing a still valid and all-encompassing perspective of the *real* world.

Popular Secularizations as Religious Structures

Euhemeristic historizations, created with greater or lesser artistic finesse, show themselves to be a specific religious structure of noteworthy *popular* appeal. These euhemeristic narrations relate to other popular historicizing efforts of their time. We know of humanizing and devout descriptions of the life of the Lord, especially in Christmas songs, and of Mary legends with miraculous and almost romantic details. A couple of lines in a traditional Dutch song about the Lord's childhood go:

> He ate porridge from a bowl; he did not mess himself.
> He fell on the ground, and he did not get bruised.[37]

These historicizing and humanizing documents should be considered religious structures as worthy of attention as any other. Dismissive labels like "pseudohistory" found in our scholarly tradition are misguided. Narration—the stories that at first sight might seem to do nothing but drag the gods down to a human level—occurs as *a vehicle of the sacred*.

Euhemerism Later

Later euhemerism turns the focus ever more on the *human* aspect. In the course of time euhemerizations such as those of Saint Augustine come to be seen as not even human enough—for early Christians saw the human origin of the pagan gods primarily as sinful and demonic, and the closer

---

37. The Dutch original runs:
    't At pap uit een pannetje, 't en maakt hem niet vuil,
    't Viel op de aarde, 't en had er geen buil . . .
This type of literature, in the form it was given in the Netherlands in the Middle Ages, has been described by van der Zeyde, "De letterkunde in de Lage Landen."

SECULARIZATION AND SANCTIFICATION: EUHEMERISM 51

we get to our own time, the less intellectually acceptable the notion of the demonic becomes. Only "the human" remains, and Euhemerus comes to be viewed on that narrow basis. The "demonic" falls by the wayside as a mere distortion by people who did not know what human reality entailed. And then too, the "sacred" becomes less intellectually accepted. Euhemerus becomes a skeptic, a cynic, and a secularist: an early modern man.

The mere human-ness to which later scholars reduced much of religion comprised all the mental functions those scholars associated with human beings. Moreover, those scholars deemed the mental functions of all people everywhere to be within the scope of their own comprehension. Thus they arrived at new certainties about religion different from those of any earlier euhemerizers. They sought to find, and became confident that they knew, how religion *really came about*.

The watershed between early and later euhemerism is the Enlightenment period.[38] "Early euhemerism" is still practiced; transitional forms abound; and what we allow ourselves to call "later euhemerization" becomes a prelude to modern scholarship.

Many eighteenth-century scholars dealing with religion had as "naïve" an idea of history as Saxo and Snorri. It was not unusual to begin a discussion of religion, as Fontenelle (1657–1757) did, with the question of how the original (biblical) revelation was lost in the history of the other nations. Perhaps in some cases where scholars appear to take all the Bible as history, just as Herodotus took Homer, we might suspect bowing and scraping in the direction of the clergy. We have a man, however, David Hume (1711–1776), who was not known for servile compliance, in whom we also see, perhaps more clearly than in anyone else at this time of transition, an acceptance of the "naïve" side of the euhemeristic procedure. At the same time there is something new in Hume: an unmistakable interest in general theories concerning the origins of the mythical world. If we may use the words historization and humanization for early euhemerism, here we are justified in speaking about the beginnings of system and reduction.

We might consider Hume's *Natural History of Religion*: a small treatise, not interested in rendering or preserving mythical themes but devoted to a general analysis of religion. Hume discusses early religion principally as a matter of "uninstructed mankind" incapable as yet of

---

38. For an interesting general discussion of euhemerism during the Enlightenment, see Manuel, *The Eighteenth Century Confronts the Gods*, chapter 3.

conceiving one supreme creator. With this idea Hume is very much a child of his age. Describing a presumed original polytheism, he says: "They suppose their deities, however potent and invisible, to be nothing but a species of human creatures, perhaps raised from among mankind, and retaining all human passions and appetites, together with corporeal limbs and organs."[39]

Here Hume's depiction is akin to euhemerism's "humanization" of the gods, but it is of a negative sort, somehow reminiscent of the church fathers. In Hume's estimation, fear is much more effective in the making of gods than is joy; his own very eighteenth-century remark has it that "men are much oftener thrown on their knees by the melancholy than by the agreeable passions."[40] The determining point to be found in Hume's exposition is his assumption of early humanity's inability to conceive of a supreme creator. The presupposition of the importance of such a conception rules Hume's entire natural history of religion.

The new search for explanations of the development of religion made one certain question crucial. How and why precisely would human beings be raised to a superhuman status; how and why are human passions and appetites, limbs and organs, cast upon heavenly inhabitants? This question did not preoccupy the early euhemerists, for they were convinced of qualities *surpassing* those of ordinary humans from the outset. The question did not disturb the early church fathers very much either, for the image of demons was for them a reality: evils beyond ordinary human capacity. Hume attempts to answer the new question. He seems to realize that a general psychological observation about fear will not do; fear and the lower passions by themselves are not creative and could hardly be credited with a good many of the stories about the gods. It is surprising that Hume's critical mind did not proceed further, but simply took at face value the basic assertions of euhemerism in a rather flat way. Here is *Hume's* euhemerism:

> The deities of the vulgar are so little superior to human creatures, that, where men are affected with strong sentiments of veneration or gratitude for any hero or benefactor, nothing can be more natural than to convert him into a god, and fill the heavens, after this manner, with continual recruits from among mankind. Most of the divinities of the ancient world are supposed to have once been men, and to have been beholden for

39. Hume, *The Natural History of Religion*, 30–31.
40. Ibid., 31.

their *apotheosis* to the admiration and affection of the people. The real history of their adventures, corrupted by tradition, and elevated by the marvelous, became a plentiful source of fable; especially in passing through the hands of poets, allegorists, and priests, who successively improved upon the wonder and astonishment of the ignorant multitude.[41]

It is really striking that Hume, who took no idea from the ancient philosophers for granted but critically reexamined every single one of them, did not examine euhemerism. He simply accepted it in its negative, "improper" form, embellishing it with features such as allegory and priestly and poetical changes. Everything that is put forth about religion is arranged so as to provide a contrast between superior intelligence and ignorance. The overriding concern for this sort of general explanation of religious materials sets the nineteenth-century tone. It leans on euhemerism but crucially distorts it. The new concern can view euhemerism as nothing but a theory on the causes of polytheism. Euhemerism becomes a supposed mental process, completely separated from the worship that actually was present in its earlier forms.

Unlike every previous form of euhemerism, the later euhemerism (which we see exemplified in Hume) could no longer *deal with* myth. And once this new method, looking for the (mental) causes of religion, was inaugurated, it established a hold on scholarship.

All the typical nineteenth-century students of religion, particularly under the influence of the budding science of anthropology, concerned themselves with religion in general. It has been rightly observed that Herbert Spencer's theory of evolution of religion was flavored by euhemerism,[42] "later euhemerism" as we should say more accurately. Spencer (1820–1903) wanted to find ancestor worship the first form of religion; this implied the elevation in status of humans upon their death. The theory of "animism" as the first and basic form of religion, advanced by E. B. Tylor (1832–1917), can be understood perfectly as a notion fomented by later euhemerism. Its principal content is the ghosts of the dead.

All such theories occur after the "watershed" of the eighteenth century. In these scientific undertakings, myths figure only on the fringes. Clearly, the narration that played the central part in earlier euhemerism

---

41. Ibid., 39.
42. De Vries, *Perspectives in the History of Religions*, 104.

and that had come about on the basis of mythology was a closed book for nineteenth-century scholarship.

Yet in terms of a philosophy of culture, it must be argued that destruction of myth is an optic illusion. Is not the search for origins by nineteenth-century evolutionists itself a rejuvenated myth of the utmost value?[43] This issue will not let go of us. It will return when we try to assess secularization in modern history.

Within the scope of the present discussion, however, it must be said that later euhemerism was much more destructive than earlier euhemerisms. We may remember that the church fathers were able to transform the gods into demons; they did not have to deny their very existence. By comparison, many missionaries of the nineteenth century, who were contemporaries of the great evolutionists such as Spencer and Tylor, were also, like them, thoroughly modern, post-Enlightenment men. They did not have that facility to transform possessed by the early Christians. They could only say of the gods of this, that, or the other people in the wide world that they simply did not really exist.

Later euhemerism has been a harmful virus to our understanding of human beings, spawning in turn other unsound theories. It has been destructive in its reductionism, and has robbed people of their reality, of the minimal basis for any human self-esteem. Endeavors to establish a worthwhile contact with people whose life was oriented toward those gods that were explained away have often failed. Endeavors inspired by misdirected theories only helped in creating a vacuum, the very vacuum in which many of our academic doings in the study of man are going on today.

"Secularization"

One might look upon this essay in part as an endeavor to defend the real Euhemerus. Based upon all we know, Euhemerus himself, and after him, figures like Snorri Sturluson, were not reductionistic in their intent. If they did have an interest in theorizing, their theories were a far cry from theories we work with today in the study of religions, societies, cultures. Their narratives had a preserving power that bears no resemblance to later euhemerism in its blanket explanations of tradition.

---

43. See Eliade, "The Quest for the 'Origins' of Religion."

Nevertheless, one point must be emphasized because of its significance for our discussion: euhemerism even in its earliest form is a type of secularization. It always arose in conjunction with some distinction between a truly important notion of divinity and divinities of a lesser, more popular sort; and these distinctions were the result of irrepressible changes that could not be ignored in the circles of Xenophanes, Aristotle, and Euhemerus himself. Travel, trade relations, the development of philosophy all contributed to new complexities of understanding that demanded new ways of looking at things.

For our discussion of secularization, a corollary should be added: the narratives accounting in a new way for the old gods may appear to us as a degradation, but that is not how the euhemerizations offer themselves in their context. No doubt they somehow reflected the differentiation between an elite, who had knowledge of true divinity, and the crowd, who did not; that distinction had entered the "spirit of the time." Yet the "less significant" deities did not lose their sacredness. Rather, the narratives transformed it. Thus this secularization process had as its other aspect: sanctification. The new sanctification was not identical with the ancient sanctification that made Zeus supreme over other members of the pantheon (as in Hesiod), but the new sanctification was sanctification nonetheless.

Euhemeristic procedures after the Enlightenment period were a further development from earlier ideas, yet different, unique. They are related to early euhemerism only by misunderstanding euhemerism as skeptical inquiry. They are more closely related to the euhemerism of the church fathers, which was concerned with the derogation of pagan religious tradition. The eighteenth century gave this concern a new direction; it was no longer felt exclusively for the sake of the true religion, but also for the sake of the new ideal of rational clarity. The theories of the nineteenth century aim explicitly at complete, documented exposition of the evolution of religion in the light of reason. The originators of those theories, men like Spencer and Tylor, certainly would never have called their own method euhemeristic, for they were well aware of belonging to a new, scientific age.

The interesting thing, though, is that what seems sheer "secularization" in the sense of a complete loss of the religious, on closer inspection proves to be not so very "secular" after all. Instead, there is *a shift to a new world*. Not profanation, but a constant coming to terms with the world in which people find themselves living. Our study has only been able to identify "secularization" as a normal transformation in which all religious traditions find themselves. It is a sign not of their imminent demise, but of their continuing life.

4

Secularization in Modern History

The Problem of Losing the Sacred

But are there not periods that relinquish religion altogether? Granted that euhemerism showed an interesting series of deviations-cum-preservation on an ancient set of religious certainties; isn't the existence *we* share, this latest product of modern history, isn't this age doing what it wants—without preserving "the sacred"? Many among us know that the philosopher said, "*God is dead!*"

(Not all who quote these words of Nietzsche pay much mind to what they contain. Nietzsche is often repeated as if he had said "God does not exist" or "God has become outmoded," neutral statements that the average self-satisfied atheist can make without much fervor. However, Nietzsche did not propose a thesis, but made an announcement and marked it with an exclamation point.)

The popular question and conception is quite straightforward: is there not a process of secularization in our day that is about to score a final triumph over the myths, symbols, and rituals of the past? And whether one rejoices at this, sheds tears, or is indifferent—isn't it occurring before our eyes?

Serious scholars are cautious about their terminology. Still, even serious and influential scholars can resort to hazy expressions in their endeavors to outline what we all think we sense: a loss of the sacred in our time. Typically, the sociologist Peter Berger speaks of "the diffusion of modern consciousness in what is commonly called the Third World," a topic to which he devotes a large part of one of his best-known books.[1]

Earlier, in the nineteenth and into the twentieth century, many scholars sensed a progression from "the simple" to the complex, and "saw their own religion as the culmination of a development."[2] But whether the culmination is religious or "secular," in all cases it refers to a particular state of erudition that deems itself capable of mapping the direction of the world's meaning from start to finish.

We must always question these first assumptions. We must ask whether our impression of a world evolving *in toto* towards secularity or modern consciousness is a genuine insight. We must think further about secularization.[3]

In regard to this modern consciousness that appears to us so devastatingly unleashed on the entire world of traditional religions, we might also reflect on these words of the historian of religions Noel Q. King, who wrote at the beginning of a book on religion in Africa:

> Suffering, according to all the great religions, is the stuff of human growth, and Africa has accumulated capital in the world bank of suffering that none, not even the Jews, can surpass. She has undergone invasion and subjugation by colonialism, which has reduced some of the richest people in the world to destitution.
>
> In 1960, the *annus mirabilis* of African freedom, the death-knell of the colonial insult was ringing, and new African countries were everywhere proclaimed. Those of us who were so fortunate as to be there—"to be young . . . and in that dawn to be alive . . ."—were confident that the whole world would pay attention and turn respectfully to learn from this person who, even when stripped naked, sold down the river by black and white brothers, and maltreated, still retained immense dignity, inscrutable wisdom, and—mysteriously enough—love and forgiveness.[4]

1. Berger, *The Homeless Mind*, vii.

2. Burkert, *Homo Necans*, 73.

3. With respect to the *intellectual* history of our "secularization," a helpful work is Turner, *Without God, Without Creed: The Origins of Unbelief in America*. Despite its title, it covers a good deal of European history as well. For developments in the United States especially with respect to problems faced by courts of law in comprehending religious issues, see Carter, *The Culture of Disbelief*.

4. King, *African Cosmos*, 2. Scholarship must open our eyes to more than just what is absolutized on the screen of our "modern world." In the work of classicists,

"The Sacred" and "The Profane"

When a religious tradition considers certain things "sacred"—by whatever near equivalent it refers to those things—how did that sacredness originate? The nineteenth century was obsessed with questions of this sort. They were identical with the quest for the origin of religion itself. The obsessive nature of this quest has since subsided. We are now even able to look at this obsession as in some sense a "religious" phenomenon.[5] We have separated ourselves from our scholarly forebears quite strikingly by no longer searching for single, absolute beginnings. We are more aware of the limits within which we conduct our inquiries. The overwhelming variety of religions and sacred structures would lead us today to make some assessment along these lines: almost everything seems to have been able to take on a sacred quality to people at one time or another. *And by the same token everything seems to have been subject to a process of losing sacredness.*

Something profane can become sacred, and vice versa. "Sanctification" and "secularization" are the historical processes that must be understood in order to understand the terms "sacred" and "profane."

"Secularization" and "Sanctification" at the Present Moment

Discussions on secularization are usually marked in the first place by the bias of the participants. Even before arguments are spelled out, it is palpable that some consider secularization a hopeful development and that others regret it. Always, the debate moves between hope and fear.

Some say secularization began in earnest with industrialization and urbanization. Quite commonly it is said that the process of secularization is linked with the rise of modern science. Where this opinion is held, "secularization" often seems to be viewed as a single process affecting the entire world. Then it is seen more as an absolute category—almost like "space" and "time"—than a descriptive term for specific happenings or documents. And frequently, then, it is referred to as if it were an

---

Africanists, and many others, discipline is built up slowly; and lo and behold, it discovers that religion is still there.

5. Eliade, "The Quest for the 'Origins' of Religion."

irreversible process, whose implication is that the world is destined to become less and less "religious," until at last no sacredness is left.

That there is a process whereby the sacred loses its force is not in dispute. But how should the historian of religions broach the manifold issues involved? The generalization that we also have evidence of reverse, sanctifying processes will not wholly satisfy us. The incontrovertible fact that certain things have acquired or are in the process of acquiring sacredness does not have sufficient "bite" to counterbalance the broad sensation of a loss of religious belief. Furthermore, it is a source of much distress that some of the examples we find before us of new acquisitions of sacredness involve extremisms in Christianity, Judaism, Islam that often are linked to violence and hate-mongering; we cannot forget that the wars of our time have conspicuous religious components. Many would deny the "sacredness" of such developments. And, of course, an array of scientifically intended psychological vocabularies makes short work of any possible religious meaning when movements are scrutinized by the media. Thus for many of us, our jargon and our disdain cut off the suggestion that something religious could be basic to what is happening before us.

Secularization as a Concealed Process

A religious tradition, with all the views and reasonings it involves, can lose its self-evidence. As a result, people within the tradition may justify and preserve it by devising new reasonings that are as much evidence of a process of secularization as any of the phenomena we normally think of as "secularization" (such as confrontations and outright denials of traditional authority). In this sort of situation, the process of change that is occurring is not apparent as such.

It seems to me that some of the most important evidence of secularization-in-progress comes from elements that we catch unawares in a document as being unknowingly at variance with time-honored traditions of thought. As a rule, we can only see such evidence in hindsight; the historian, not the sociologist, will be the one who notices it.

There is a tragedy by the Dutch playwright Joost van den Vondel (1587–1679) that depicts the fall of King Solomon. The simple plot is adapted from the biblical story. Solomon, at the height of his glory, is induced by one of his pagan wives to build a temple to Astarte. God demonstrates his anger in a frightening thunderstorm; but when Solomon sees the magnitude of the error he has committed, it is too late. The play concludes with Nathan's prophecies of the disasters that will overcome Israel.

There was probably no religious or political struggle in the golden age of Holland in which Joost van den Vondel did not make his voice heard. However, he was not a "party man" for any of the political or religious factions. He embraced Catholicism at the middle of his life, but a play like his *Salomon* speaks about the duty of a ruler before God in a language that would not be foreign to a follower of Calvin. The sins of the king affect the world and its course of events, hence God's creation and purpose. At the end of the play, the chorus cries:

> O King, who lost thy wisdom,
> What cleansing, what forgiveness
> Can wipe away these doings
> That no Hebrew can speak of
> Without horror . . . ?[6]

And the chorus deplores the heathens' joy over Israel's failure:

> What heart will not shrink
> At the Heathen's scorn?
> How the uncircumcised will rush out
> From their towns—
> Whole families, men and women—
> To look upon this shame . . .
> The wisest of all Princes
> Fell to Baal.

There is the tone here of confession of sins—for in the acts of Solomon all are involved, in the history of Israel and of the church—and this tone is unmistakable in the concluding lines:

> Alas, an age is over.
> It left us corrupted.
> How the Law has been defiled
> By what Solomon built.

---

6. This is my translation of these passages from *Salomon*.

These lines and their view of events in the time of King Solomon have nothing to show us yet with respect to secularization. Vondel, as the poet he was, transcending the partisan arguments of his day, found his imageries in a tradition that Catholics, Mennonites, Remonstrants, and their Reformed enemies shared, and also that those in authority who were only mildly interested in religious matters could recognize.

But turning back to the first act of the play, we find an unexpected thought woven into a discussion between a Hebrew scribe and a pagan court priest. When the priest, Ithobal, mentions his pagan goddess, the scribe exclaims:

> The unchaste one, ravished by
> Adonis—a sprout of royal incest!

Ithobal ignores the insult and explains that indeed Astarte was loved by Adonis, until he was killed by a wild boar. The death of Adonis, he adds, is the reason

> ... our maidens still bewail
> His corpse each year,
> When the seasons change the rivers into blood
> Flowing in torrents from the cedar forests of Lebanon—
> A miracle that should persuade the Jews,
> Convincing one and all to worship with us.

Then follows the passage that concerns our discussion—presenting us with a sudden glimpse of a secularization process in occurrence. Listen to the rationalistic tone of the scribe's response:

> ... the color of streams comes from the soil.
> When the water descends, running its course
> It mixes itself with the earth and takes its shades.
> They mingle as do elements that agree.
> Thus Adonis seems red.
> The sands come down from Lebanon,
> Chased by the wind.
> Then the dust paints the streams.
> Is this a miracle?
> And upon this do you build Astarte's feast and church?

Ithobal objects that the goddess is venerated in many lands, but then the scribe adds another observation:

> She is offered sacrifices only because people lack discrimination.
> Blind men promote the blindness of a nation because they profit by it.

The flatness of thought of this argument is obvious, in spite of its poetic dress in the original. What you think of in such exalted terms, the priest is told, is an ordinary process of nature. Here is naturalistic secularization *in statu nascendi*. The second statement, about profit mongers behind a cultic tradition, is quite striking and closely resembles Voltaire's well-known reasoning about religion as deceit by priests but antedates it roughly by a century.

It is essential to bear in mind that neither Vondel himself nor any of his contemporaries were disturbed by the lines we have just cited. Catholic or Mennonite, Reformed, Remonstrant, they would have seen only orthodoxy in that little lecture given by the scribe. And yet here, early in the seventeenth century, a particular secularization process that we know so well from the eighteenth-century Enlightenment was already "sneaking up" on a civilization.

The Choice of Words

It may be helpful to devote some more attention to the use of words. The words that are needed to describe and interpret what happens in desanctification or secularization processes are not always easy to select, but most of the time we insist on a hurried explicitness that can seem to sum up the jumble of events that make up history. The patience required by the many particulars of history is a rare commodity.

Our culture of video monitors prefers the quick view and is not much marked by historical awareness. Our academic, intellectual disciplines too would prefer quick concepts to describe a general process or the stages in a process by which "the sacred" loses ground. The search for the all-encompassing concept tempts us in the study of secularization processes to look for terms like those in biology that deal with natural processes of extinction, as if the loss of the sacred were like the loss of the hairy mammoth.[7]

---

7. It is interesting to notice the enthusiasm expressed for David Sloan Wilson's book *Darwin's Cathedral* in the *Council of Societies for the Study of Religion Bulletin* of April 2002. No one raises the question of whether the successes of biology suffice to

It is important to say quite clearly that when we speak of the ways in which secularization occurs we deal with *history*, and not with biology or geology. Consequently, we must not adopt a vocabulary that will mislead us and make us believe that we are establishing natural laws. The "concealment" of secularization does not refer to evidence that we simply have not uncovered or not yet sorted out. It relates to the nature of history, hence to human life. Thus even the best scholars are succumbing to a dangerous temptation when they pronounce scientific-sounding phrases or offer easy-word solutions for the disorientations any secularization brings to human beings.

And now let us look, at some greater length, at a phenomenon we all somehow sense is linked with our own secularization. This will be a case where our choice and use of words has truly failed us.

Fundamentalism

Fundamentalism: the subject seems within everyone's reach, and in America just about everyone has a reaction to it. Fundamentalists can irritate academics like almost nothing else. Precisely for this reason, the subject may do us some good in showing the ease with which we use unwarranted vocabularies and speak unjustified words.

Fundamentalism is the name given to a most particularly American movement in various Protestant Christian churches. Among many intellectuals, "fundamentalist" has become a loose term used in denigration—but the important thing to keep in mind is that a large number of Christians, beginning in the nineteenth century, wanted to return to the *fundamentals* of biblical teachings.[8] The American fundamentalists are in

---

come to terms with problems in the history of religions. Is it necessary to repeat that a science is scientific only insofar as it uses methods that are adequate for its object of study?

8. For the use of the term "fundamentals," really only introduced in a "technical" sense in the twentieth century, see Ahlstrom, *A Religious History of the American People*, 815–16; and Marsden, *Fundamentalism and American Culture*, 118–23. The latter is essential reading for an understanding of the simplicity of thought among fundamentalists, if focused on "objectively" and "from the outside." Marsden's work on fundamentalism is one of the best we have. Important studies have appeared in the series called the Fundamentalism Project: see especially the first volume, edited by Marty and Appleby, *Fundamentalisms Observed*, a study conducted by the American Academy of Arts and Sciences.

some way part of a wider world movement in Christianity—an essential detail that can escape American historians.

Beginning in the Napoleonic era and with the birth of constitutional monarchies in Europe, many people became urgently concerned about the heritage and the very reality of the Church; too much change was taking place all at once in the political landscape of thought. This general religious movement, which was genuinely universal, springing up spontaneously in different places, a movement of zealous endeavors to *preserve* rather than merely react, is an integral part of Western civilization, and one that receives scant attention in college courses that bear the name. A most striking feature of the whole movement was that it was carried by masses of poor individuals who by upbringing made up the churches. A good many of these people had migrated to the United States. Was their motivation in emigrating "religious" or was it "economic"? The suggestion that we should determine one way or the other is historically nonsensical. In the course of the nineteenth century, several waves of Dutch migrants to America did come from poverty-stricken areas of the Netherlands, yet their major leaders were always pastors. Southern Illinois and the state of Michigan would not be quite what they are now were it not for those immigrations.

In its development through the nineteenth and twentieth centuries, the movement toward religious preservation was certainly multifarious,[9] and came to comprise among its adherents a number of articulate theologians.[10] Nevertheless, the essence of the movement was and remained the "ordinary" believers—and let us keep in mind that their "ordinariness" was identical with the very force that had carried the Church for many centuries. The first voices we would identify as "fundamentalistic" came from rural communities.[11] However, industrialization and urbanization in the twentieth century did not alter the drive to assert in a simple, unmistakable way the certainties of traditional faith.

---

9. An illuminating article on right-wing Protestants and the theological variety among them is Covell, "The Christian Gospel and World Religions."

10. See Ahlstrom, *A Religious History*, 815–16; and Sandeen, "Fundamentalism and American Identity," 289. Of special importance in showing the intellectual quality of the theologians involved, see Weber, "The Two-Edged Sword."

11. The classic study by Niebuhr, *The Social Sources of Denominationalism*, 184–87, sees fundamentalism as essentially a rural phenomenon and as a passing phase toward urbanization and increased education.

The reasons why America gave such a special platform to this movement are not difficult to see. America broke radically with any tradition of a state church. This was part of her Revolution. Moreover, in place of the many divisions and hierarchies she broke from—religious, professional, intellectual, social—America offered the ideal of the individual, the individual participant in her democracy. And furthermore, it comes as no surprise that we find a glaring lack of academic sophistication in many of those who have given Fundamentalism its power in America. The United States never educated its religious leaders in the formal way that in Europe was the rule. With the exception of a few old institutions in the northeast states, no university had a theological faculty. And even in the places where theology was taught, it came to be part of a professional school, not infrequently separate from the main buildings and programs of the college and the "real" graduate activities. This arrangement, a product of the nineteenth century, is visible to any visitor to the campus of Yale, Princeton, or Harvard.

Across the nation as a whole, during the hard and often cruel conquest of the West, the education of pastors was far removed from critical intellectual inquiry. Moreover, democratic procedures in towns, states, and the nation further stimulated the ideal that the individual participant in politics and also in religion was of the utmost value. This was the social and intellectual novelty of the United States that so intrigued and disconcerted Tocqueville. The backbone of democracy in the American Republic is virtually identical with the religious organizational system of Congregationalism.[12] The buddy-buddyness with which a parishioner in an American Congregational, Baptist, or most definitely any Holiness church can address his or her pastor is rooted in America. Such familiarity would have shocked European churchgoers early in the nineteenth century, and still surprises them today. No doubt the anti-intellectual attitude of the American public is historically related to this feature of its Protestant churches. The churches seldom ask that pastors be learned; and indeed, if they are, they easily arouse suspicion.

The superb scholar of American religion Herbert Wallace Schneider spoke of Fundamentalism as a particular form of "stubborn religion."[13] He

---

12. See chapter 13, "The Enduring Validity of Congregational Polity," in James Luther Adams' splendid book, *The Prophethood of All Believers*. See also the elaborate study touching on the same subject, by Nathan O. Hatch, *The Democratization of American Christianity*.

13. Schneider, *Religion in 20th Century America*, 14.

acknowledged its enormous influence. Its leveling impact on informed, intellectual discussion is indeed difficult to miss; Schneider, and most other scholars, looked upon it very critically. Of similar importance to note, however, are the equal and opposite reactions to this "stubborn" impact which we find in the mentality of academic folks. The caricature-like excesses of simplistic exegeses often seem to be the only real image of religion that comes to the mind of many learned men and women. Similarly, the habit of Americans in using the name "fundamentalist" for Islamic groups of which they have no knowledge reflects a wide distribution of ignorance.

"Fundamentalism" is really hard to pin down with respect to datable and evident events. As we have indicated, its gradual birth took place in the first half of the nineteenth century. Its most crucial general characteristic from the earliest days onward was the vociferous affirmation of the literal truth of the biblical text from beginning to end. (Only recently has the emphasis on the exclusive truth of the King James text been diminished.) Also, in many fundamentalist quarters expectations of the end and renewal of the world have always been strongly expressed. This of course was a continuation of earlier theological teachings and discussions derived from the Bible. Yet the actual content of these expectations is hard to do justice to under one definition. The different levels of education among ministers, the differing evaluations of events of the day (was the world proceeding in a proper way, as ordained, or were the times depraved and signaling gruesome changes before the millennium could arrive?)—such things as these must have made for very different interpretations of biblical passages. "Fundamentalism" is unthinkable without words spoken, shouted, hammered in, by uneducated preachers on the frontier as well as by better educated ones in the Eastern part of the nation. But without having before us all the texts of all the sermons, we cannot know as much as we would like about eschatological teachings and congregational experiences. Thus the most easily discernible feature of Fundamentalism remains its biblical literalism. And indeed, what helped to bring about some measure of unity among the large mass of fundamentalists was biblical literalism in its combat with Darwinism. All felt called to this front, where nothing less than the straightforward text of the Bible was at stake.[14]

---

14. For a brief account of the famous Scopes trial, see Ahlstrom, *A Religious History*, 909–15.

Beyond what has just been said, there are other features of Fundamentalism that are important to understand. Three such features have become apparent only slowly—as is usual in the study of history, through hindsight and a lessening partisan malice.

First of all, Fundamentalism's characteristic literalism, although a feature in recent Church history, does not belong exclusively to Church history and certain "simple believers." It is an *obsession with factual reality* shared by very diverse groups.

The first half of the nineteenth century, the era of the beginnings of Fundamentalism, was also the era when philosophical positivism made its appearance. That movement and the name we give it derive from the young Auguste Comte's important and influential work *Cours de philosophie positive*, published in six volumes between 1830 and 1842. Other thinkers of the period, notably the social philosopher Herbert Spencer in England, displayed the same obsession with factual reality. With respect to religion their reasoning led to the conclusion that the entire religious world was not real and called for unmasking by real, or positive, intellectual and empirical analysis.[15] (From a very different perspective, the German theologian Ludwig Feuerbach arrived at a position equally critical of the traditional reality of religion.)

We have mentioned Auguste Comte. Comte's theory, laid out in the *Cours de philosophie positive*, has its foundation in a "great law" of three stages of human thought.[16] The third and crowning state is *positif* and represents a final evolution. The first stage is the "theological or fictitious." The label tells the story; for Comte, this was the long phase when human imaginings were devoid of positive reality. In other words: religion. A transitional period Comte calls "metaphysical." It is a "general modification" of the first state; supernatural fictions that served to explain the

---

15. In 1957 the celebrated British thinker Bertrand Russell wrote a preface for a bundle of essays he had published over the years. The title of the collection is *Why I am not a Christian*, and Russell's reasons are given systematically: religion is a matter of beliefs; the things believed do not exhibit anything resembling proof; not only is there lack of evidence for the things believed, but many of the things done are stupid and cruel, from burning of widows in Hinduism to the burning of heretics at the stake in Christianity. Russell's reasoning is presented as a factual demonstration of the wrongness of religion.

16. For an excellent overview of Comte, see Comte, *Introduction to Positive Philosophy*. The book is a translation by Frederick Ferré of the first two chapters of Comte's long work, in which two chapters Comte presents in summary his method and his theses.

world's phenomena are replaced by abstractions (here we are speaking of Western philosophy). Only the third, the positive state, rouses the human mind to its endeavor "to establish the actual laws of phenomena." In short, of the three stages: "The first is the necessary starting point of human intelligence; the third represents its fixed and definitive state; the second is destined to serve only as a transitional method."[17] In his later years, Comte anticipated a *culte de l'humanité*, a cult of humanity; the religiosity so named would not stand in contradiction to the positive sciences, for it would bear no taint of mankind's first two states.

To be sure, Comte's was just one of a number of developmental theories, and Comte has stirred no major interest among historians, who have paid more attention to Hegel and Marx. However, Comte may have expressed more typically than the others the mood of reliance on scientific progress and unconcern for questions of religion or philosophical reflection. Here is Comte on the highest stage of human development: "in the positive state, the human mind, recognizing the impossibility of obtaining absolute truth, gives up the search after the origin and hidden causes of the universe and a knowledge of the final causes of phenomena. It endeavors now only to discover, by a well-combined reasoning and observation, the actual laws of phenomena—that is to say, their invariable relations of succession and likeness."[18]

I think it is important to see that we have in these words a sense of a succinct opposition between "fiction" and "reality," between error and truth. The idea of this opposition impelled the entire nineteenth- and early twentieth-century world of thought—and may still be found today. When one takes on the task of reading through the literature of missionary societies, one confronts that same distinction: the illusions of the savages, believing in gods that do not exist, in contrast to the reality of the gospel. No previous age condemned human thought as illusion and fiction with such ease. We may recall—perhaps with new respect for people who were able to take other people fully seriously—how euhemerism did not rob any deity of its reality.

The effects of nineteenth-century innocence and confusion are still with us, and they still make honest confrontations unnecessarily difficult to achieve.

17. Ibid., 2.
18. Ibid.

In the grand scheme of the conflict between "believers" and "intellectuals," an examination of the words each side has used is illuminating. In this war of words that has dragged on for close to two centuries, the most foolish animosities have arisen alongside "fighting words." Fundamentalists in our own day have used the term "secular humanist" to describe their opponents. The name "humanist" by itself of course contains no insult for anyone who knows a bit of history and does not mind being included in the great tradition of the Renaissance. But the person launching the attack, with particular contempt stressed on the adjective "secular," pronounces "secular humanist" with a real sting.

"Supernatural" is part of the standard vocabulary in the social sciences. A "primitive" (or more recently, "nonliterate" or "tribal") people sets store by "supernatural" beings and "beliefs." And in this situation fundamentalists too are "supernaturalists"—the virgin birth and the creation of the world in six days serve as evidence—"supernaturalists" in the same pejorative, dismissive sense in which their opponents are "secular humanists." "Supernaturalist" and "secular humanist": here we have a pair of "fighting words," each intended to wound the opponent.

The labels and dismissive conversation-stoppers must be seen in a deeper vein as part of our commonly shared sense of an opposition between fictive and real, between error and truth. It is also extremely important to understand that in spite of the fighting stance between the two sides, the scholarly critical side and the side of the ardent renewers of the churches, *the thirst for factual reality* has always united them.

By and large, when the debate was beginning in the nineteenth century, the two sides were ignorant of each other. Certainly Comte and Spencer would not have had the least interest in sermons of American preachers. But soon, in the reverse direction, through popular tracts and by word of mouth, the general drift of new erudite and scientific ideas did reach many among the masses, particularly in the American Far West. And often those receiving the news felt not enthused, but threatened. And they reacted in kind. The point to be registered is that biblical literalism was an answer to the bothersome notions being raised in intellectual circles. It countered with equally "positive" theses. This activity has not struck many historical theologians as being of great importance. And yet it is a crucial thing to understand if we want to see what happened to religion in the nineteenth and twentieth centuries.

Augustine, Thomas Aquinas, the Protestant scholastics could not conceivably have dealt with the biblical texts in the literal way that now became common. The fundamentalists framed their religious answers on the level of factual realism that prevailed in their day. If *The Origin of Species* suggested as fact the slow evolution of man, the biblical account of Adam and Eve was there to be taken as an equally real counterargument.

This fixation with factual reality possessed by Fundamentalism leads us to another feature of the movement. It is that quality of *concealment* we have already spoken of in connection with secularization movements in progress. Indeed, the fundamentalist movement is an example of concealed secularization. The ways of the world, to be sure, are seen as opposed to it, but the price paid for placing itself in opposition to the way of the world is participation in that same world. Even the certainty of being different (in biblical terms, "the remnant that will be saved") confirms this participation in the inflection it is given by fundamentalists; the Church becomes a social entity whose reality is as demonstrable as any scientific fact. The splintering up of American Protestants into a multitude of different churches allows for one more affirmation: this group that you can see right here (the smaller the more visible upon inspection) is a *fact*. Similarly, the virgin birth becomes a literal fact to be affirmed as the one biological exception to a biological law. Historically in the long line of Christian theologians none would have spoken of the meaning of the birth of Jesus in biological terms, or the meaning of the Church in sociological terms; but in the new world we now have entered such basic deviations from orthodoxy become possible and unremarkable.

Thus Fundamentalism, *qua* literalism, is a secularization movement in a double sense of the word. First, the movement is a secularization in relation to traditional churchgoers of previous ages, for the turn toward factuality does indeed mean a hollowing out of faith, a loss of sacredness. One's faith becomes simply a person's opinion concerning matters assumed to be factual, empirical, and verifiable. The mystery of salvation becomes definitely reified, transformed into a "thing." Second, Fundamentalism is literally secularization in the sense of "conforming to the world," as it comes to terms with contemporary aims and assumptions and vocabulary for what constitutes "reality." It conforms to the world unintentionally, as Vondel did in the seventeenth century when he placed a rationalistic argument in the mouth of his character in *Salomon*—such techniques being the latest procedure of the learned world at the time.

There is a third feature of the fundamentalist movement that is important to recognize; it deserves to be called the *legitimacy* of the crowd of believers tying their salvation to facts of a positive, scientific tone.

A rather hidden historical point is that the life of the churches was not carried on altogether by great theologians. The pious in the pews continued and continue to be the mainstay, a historical force that for all its obscurity "on the record" is not less real. The essential fact of the "priesthood of all believers," or rather their prophethood, remains an undeniable part of historical reality.[19] This in itself gives historical legitimacy to the fundamentalists. Furthermore, what we have here is not merely an aspect of historical reality, but also a clearly identifiable Christian symbol, too easily hidden from view by the "problem" of Fundamentalism. *It is the symbolism of the Church as the body of Christ.*

Certainly a most original contribution of Western civilization to the world is "materialism"—if one word may sum it up. Whether or not one likes this term or what it represents, it stands for what most of us without objection normally think of as physical reality. In the perspective of the general and comparative history of religions, Fundamentalism's re-creation of the church into something too literally "real" to fit with the creed of the fathers tells us that Fundamentalism is a clear product of Western civilization.

It is instructive that perceiving Fundamentalism's root means rediscovering a central core of Western religion in its latest great transformation. Each religion turns around a central cluster of symbols. Elsewhere, further removed from ourselves, the transformations and offshoots of these central symbolisms seldom come to irritate us; yet with fundamentalism in biblical religion, they so often do.

We must recognize, however, that Fundamentalism is part of *our* Western religious development. It is also part of *our* secularization processes. In its intellectually most bothersome features, it originates from the wellsprings of Western existence in the nineteenth century.[20] We have to keep in mind that the physical sciences and biology had developed for a couple of centuries, and in the nineteenth century became part of the curricula of secondary schools—a total novelty. Another new development had begun at the end of the eighteenth century: as fewer people attended their churches and the ranks of the clergy diminished, the laymen took over. One can very well see this as one of the great miracles of American church history. Nevertheless, the price paid for this miracle

---

19. The term is used for the title of Adams' work, *The Prophethood of All Believers*.

20. In an interesting article called "What Is Fundamentalism?" Karen Armstrong speaks of fundamentalism's "symbiotic" relationship with secularism (Armstrong, "What Is Fundamentalism?," 15).

was considerable. As the influence of laymen increased, the education of priests, ministers, and pastors deteriorated. On the contemporary scene, of those who provide guidance to souls, not many have access to the principal biblical languages, Hebrew and Greek. In most seminaries and divinity schools the biblical languages are optional. Until not too long ago, a standard caricature of the fundamentalist was the person who said: "If the English of the [King James] Bible was good enough for Jesus, it's good enough for me."

Secularization Is Inevitable

The example of Fundamentalism supports the thesis that secularization cannot be avoided—remembering the primary meaning of the word itself: coming to terms with the *saeculum*, the world, the age we are in. After all, there is no other world for anyone at any time. Yet even if we cede that the process is inevitable, problems of history remain. How does secularization proceed? In what manner do individuals serve as its agents? How do we inherit what makes us who we are, and yet change?

The early Renaissance figure Nicholas of Cusa (1401–1464), also known as Cusanus, was a protagonist in the development of thought in astronomy; he always plays a role in historical surveys of science. And since religion and science are popularly presented as antagonists, Cusanus plays his role these days in discussions on the secularization of the West. His work has figured prominently in a number of important publications, and translations have made him more widely accessible.[21]

Nicholas of Cusa, mathematician, astronomer, philosopher, theologian, cardinal, lived in the dawning of what we now see as the "scientific world." Of course, he never dealt intentionally with any problem of religion versus science or of "secularization." Nevertheless, as we look back on him, many of his pages shed light on our more and more "secular" history. I would like to turn to some of his thoughts about the sacraments to begin making this point.

It was one of Cusanus' assignments as Cardinal to occupy himself with the theological problems stirred up by the Hussites—who were

---

21. In addition to *Nicolas de Cusa Opera omnia*, critically edited by Hoffmann and Klibansky, and the reprint of the Strasbourg edition of 1488, edited by Paul Wilpert, eloquent signs of renewed interest are *Das Werk des Nicolaus Cusanus: Eine Bibliophile Einführung*, edited by Heinz-Mohr and Eckert; *Nikolaus Cusanus*, a fascinating book by Karl Jaspers; and *Nikolaus von Kues: Philosophisch-theologische Schriften*, the study edition in Latin and German edited by Leo Gabriel.

precursors of the Reformation of Luther and Calvin. Among other things, the Hussites insisted on a communion celebration at which laymen received not only the bread, but also the wine (*sub utraque specie*, communion celebrated "under two kinds"). In his *Epistolae ad Bohemos*[22] Cusanus dealt with this problem at length.

Cusanus' concern for the unity of the Church marks these letters. This concern, which he held throughout his life, was clearly fueled by the existing conflicts, and no less by his own church-political career. However, it would be wrong to think that any of these worldly concerns dominated Cusanus' thinking. For him, unity was ultimately a mystical matter. Furthermore, Cusanus was a mathematician, and as has often been the case with mathematicians, he was fascinated with the mystery of the number one. His most famous work, *De docta ignorantia*, which is among the most splendid documents of mysticism in Western spirituality, may well be said to turn around the mystical reality of "unicity."

Looking at the approach Cusanus takes with the Bohemians regarding the sacrament of communion, we should reiterate that we are not about to find in him any conscious abandonment of the past. Nevertheless, a theme is developed that captures our attention. With some justification several readers of Cusanus have summed it up thus: You Bohemians should not be under the illusion that communion under two kinds will give you more grace than one.[23]

This thought arrests the modern reader because he can take it to the next step, for he knows what happened in the centuries after Cusanus. The modern reader concludes the picture with the kind of thinking that became habitual for a great many of us; since two kinds do not convey more grace than one, it makes no difference to the state of my soul whether I take one or the other type of communion either—or, for that matter, none at all.

Let me back up and go over the point again, this time looking at the broader thoughts Cusanus expressed concerning the Eucharist. I think we will find even more strikingly that Cusanus is paving the way for something new—without ever intending to do so.

The writer of the letters to the Hussites is well aware that the early church knew communion in "two kinds," and that in the course of events

---

22. Although the letters appeared as separate texts in the Basel edition of 1565, they actually seem to have been composed as one single work, *De usu communionis*. See Sigmund, *Nicholas of Cusa and Medieval Political Thought*, 33.

23. For a summary along these lines, see Bett, *Nicholas of Cusa*, 23. Bett is following Düx, *Der Deutsche Cardinal*, 154–55.

the custom changed. He is aware that throughout the history of the church, customs changed under various circumstances. And he abhors all tendencies to attribute an absolute, universal validity to these *particulars*, even when—as with the preferences of the Bohemians—they are taken straight from the New Testament texts. Cusanus likes to quote Augustine in support of his central ideas. For Augustine, to perform the act of the Eucharist only outwardly, without regard for Him to whom sacrifice belongs, is to eat and drink to one's own condemnation. For Cusanus, there is the outward act of taking the Eucharist and there is the essence of the sacrament, which is given with the sacrament yet is beyond it; and, for Cusanus, this *beyond* is decisive. Salvation, the *salus* of souls, is the crucial thing. And there is an infinite difference in importance between this and the forms of the cult. Cusanus makes vivid references to baptismal practices in the early church. The apostles baptized sometimes in the name of Jesus, sometimes in the name of the Trinity; differences occurred in the sacrament of baptism between the Greek and Latin churches. But none of this cultic diversity affected the *salus* of souls.

Here is a characteristic of Cusanus' thought which I believe begins to lead to a loss of self-evidence in cultic acts. While Cusanus insists on the *transcendence* of the divine beyond, in a more concrete sense God's power begins to fade. At issue is not the *omnipotentia Dei* or the *potestas absoluta Dei* of the theologians, but the availability of God's grace—most evidently for "the believer." For him or her, of course, nothing *but* the almightiness of God had infused the sacraments in a completely immediate way. Precisely this certainty is now at risk. A threat to "the sacred" has appeared.

Everything in Cusanus' thought is determined by a basic distinction between the divine, seen as the transcendent that holds the mystery of the absolute unity of all there is, and the empirical, calculable world characterized by multiplicity. In an earlier work, the *Concordantia catholica*, Cusanus uses an imagery to distinguish between the church in the world and the heavenly church. Like others before him, he depicts the church on earth as *ecclesia militans* and the heavenly church as triumphant and the eternal ground of the worldly church. But in a further elaboration, Cusanus uses images not unknown before him in an almost empirical schematization that represents something new. At the summit of the eternal church is God Himself, and on the second level, the angels, and on the third, the blessed souls. In precise parallel to this tripartite division, in the church on earth we find the sacraments, the priests, and the people. Of course, Cusanus is not saying that what is God in heaven is "merely" the sacraments here. Yet the very need felt by Cusanus to clarify the relationship seems to open a way toward the entire process we refer to as "desacralization." Could Cusanus have intended any of this? That is out of the question.

Quite consciously Cusanus utilized philosophical ideas he had learned from classical authors. They provided him with the tools he needed to go beyond limited formulations. (In his letters to the Hussites he wanted very much to point out the danger of setting demands that arose from limited thoughts.) It seems as if he liked to quote from ancient pagan authorities *in order* to construct a truly universally valid metaphysical framework—not simply to examine all things and then discard them as erroneous, but to embrace them in their real scope within the whole.

It may be said that while Cusanus was not the only medieval or Renaissance thinker to make use of classical philosophy, his metaphysical drive in doing so is probably not equaled by others. Approaching the end of his life he sums up his thought once more in a great work, titled *De venatione sapientiae*, "About the Hunt for Wisdom." *Sapientia, sophia*, wisdom, differs from *scientia*, which comes close to such terms as "knowledge," "erudition," "science," or "research" in our present vocabulary. The title Cusanus gave his conclusive work makes clear that he wanted to see his treatise truly as philo-sophia, the desire or love for wisdom.

Of course he knew the word *fides*, faith, as well as the one he preferred here; his preference is noteworthy and characteristic for the structure of his work. But again, it would be impossible to call Cusanus a "secularist." This great prince of the Church did not make the least attempt to trade what mattered most to him for a "positive" certainty. His work is a constant denial of thoughts that might lead one astray, and a constant rejection of premature conclusions. Karl Jaspers has rightly located the genius of Cusanus in his tireless metaphysical speculation—the principal reason why he did not create a "school."[24]

It is precisely this tireless activity that pushes some traditional certainties of religion further to the fringes than one would expect, and much further than anyone in the fifteenth century could have foreseen. Also, there is a strong Neoplatonic strain in Nicholas of Cusa, and this too is related to the spaciousness, the "modern feeling of life" we sense in

---

24. Jaspers, *Nikolaus Cusanus*, 31–34, 226–88.

him. A strong Platonic bias cannot be conducive to the self-evidence of religious particulars, any more than to other particulars.

In his chief work, *De docta ignorantia*, Cusanus sets forth that the cardinal and first manifestation (*emanatio* is the word he uses) of "the absolute maximum" (the transcendent, eternal and absolute unity, God) is the *universe*. It is not God's son, the Logos, as one might have expected. The incarnation is rather a special *emanatio*, quite distinct from the emanation of the world. The incarnation is a *coincidentia oppositorum*, a coincidence of opposites. It must take place through man. In the universe, man alone has this mediating function, since he participates in lower (sensual) and in higher (intellectual) life. This perfect mediation is realized in Jesus Christ, according to Nicholas of Cusa. The view of man implied in Cusanus' reasoning veers away from the prevailing sensibility of the Middle Ages, because Cusanus clearly shows us an image of man that is not set apart, not different from nature, but part of nature. (Doesn't this begin to resemble something we moderns recognize?) Cusanus explains that the incarnation had to occur in the way it did because of man's place in nature. (Could we recast this in a thoroughly "modern" way? God is beyond, we are here, and Jesus Christ is the proposition that unites us.)

Cusanus' writings contain a tendency toward abstraction that the Christian religious world had not known before. The incarnation had to be spoken about in a new way. The sacraments had to be spoken about in a new way that seemed to make their concreteness less concrete, their self-evidence less evident, and their efficacy more questionable. Cusanus' views are literally of cosmic proportion. His expositions were bound to break through the isolation of the facts of faith, just as they transfigured every provincial or pompous idea one might have of the uniqueness of Christian history.

In *De pace fidei*, Cusanus depicts a council meeting in heaven where the issue of unity is discussed by spokesmen for all the religious divisions on earth. It cannot be by accident that the word *fides* occurs in the title of this work. Might the word be meant as a synonym for "religion"? We do actually have some sort of dialogue here among the world's religions. But one would not normally have come up with the word *fides* for a meeting attended not only by a number of Christian partisans, a Jew, and an Arab, but also by a Persian and an Indian: a truly interreligious disputation. The term *sapientia* could perhaps have seemed appropriate. Paradoxically—his favorite way—Cusanus made his own switch in terminology. He uses *fides* where *sapientia* would have seemed natural. His speculation, so it would seem, does not cease at anything. And when the movement of his thought becomes most expansive (and indeed moves over the whole earth in this case), he also turns his speculation very close to home.

At the meeting a Bohemian is present. And it is Saint Paul himself who speaks to the Bohemian about the Eucharist. Do his words echo the reflections of Nicholas of Cusa?

> In so far as there is faith, this sacrament, in its empirical character, is not of such necessity that without it there would be no salvation. For it is sufficient to believe for the sake of salvation and so doing to partake of the food of life. Therefore no unexceptional law has been laid down about the distribution, whether, to whom and how often it should be given.[25]

No law has been laid down to which we may not take exception. This speech placed in the mouth of Paul is in harmony with the entire philosophical oeuvre of Cusanus. "The absolute maximum" remains transcendent, and while it is the source of the universe and everything in it, it must not be considered as if unequivocally present in anything in particular.

No vagueness in thought—and yet an almost unbearable "distancing" of God's involvement and availability in human life. Among the hearers of Cusanus—and we may remember that he indeed made no school and can be said to have had hearers rather than disciples—some concreteness, some sense of the means of salvation *right there*, was doomed to recede.

If we register this as a beginning of a secularization process, we have to repeat that nothing "irreligious" was intended. The process has nothing intentional to offer, but to us, looking back, it shows at every turn an inevitable necessity. At first consideration such inevitability of secularization may offer little comfort to those in our midst who regret "the loss of the sacred." And yet, this inevitability is an aspect of the very life of any religious tradition. It is exactly because a religion is alive that it must come to terms with the existence, the phase of the world's life it is in.

As to Cusanus' intentions, he was adamantly opposed to all naïve reification of religious facts. It was necessary (and perfectly proper to his mysticism) to state one fundamental idea in an endless variety of ways—the "real" thing being behind all given forms. However, with this sentiment, which made a great deal of sense in specific contexts, a new reading

---

25. Cardinal Nicholas of Cusa, *De pace fidei*, 18.

became inevitable, to wit: the "real thing" is unattainable any way. Our world has proceeded to embrace this proposition along many paths.

It goes without saying that Cusanus had "intentions," and that none of his lofty pages that still move us today could have been written as if "by accident." Trying to do things "intentionally" is something he of course had in common with all of us more pedestrian strugglers for "sense." And more than most, he truly enlarged the framework of ideas in which the religious tradition wherein he excelled could come alive. Latecomers such as we ourselves now find a spaciousness in the world he helped create beyond the geometry he consciously projected.

I want to suggest that there is an inner conflict in this instance of secularization, as there is in all likelihood in all secularizations. The world of Cusanus, which turned into our world, continued to develop, to renew itself at the same time because of him and in spite of him. The two seemingly contradictory qualifications of change, intention and inevitability, give us somewhat of a historical measure of man. And there is consolation and a comic relief in seeing the *real* limits of the effects individuals are responsible for.

Secularization and Mythification

We are in a position now to propose some observations on evidence we have looked at, and no doubt many a student of history will have his or her own examples to add to their persuasiveness.

Secularization, as a process in which religious certainties are undermined, is concealed during most of its occurrence. Thus I believe we may assert that one does not "program" secularity. Neither the poet Vondel nor the mystic scientist and theologian Cusanus was out to discredit traditional religion. Only hindsight enables us to see the relationship between them and certain things that happened after them, such as the "démasqué" of priesthood in the Enlightenment or the loss of self-evidence of the sacraments. The example of Fundamentalism confirms the same concealed nature of secularization processes; its biblical literalism cannot be comprehended except as made of the same material as the reification in philosophical positivism. As in the other examples, secularization continues to show its basic meaning: coming to terms with the world surrounding the religious movement. At the time of the events under investigation, no one could have an inkling of where to look in Vondel's or Cusanus' work, or in the beginnings of what became the multiform movement of Fundamentalism, for ideas conducive to a religious decay. So much the less could anyone have made use of such ideas to undermine traditional religion on purpose.

Secularization can mean only secularization of specific religious facts, and especially after discussing Cusanus we must emphasize that *secularization is a necessary process that makes room for what is newly felt to be the real world*. This means that a full-scale religious renewal is not possible except through secularization in its basic sense! Such a conclusion is neither paradoxical nor mystical. It is an ordinary fact of human existence. That which our time with all its techniques and means of perception forces us to accept as the real world conquers and transforms the past that educated us. It is a process of negation and acceptance in one. We do not have the option of taking only the negation. In other words, we cannot insist on seeing secularization as liberation *from* the bonds of tradition. (We should be willing to admit that an astounding number of modern intellectuals like to imagine a total freedom from religious inheritance or indebtedness.)

Humbling though it may be, history really teaches us a lesson here. It is just as impossible for a human being to invent a secular world as it is impossible to invent a religious symbol.[26] Secularization resembles religious symbolization in that in spite of all tinkering no one can produce it at will.

Secularization is not the fruit of anyone's brainstorm or the creation of a few individuals of like mind. Just the same, some individuals may be seen by later generations as its precursors or eminent spokesmen. The case of Cusanus shows dramatically how inevitable the process is and also how the intentions of an important figure and the subsequent course of history are not in harmony.

Thus the subject is surprising at every turn, yet not elusive, but within the compass of our understanding. What we are looking at is the historical transformation of religious phenomena. The endless flexibility of religious symbols is nowhere more evident than when people make their attempts to come to terms with the *real* world. In short, secularization and symbolization (or the creation of myths) should be seen as two aspects of the same events.

---

26. Cf. Bolle, *The Persistence of Religion*.

The Surpassing of Authority

We observed at the start of the present essay that while as a group we think we sense an irreversible secularization overtaking the world, individuals might greet that prospect with joy or sorrow, relief or anxiety. As we speak among ourselves within one more or less coherent cultural complex, our collective attitude toward secularization can only be called ambivalent. Taken as a phenomenon in itself, what does this ambivalence show? Perhaps the confused emotions and mixed interpretations are simply the way human beings cope with the shift from "the past"—always conceived as carrying "the tradition"—into the present and future. If indeed the source of our ambivalence is as basic as this, then we will find this peculiar "ambivalence" accompanying secularization processes in other cultures, too.

Systems depicting a golden age and a present deterioration are found everywhere. The Indians have described four ages, called *yugas*, which the world passes through. The first had by far the longest duration; of the subsequent ages, each is shorter than the one before. (People have the sensation of "time moving faster and faster.") Of the four *yugas* only the first was perfect, with the others becoming progressively worse until, alas, we find ourselves with the authors of the texts in the last and worst of all, the *Kaliyuga*. The Indian speculations have been dealt with many times, but one peculiarity is of special interest for our discussion, because it holds up the mirror to our ambivalence about "our" process of secularization.

All Puranic and Tantric texts that elaborate on the deterioration of the world do something else at the same time: they add that the present age—the very worst—has been given an extraordinary grace. It is evident to the authors of the texts that former ages were excellent because, among other things, everyone performed the prescribed sacrifices. In the present age, these sacred duties are not only neglected, but have become impossible, for the economic wherewithal has dwindled as badly as the necessary learning. Therefore, the time has arrived for special means of final release. And the god or goddess has seen to it that these means are revealed. The Tantric texts often emphasize that this new way is easy and fast. Is there not a striking ambivalence in all of this?

The mixed feelings we suffer regarding secularization might be contrasted unfavorably with the ambivalence found in the Indian texts. After all, the Indian *yugas* have nothing in common with trendy certitudes or with mournful sentiments about a "decline of the West." The Indian world-ages have a clear, unmistakably mythical intent. They are meant to provide an orientation in time, which is not contradicted, but complemented by the new means of realizing *mokṣa*, "final release." But despite what is perhaps its greater maturity, I do not see any convincing reason why this ambivalence could not be regarded as a sign of secularization, as elsewhere, in the sense of "coming to terms with the present age." As a matter of fact, a case could be made for the Indian division in periods as a secularization process far more thoroughgoing than some of our own mercurial versions. In the Indian texts, it is not necessary to make either the truth of yesterday or the truth of today into an absolute and therefore to waver between the two; they are both absolute, held together by a conception of history that provides room for the real world of experience.

The conceptual insight on the part of the Indian texts is indeed liberating. After all, at the present time, priding ourselves on an unprecedented, worldwide, and instant technology of communication, we still suffer enormously from a basic hindrance to understanding that is as old as humankind. We imagine that our past experience has given us all the means to arrive at a full understanding of the entire present world. Fundamentally, this is the great hindrance each religious tradition at its own "cutting edge" has had to fight. When we speak of the Old Testament prophets, the figures of Jesus Christ and Muhammad, we are speaking of such cutting edges. In each instance a wider view and a more encompassing community were the issue.

Am I saying that the Old Testament prophets, Jesus Christ, and Muhammad are documenting secularization processes for us? I am most certainly saying exactly that. If it sounds strange, then I suggest it is high time we get rid of our stereotypes about what is "religion" and what is "secularization" and do some real thinking about the actual constitutive elements in each process. The mutual exclusivity of secularization and religious renewal is a figment of the imagination, comparable to other uncritically accepted divisions we have had occasion to refer to in this book—(as, for instance, between a mythopoeic period in which people composed myths and a following period in which people stopped composing myths).

In order to begin speaking about secularization and religious renewal as two aspects of the same thing, we might say that the crisis in great changes in human orientation always involves a surpassing of authority. It is, as we said, that shift from the past into the present and future. And of course, viewed thus, as the surpassing of authority, both secularization and religious change are easily understood as tending to produce ambivalence.

A Role for the History of Religions

One contribution of religiohistorical study should be the help it renders in overcoming invalid fashions of thought. Fashions of thought, often appearing simply as figures of speech, can obscure our understanding of peoples and their religions. Many recent fashions of thought relate to the issue of secularization. A notion that emerges frequently has it that we can look at religious processes from a superior or a nonreligious point of view. This idea, though typical of nineteenth-century intellectual history, did not end with the nineteenth century; it has only acquired new guises. Indeed, the question proposed in the opening of this essay: *is there not a process of secularization in our time that is about to score a final triumph over the myths, the symbols, and rituals of the past?* was really no more than a fashion of thought, a pervasive fashion of thought.

The historian of religions remembers that his discipline is the fruit of our particular secularization. The History of Religions is a child of the Enlightenment. It owes its existence to particular cultural configurations in which particular religious traditions became problematic in particular ways. Understanding this leads us to take that secularization process in which we "live and move and have our being"[27] and in which our own way of questioning arose, quite seriously—however, *without absolutizing it.*

Our "secularity" does not separate us from the people in our documents (and by "documents" I include what we find in the news). It shows our humanity in common.

All traditions speak of peace. Most human beings desire it. But it is extremely important to be aware that people think about peace within their own tradition, and each tradition speaks of "peace" in its own way. So that actually the human voices speaking about peace are not all saying the same thing and are not all accessible to one another. These voices do not come out of a timeless beyond. They come out of those processes we have referred to as "sanctification" and "secularization." And it is the goal of peace—that most widely desired *salus* of the human race—that

---

27. I hope this free borrowing of Saint Paul's words is justified by the borrowing, in a very similar context, by José Ortega y Gasset in *An Interpretation of Universal History*, 49.

demands our most careful and thoughtful efforts to make these voices more properly understood.[28]

28. Secularization processes and their interdependence with religious traditions have not been neglected by design in the history of religions. They have been overlooked as a result of other preoccupations, such as the quest for "the essence" of religion or for a comprehensive phenomenological view of religion, or simply the effort to preserve the study of religion in our universities. Add to this the fact that much of the religiohistorical arsenal of terms and problems has been drawn from the study of those religions that were called primitive, where for too long the study of *change* was deemed unnecessary or was negligible, and it becomes understandable that the actual historical transformation of religious phenomena has not been given due attention by general historians of religions.

A case in point is the minimal interest historians of religions have shown towards modern times, except when it comes to outlandish phenomena (such as Swedenborgianism, the subject of a famous scholar's study composed during the years of the Second World War—for which no one in the Third Reich would have made him a reproach), exceptional individuals (Gandhi comes to mind), and sundry curious organizations and artistic creations, most of them out of the mainstream of history. But why did not some historian of religions try his or her hand at the subject of post-revolutionary Russia? A number of facts and documents concerning religion in the Soviet Union were recorded during the Cold War in *The Church and State under Communism*, prepared by the Law Library of the Library of Congress. Why did not some historian of religions try to look at whether the secularization of the Soviet Union was different from the secularization in, say, the United States in the same period? I cannot think of a good reason why so many documents and obvious questions were ignored. Historians of religions might see more sharply than many other specialists the oddness of the premises of the Soviet leaders in their endeavors to finish off religion. One such premise was that religion was essentially a matter of organization; it followed that religion could be rendered powerless by enforcing organizational change. Another assumed that religion was the worship of God—which must have sounded perfectly obvious but raises interesting questions with respect to the Buddhist inhabitants of the Soviet Union. These premises and many others contained only fragmentary truths, and the fruits of antireligious propaganda were not forthcoming. For the historian of religions the great fascination of the subject might lie in this limited nature of Soviet secularization efforts, as conditioned by specific religious traditions, and even more in the way the *actual* secularization process of the period (distinct from these intentional secularization efforts) crossed national borders freely and was ignored as it did its work.

Not altogether unrelated, and of equal importance is the strikingly American sort of secularization that is by and large restricted to the antireligious attitude of some American intellectuals. How is it related to the religious structures preceding it? Does it show different faces in different population groups? To what extent might it be a reaction to a perceived "lower class" membership in American Protestant communities? These and many other questions need to be raised by serious historians in order to understand more about the world and its many—often unnecessary—misunderstandings.

Part Two

RELIGION AND POLITICS

The Way is eternally nameless.
If feudal lords and kings preserve it,
The myriad creatures will be transformed
By themselves.*

—LAO TZU

---

* This observation from the *Tao Te Ching* cannot be resisted in a discussion of religion and politics. From its perspective in Chinese tradition, it suggests that if political folks were able to preserve the nameless Ultimate, an enlightenment of all creation would occur (Mair, *Tao Te Ching*, 105).

5

Early Kingship

Spirit and Power

In speaking of religion and politics I am conscious of addressing a "Christianity-affected" world. The major political divisions and dominant frames of reference come from the involvement of Western, "Christianity-affected" powers, and as a result most political discussions are conducted in a language that originated in the West.

Of course, the "Christianity-affected" point of view is not a homogeneous entity, and does not necessarily identify itself as "Christian." Indeed, it includes anti-Christians, self-styled secularists, and atheists. It includes as well many a non-Western, non-Christian intellectual who has acquired the patterns of expression deemed necessary to speak of global political matters. What we need to keep in mind, then, is simply that in an endeavor to detect "structures" of religion and power, we must make a conscious effort to think and speak in a way that does justice to all the human realities we encounter.

The historian Leopold von Ranke observed: ". . . no state has ever subsisted without a spiritual base and a spiritual substance."[1] Although that is a general statement, it describes what we know from all *particular* documents at our disposal. We know of no state that has not seen itself as justified and grounded in moral and spiritual realities prior to its own existence and beyond itself.

---

1. These words by Ranke may be found in one of the fragments from his literary legacy. See Stern, *The Varieties of History*, 60.

The moral and spiritual realities invoked by states do not all come out of one single source. We can expect to find each and every state closely connected to some specific religious tradition.

I propose in the following essays to look at evidence that can inform us about how structures of religion and structures of power occur in pairs, how sacred models give rise to particular political and social forms, and how the underlying sacred paradigms determine how social structures and structures of power are *experienced* in the actual lives of human beings.

The Ancient City

With the early cities, kingship came into being. Kingship is not a primordial feature of human existence. Kingship, together with all it involves, is historically delineated. It is a cultural product that appears with the presence of urbanization. Specifically, it appeared in the period between the first establishment of enduring settlements in the fertile regions of the Near East and the rise of Sumer. The time it needed to take on its definite shape was not all that long. Henri Frankfort suggests that a few generations sufficed; and Lewis Mumford believed that the development of *all* the urban institutions, including kingship, would not have required more than a few centuries.[2]

As soon as we enter the ancient city, we enter a conspicuous religious territory, and we find the beginning of historical documentation for the relationship between religion and power. Mumford has discussed the peculiar dimensions of the citadels characteristic of all early cities archaeologists have brought to light, from Mesopotamia to the Indus Valley. The citadel of Khorsabad in northern Iraq, for example: its walls have a thickness of seventy-five feet. "Significantly out of all proportion" to any means of assault that existed at the time, this surely speaks of more than self-defense. Why such walls as these? Mumford answers that men would exert themselves so extravagantly only for their gods.[3] It is interesting that the archaeological evidence lends credence to writings that otherwise would seem like fiction. The book of Judith, probably composed

---

2. Mumford, in his celebrated study *The City in History*, 33.
3. Ibid., 37.

in the second century B.C., tells that the ramparts of the ancient city of Ecbatana were fifty cubits wide (a cubit being about twenty inches).[4]

There is no doubt that the kings of ancient cities were leaders in war; most often this was probably their primary function. But at the same time Mumford's conclusion that the walls that fortified those rulers and their armies were also built for the gods is difficult to escape. Mumford leads his reader to a further conclusion that is most uncomfortable: in the ancient city we enter our *own* world; religion and worldly force are together; war has become a permanent institution. War itself is an institution the ancient city and its religion produced.[5]

We have already suggested in this book that religion is more than the individual's inner stirrings. We must also bear in mind that religion is not necessarily "nice." Perhaps the most disconcerting thing of all to ponder is that we cannot remove ourselves from the religious situation in which we exist. Our civilization has created its precise forms and details. It is not an external, ceremonial state from which good intentions might serve to extricate an individual. It is the situation in which we are born and have been taught to speak and feel and orient ourselves, and in which our good deeds and transgressions are measured within us and over us. Man is a religious creature, even though we are not required to take delight in that proposition.

In the same way, it does not make sense for us to ignore or to protest the inseparability we find between religion and power-in-general. The design of the ancient city set a stage we have not left ever since. The question of whether we would *like* to have spirituality and power bound together does not arise. They exist together in the religiosity that is characteristic of our world. The outrageous walls of ancient citadels have their parallel today; we live with gigantesque military nation-camps that possess many times the quantity of weapons sufficient to destroy the earth.

---

4. Judith 1:2.

5. Mumford, *The City in History*, 45. It should not need to be elaborated that war as an institution, born with the city, differs from other forms of violence that in comparison either are more general, "ethological," belonging to the world of nature, or are related to specific nonurban or preurban cultic forms. For the former, see Goodall, *The Chimpanzees of Gombe*; for the latter, see the headhunting customs discussed in van Baal, *Dema*.

The Hittite Kings, Alexander the Great, Egypt

The most ancient historically traceable structures of power and spirit become quite difficult for us to reconstruct. A brief look at one case, from the Hittite kingdom, may provide an impression of the complexities involved.

At its climax, the Hittite empire extended over a large part of Asia Minor and Syria (fourteenth–thirteenth century B.C.). Its beginnings were approximately 2000 B.C. and it endured to about 700 B.C. With regard to the development of the civilization and culture of this empire, most everything is hard for us to understand. Our fascination—as well as a major problem—begins with the complexity of Hittite origins. The radiant Babylonian culture was certainly a strong influence on the Hittites. Much earlier, however, other traditions had made themselves felt. Among these was the earliest culture of which we can claim to have some knowledge; within the "Hittite realm," on the central plain of Anatolia, stand Çatal Höyük and other excavation sites which have brought to light the ruins of highly developed extended villages that had their origin in the seventh millennium B.C. To speak of an "influence" from this ancient hearth of organized human existence seems almost disrespectful. One scholar has observed that "Anatolia presents to us a remarkable continuity in religion," a lasting continuity until Christianity became implanted.[6] Hittite civilization is striking from the perspective of world history because it blended and preserved a multitude of Indo-European and Semitic elements, languages, and tribal customs.

The aspect of this civilization that interests us here concerns the king in his relationship to the celestial Sun God.[7] The Hittite king was addressed as "My Sun." There is a record that even before the empire flowered the expression "Our Sun" was in use. It seems that according to the tradition, upon their death the king and royal family members became gods.[8] However, the imagery and mythology available indicate also that there was closeness between the living king and the Sun God. We are unable to fully reconstruct the nature of this link. We do know that what tied the king to his divine counterpart was his political function, and most especially his function as leader in war. An assembly of the gods played a crucial role in deciding issues relating to justice, and

---

6. Vieyra, "Les religions de l'Anatolie antique," 258.
7. See for the following especially Houwink ten Cate, "The Sun God of Heaven."
8. Otten, "The Religion of the Hittites," 322.

to any breach of treaties,[9] which last was of the utmost significance for decisions on whether or not to go to war. In these matters the close link between the king and the Sun God was vitally important. On occasions when these matters relating to war were to be decided, the assembly of the gods was invited to be present, and not only the Hittite gods but likewise gods of the opposing tribes or nations. Although our records on what ensued are unclear, we can see an identity between religion and the functions of law. We should clarify this further by stating that we see an identity not of religious "dogma" or "conviction" but of religious *conduct* and the functions of law.

How can we make something clear that is indeed evident in the documents in spite of our fragmentary grasp of them? How can we make an *instituted experience* clear to our present-day mental habits? Religious conduct of the sort just described has nothing to do with imposed dogmas or with "beliefs." It is rather a matter of things that needed to be done in the only way they could be done. Hence it was a matter of experience, and not "experience" in the sense in which our contemporaries normally interpret it—something felt by individuals in their private inner life—but again, something that must be done because it cannot be sensed otherwise.

We have an ancient Hittite record that when for whatever reason the king's continued life is uncertain, he bows down before the celestial Sun God in a daily ritual, imploring the god in prayer to spare him from a fate among the shades—the fate in store for mortals after death.[10] Although the interpretation of this prayer is uncertain on several points which scholars debate, there is no doubt overall that the king's function as a ruler in this world is of crucial significance in Hittite religious expressions. Our knowledge that this was the case must be brought to bear when we look at the prayer. The king, perhaps in ill health, perhaps threatened by enemies, says to his heavenly counterpart: as king, I belong to the *divine* realm; maintain me there. It is a plea not to die, of course—but not with the modern "private," "experiential" connotation. The prayer begins with the words: "Oh Sun God of Heaven, my lord, what have I done? You have taken the throne away from me and given it to another . . . But me you have assigned to the shades. I have made my appearance before the Sun

---

9. Houwink ten Cate, "The Sun God of Heaven," 19.
10. Ibid., 27.

God of Heaven, my lord: admit me to my Divine Fate, to the gods of heaven and release me from my residence among the shades!"[11]

Modernizing, "existentializing" this prayer would no doubt be an error; it would force ideas that to us are familiar upon documents that speak an altogether different language. We must attempt to read this prayer in the light of what we do know about Hittite kingship as the counterpart of a particular god. The prayer is in the form of a fixed liturgical item for circumstances that can occur in the experience of kingship as an institution. It does *not* make the king like any ordinary mortal. Rather, it shows the king as *the function* which he must fulfill and which relates him to the Sun God. Similarly, the Hittite "Sun God of Heaven" functions also in the mode we would call "political" by heading the divine assembly that decides on the fate of the land.

This seemingly remote context of religious practice tying together the actual world of power and the gods is also visible in biblical texts. In their prayers, the kings of Israel and the psalmists remind God of his promises not to abandon Israel and of the covenant he made between Himself and his people. *You know my fate; You know your promise; Remember it!*[12] Thus the biblical texts may serve as a bridge for our understanding. They are a great deal closer to the fragments from the Hittites than they are to our contemporary world.

The career of the empire-builder known as Alexander the Great (356–323 B.C.) was an entirely new phenomenon, both from a religious and from a sociopolitical standpoint. It meant a complete break with the religious self-sufficiency of the *polis*. Alexander accomplished quite dramatically, on a worldwide stage, what the cult of Dionysus and the mystery religions with their initiations and their esoteric awareness had accomplished for individuals. In both cases, traditional limits were widened to an extent for which no paradigm existed. It was but natural that popular esteem and tradition would associate Alexander with Dionysus. Dionysus was much more than a god related to one place in particular, as Athena was to Athens or Zeus to Dodona; even Aphrodite, whose cult was widespread, had her special places of worship.[13] Like Dionysus' saving power, Alexander's power to rule seemed to reach throughout the universe. The great Italian scholar Raffaele Pettazzoni, who broadened

---

11. Ibid., 24.
12. For example, 2 Chr 1:9; Ps 77:8; 105:42.
13. See Nilsson, *Geschichte der griechischen Religion*, 1:523–26.

the framework of scholarship on myth, ritual, and kingship by pointing out many inner relationships of social, religious, and political realities, has expressed it thus:

> Every social order is, in effect, a system of collective forces that are felt as superior to man, and are sacred. Their sacredness resides most particularly in the person of the founder, and people express that sacrality by divinizing him and by sanctioning this divinity through a cult. Alexander was already the founder of a city and for that reason was a *heros ktistes* or *oikistes* and Alexandria venerated him in that capacity. However, he was now also the creator of a new state, the empire, different from the *polis* as well as from the national monarchy. This empire, in its turn, demanded its religious consecration, and that meant the consecration of its founder.[14]

A great variety of regions and nations, each from its point of view, recognized this new phenomenon. The Greeks, the peoples of Mesopotamia and of Egypt and also of a number of smaller states and tyrannies, found their own preparation in their own heritage for a new *proskunesis* (worship).[15] Among the lands that came under the sway of Alexander was Persia. One might argue that in a sense the experience and history of Persia had anticipated Alexander. Darius (550–489 B.C.), king of Persia, and called "the Great," who preceded Alexander by two centuries, is known to us through his self-glorifying inscriptions. This very large region, Persia, was itself a conglomerate of states rather than a strictly organized monarchy, and hence presents almost a model for what would come to pass through Alexander all over the world. Persia too saw in this new ruler the revelation of an all-embracing unity of the whole world. We could indeed call this a religious awareness, as Pettazzoni suggested. And yet it would have been difficult to explain to the Persians the religious quality of the *proskunesis* they engaged in. They did not look upon it as a religious act per se. For them, a ruler, especially while alive, was not a god, any more than rulers were gods in Mesopotamia or any another region. However, the Persians had cultivated display surrounding their rulers more than any other nation. Their ceremonies and pageantry helped to create an atmosphere of religious adoration, and rather awed the Greeks in that vein, even though the Greeks for their part were not inclined to divinize

---

14. Pettazzoni, *La Religione nella Grecia antica*, 252.
15. The final chapter in Pettazzoni is quite illuminating on this point.

kings.[16] Persia seemed prepared for Alexander by custom, tradition, and memory.

All such items of history speak to our imagination and yet they are not really easy to grasp over the long span of time that separates us from an event like the formation of Alexander's empire. We "moderns" may be inclined to attach significance to matters that did not carry a great deal of weight in their own day. For instance, we may feel a certain kinship with Alexander when we hear that he did not like being made into an object of worship. Unlike the rulers of the Achaemenian dynasty of Persia, and some other early kings, he never called himself "king of kings." Nevertheless, accuracy demands the observation that Alexander was a man of the ancient world, different from us precisely in not resisting the idea of his own divine nature so very much. His personal character seems romantically inclined; modern scholarship likes to point this out in explaining his career; and no doubt scholars are right that he "possibly felt himself an instrument of the gods."[17] Yet again, though, a difference in significance; his age did not do what we are used to doing: separate in some absolute way the concept of a god from the concept of the human world. The notion of one transcendent deity had not made its impact yet. That was part of later historical events, in which the key role was played by ideas rooted in Israel and channeled through a large part of the world by Judaism, Christianity, and Islam. Universal kingship of the type associated with Alexander certainly amounted to a new religious phenomenon, but let us pay attention to what exactly made it new; it was not an elevation of the divine over the human, of the type that comes to mind for us, but the togetherness of what we might call "the universally religious" with the political element of supreme universal power.

With respect to a ruler like Alexander, let us make another cautionary aside. In all probability there has been too much talk about *sacred* kingship. Our fascination with the religious aspects of such kingship, so distant in time, should not make us forget that the worldly power of kings was indeed worldly, and was exercised to the hilt; it was not a secondary extension of royal "sacredness."

Historians are not the only ones who may come to a premature understanding because they see what they would like to see. Among

---

16. Ibid., 260–61.
17. Tarn, *Alexander the Great*, 124.

theologians, errors of understanding occur because of a desire to find evidence in history for the truth of the biblical revelation.

Thus, interestingly enough, just as a "secular humanist" might feel an (imaginary) kinship with Alexander, who is pictured as if he were a "modern," "secular" man, so a believing theologian might be overeager to picture in the Egypt of the pharaohs sacred kings who are removed from the human realm and worshiped, whereas in the Hebrew books of Kings he might feel satisfaction in seeing rulers who are presented as human beings. However, we shall certainly have to point out ambiguities when we discuss the status of kingship in the Bible. And in looking at the pharaohs, honesty must compel us to avow that we are far from understanding what they represented in the living minds of the inhabitants of Egypt.

It is always Egypt from which the paramount examples of divine rule are drawn in our discussions. We feel we know ancient Egypt as well as we know familiar corridors in a museum. But we ought to be much more circumspect with respect to that land, and the first thing we need to realize is that we have great difficulty explaining what "divinity" meant there. Erik Hornung has discussed in detail the peculiarities of Egyptian notions of "godhead," beginning with the insight that the contradiction between divinity as one or as many was not essential for the Egyptians.[18] Even earlier, the Egyptologist Siegfried Morenz emphasized the very significant detail that the Egyptian gods are not revealed but seem rather more like necessities, inevitabilities, or exigencies that people experience in their lives.[19] The forces the Egyptians felt exerted upon them were of course not necessarily forces we are familiar with. Their world was extremely complex in its organization, and that complexity was hierarchically arranged in a manner for which we have no equivalent. But the majority of those needs and exigencies were "here and now," in this world, rather than beyond the world of our senses. Hence, for various reasons, the distance between people and their "god" ruler, whose function was necessary for the existence of the realm North and South (the complementary set making up the whole of the land according to the texts, mythical and realistic at the same time), had little to do with the transcendental distance we tend to imagine.

---

18. Hornung's *Conceptions of God in Ancient Egypt* is a brilliant exposition of this state of affairs.

19. For a discussion of the nature of Egyptian gods, also of Morenz's suggestions, see Derchain, "La religion égyptienne," 78–79.

Something else should be considered too, if we want to avoid misunderstandings. The elaborate funeral rites for pharaohs, of which the pyramids are the lasting monument, are not to be seen exclusively as demonstrating a chasm between the ruler and the ruled. Of course, the pyramids and the powerful rituals behind them are of great significance, but not simply for separating "divine" rulers from "profane," ordinary men; on the contrary, in the course of Egyptian history we see that the royal funeral rites came to be performed for more and more Egyptians.[20] The symbolism of the pharaoh's funeral rites was not directed only from the king to god; it spread outward and permeated the lives of the people.

The point to be registered is that the religious symbolism of kingship is not only, perhaps not even primarily, a matter of the king's relation to God or the gods, but of his relation to other men, the people over whom he has authority. This relationship may be called a basic symbolic feature in all kingship. It is amazingly strong and persistent in an unending number of expressions through time. Every schoolchild in Holland learns in history class the final words of Prince William of Orange, "the father of the fatherland," when in 1584 he was shot in Delft, and said *Mon Dieu, ayez pitié de moi et de ce pauvre peuple.* ("My God, have compassion on me and on this poor people.") Most of us, being unaware of the antiquity and basic symbolism of such pronouncements, instead would settle here for sheer sentimentality.

An irony of history occurred during the "everlasting" period of pharaonic kingship. In Ptolemaic times, after Alexander's revolution had extended over the Mediterranean world, the ruling dynasty in Egypt was Macedonian. The Ptolemaic kings represented a change in the political landscape; the rulers of Egypt were no longer Egyptians. A self-contained order had been invaded. Although there had been dynastic breaks within the millennia of Egyptian history, the revolution of Alexander and its idea of universalism brought the irruption of a much larger and more diverse world. Still, the cult, in all its intricate relationship to the ruler, went on as before. Signs made their appearance in the temple courts of Memphis to direct that non-Egyptians, of whom there now were many, were not permitted to approach the *sanctum sanctorum*. The irony that would not have struck anyone at the time was that while the unabated cult sought new mechanisms to protect and maintain itself, the supreme ruler had become a foreigner.

20. Ibid., 125–31.

The logic of the cultic symbolism may be untranslatable into the logic of Aristotle or Aquinas, but its sense lies unmistakably in expressing an unceasing, continually rejuvenated certainty concerning the deity, the sovereign, and the people in their socioreligious relationship.[21] This equilibrium, which pervades more than three thousand years of Egyptian history, is a source of astonishment for us. The historian Toynbee, well known for his thesis that all civilization springs from conflict, indicated that Egypt was the one remarkable exception. In the words of a specialist on Egypt, the myth-ritualist[22] H. W. Fairman:

---

21. How important the *function* of the king was and remained, as compared to his personal or national origin, appears from an interesting detail: a title given to him in Ptolemaic times points explicitly to his priestly and divine nature, and apparently was not given in earlier times. See Otto, *Gott und Mensch*, 69–70.

22. Decades of scholarship have been devoted to the study of myth, ritual, and kingship. A host of philologists, historians, and anthropologists who became collectively known as the "Myth and Ritual School" experimented with a new focus of research into religious realities. Their efforts formed a healthy antidote to the abstract theories about religious evolution that had so enthralled the nineteenth century. The myth-ritualists turned their attention to the actual lives of people, their societies and their governments, most especially in the ancient Near East—where by common consent we recognize the beginnings of Western history. Some of the outstanding myth-ritualists were specialists on the Hebrew texts of Israel or on the texts of Mesopotamia and Egypt. In spite of differences, of which they were well aware—there was much they disagreed on among themselves—and in spite of exaggerations that critics rightly pointed out in their views, the work they did help enormously in breaking through the isolation in which many a specialist found himself—for they truly broadened the framework for all scholarship.

Among the myth-ritualists, it was the great accomplishment of the Englishman S. H. Hooke to have brought together researchers, guided their discussions, and edited major collections of their essays. Less after the manner of a school, Scandinavian scholars associated with the myth-ritual movement contributed important work in discovering the live texture of religious life in the ancient world. The Norwegian Sigmund Mowinckel (1881–1965) studied the Psalms in a new light; it is he who saw the significance of the figure of the king in many of the texts as participant in certain rituals, in cultic conjunction with the priests and the people. A very great stimulus for all myth-ritualists came early in the twentieth century from the work of the German scholar Hermann Gunkel, who first called for attention to the context in which religious expressions functioned (the *Sitz im Leben*). For our purposes, the most significant title of the whole myth-ritual movement is Hooke, *Myth, Ritual, and Kingship*. Keeping in mind that the myth-ritualists do not accord royal rulers all the "worldly" weight that occupies political scientists, it seems to me of the greatest importance that many myth-ritualists did turn our eyes away from esoteric speculations on the origin and nature of "the Holy" and opened them for documented interrelationships between religion and power that for too long had not been given proper attention. (A splendid assessment of the school is Harrelson, "The Myth and Ritual School," 282–85.) Perhaps

> One of the most striking characteristics of kingship in Egypt was its extraordinary stability: revolutions and conspiracies are relatively unheard of; legitimate heir, usurper or foreign conqueror, each, once something had happened to him, became veritable and recognized king, and, what is perhaps most remarkable, each quite clearly considered his predecessors, apart from such obvious exceptions as the Hyksos and the Amarna kings, as his ancestors. It is quite evident that at some point in the making of a king, in his selection or in his crowning, something happened that ensured his legitimacy, that automatically disarmed opposition and claimed and obtained loyalty, and that simultaneously made him a god and linked him directly with all of Egypt's past.[23]

The "something" that ensured each pharaoh's legitimacy was the enthronement and the rituals of loyalty. We must take Fairman's words literally that something *happened*. Egypt underwent its difficulties—but each such difficulty led the Egyptians back through that which "happened" to the stability that intrigues us. Fairman writes:

> The Egyptian of historic times did not have our doubts and difficulties. To him the kingship was not merely part, but the kernel of the static order of the world, an order that was divine just as much as the kingship was divine. The Egyptians believed that the first dynasties were of gods, followed by a dynasty of spirits and demi-gods, the Followers of Horus. It was in these times that justice and the social order were created, so that in later times texts would speak of "The Ghosts who made the sun-disk, who created all good things in their time. Ma'et (Truth), who descended from heaven to earth in their time, she consorted with the gods, there was abundance of food in the bellies of men, there was no falsehood throughout the land, no crocodile seized, no snake bit in the days of the Primeval Gods."[24]

What we are asked to understand is not that wars, upheavals, all the miseries of the human world were absent, but that they had no channel open to them except the one leading to a reestablishment of divine equilibrium. To an unusual extent, the Egyptians reactivated through the

---

the most significant single critical treatment of the myth-ritualist theses is the classicist Fontenrose, *The Ritual Theory of Myth*.

23. Fairman, "The Kingship Rituals of Egypt," 77.

24. Ibid., 75. For the suggestion of Egypt's power to conserve, see also Otto, "Die Religion der alten Ägypter," 33.

realities of life that primordial balance, that blissful "sameness," modeled in the myth of primeval gods who ruled in the first dynasties and lived in perfect accord with Justice. In matters of military and political reality, Egypt shared the world of the other early kingships—but the religious structure of the Egyptians gave their kingship its unique features.

Egypt does have parallels elsewhere. Historically, Chinese and Japanese emperors have taken actions and had things "happen" to them that seem equally foreign to us in our cultural habits. Those emperors were not asked to *do* something for the tradition; they were born into it, and at the ritual of enthronement remodeled into it. We are very far away in such cases from the idea of a "separation of church and state."

The most ancient, the most "traditional" civilizations, which are the beginnings of our own history, share neither the perception nor the conception of politics and religion as separate entities. Such separation begins much later, and is slow and painful. The origins of the "separation of church and state" do not occur in the development of political or economic power in isolation. The origins come about *as religious creations* in Israel and in Greece.

6

Israel, Early Christianity, Greece

Biblical Kingship

It is generally supposed that the Hebrew Bible does not present any sacred myth of kingship. And it is true that the religion of Israel has no myths of divine ancestry comparable to those of Egypt or Japan or the Inca. However, I am not sure students of the Old Testament always draw defensible conclusions from such a fact. Along this same line, sundry scholars, together making up a far from negligible group, would even have us believe that biblical religion is devoid of myth altogether.

A certainty like this must be compared to the preestablished opinion of the beginning student whose mind is made up about truth or untruth in religion. The type is well known to professors; no amount of information, evidence, or philosophical reasoning can shake him. The final paper he produces is filled with idiosyncratic facts and arguments. Scholars express themselves less naïvely, but still may have had their ideas in place before they began and may be eager, all-too eager, to prove what they knew before they started. What they may have in mind with respect to our present topic of religion and politics is a posited "uniqueness" of biblical ideas on kingship. And spoken or unspoken, often a feeling that the biblical tradition somehow makes more sense, or is better suited to solving problems of the real world.

But the Bible indeed does present us with a relationship of the divine and the political in which the two are cohesive aspects of one *religious* imagery. As in all other cases, there is a paradigm, a categorical imagery *that orients human beings in their actions.*

David and Nathan

The books of Samuel and Kings have a lot to say about the dubious nature of kingship. Wanting a king to rule over them, the people exhibit the desire of "the nations"—hardly a compliment in biblical speech. Eventually God Himself selects a king for Israel. Saul is anointed, but the words of the prophetic judge Samuel are borne out soon after Saul's confirmation at Samuel's hand. Upon Saul's anointment, Samuel had said to the people of Israel: ". . . you will realize what an evil thing you did in the eyes of the Lord when you asked for a king."[1] In its blunders Saul's kingship made Israel much like the nations that surrounded it.

Of all the kings who follow Saul, only David, the immediate successor, enters gloriously into legend. Tradition sings his praises and ascribes to him some of the most gripping poetry and prayers of the biblical texts. David's radiance glows down the ages, so much so that centuries later, Christians will claim the line of David in the generations of their Messiah. David's kingship is marked by victories and by the relative stability he provides for his people—a peace extended by David's son Solomon. Nevertheless, the text enlarges upon David's faults. He does what in the bitter collective experience kings are known to do. King David is not above evil desires and he takes what is not his own.

Bathsheba was the wife of a commander in David's army.[2] Smitten with her, the king of Israel dispatched the husband to a battleground where he certainly would perish. And when the husband did not return, David took Bathsheba for his wife. Then, in a most dramatic scene, the prophet Nathan pronounces God's judgment on the king. Nathan begins innocently, telling David of a wealthy man who wanted a little ewe lamb that was not his. The ewe belonged to a poor man, who loved it as his only possession. The rich man took the lamb and made it a meal for a traveler who had come to him. David is outraged by Nathan's story. The rich man deserves to be put to death, he declares, and the lamb should be paid for four times over. "You are the man!" says the prophet. And once again gloom is cast over Israel's kingship, over David himself and his descendants: "Out of your own household I am going to bring calamity upon you."[3]

---

1. 1 Sam 12:17 (NIV).
2. 2 Samuel 11–12; see also Ps 51:2.
3. 2 Sam 12:11 (NIV).

The biblical presentation of kingship as both rule and subjection to judgment seems to fit the Western tradition as it unfolded, with its problems of spirit and power in the antagonism between pope and emperor, church and state. The image in the background remained that of a divine appointment coupled with human failure. As in the biblical story, the failure was ultimately interpreted as sin before God. The biblical imagery, as if given in shorthand by the pregnant history of David and Nathan, had entered upon the historical scene and come to stay.

With the Christian tradition, the line from King David to Jesus Christ resumes the case of all kingships, ruling at once from above and on the same level with men. And Jesus Christ is called the son of God and the son of man, and through him, moreover, especially in the Gospel of John, judgment and grace are present simultaneously.

The Gospel of John narrates a special episode in the suffering of Christ. The Roman governor Pilate, John tells us, insisted on leaving unchanged the sign he had ordered affixed to the cross, written in Hebrew, in Latin, and in Greek, so that all could read it: Jesus of Nazareth, King of the Jews. The chief priest asked Pilate to use different words: this man said, I am King of the Jews. But Pilate refused, saying "What I have written, I have written."[4]

As with all myths, in this story several chords are struck at once. Obviously, the figure of Pilate *is* political power. He also has the strange role of a special sort of lasting reality (preserved in the creed of the Church, where his name is linked to the event of salvation) unexpectedly, prophetically, insisting that Jesus is King. It is of course true that as a faithful administrator in the Roman Empire, Pilate could hardly have used a better means than the punishment of public crucifixion to impress upon all the fate of rebels. But Pilate's cleverness in not allowing Jesus to be displayed simply as an individual with deranged ideas is certainly not the reason John recorded the inscription Pilate placed on the cross. Instead, the episode resumes dramatically the strange togetherness of power with grace and love that prevails throughout the book from its very introduction in the prologue: "The light shines in the darkness, and the darkness has not overcome it."[5]

"Prince of Peace," one of Jesus' epithets, indicates precisely those two things that do not exist together in the world we know. "Peace," certainly

---

4. John 19:19–22.
5. John 1:5 (RSV).

in the biblical texts, comes from God, as does justice and righteousness, while the notion of the "prince" inevitably suggests worldly dominion and power. And the Christian church sees in this Prince the object of faith, which cannot be amassed through power. The ambiguity of power and justice together does not become a problem solved, but is a mystery returning to mystery. But through the centuries, touched and moved by this myth, people feel impelled to take *political* action. Let us keep in mind as we proceed toward the conclusion of this essay that although the myth remains mysterious, it has a power that moves us to act.

Religious Imagery of Israel

How differently we visualize problems of religion and political power in our own lives than in other traditions far away from us! Yet we must realize that each of those traditions has been a *living* option with which people existed for very long periods of time. And moreover, our own situation can also be looked at as an array of religious imageries that compel us to *act* in certain ways. That we do not generally notice this has nothing to do with our religious belief or lack of it; *it is simply that we live with the presence of our religious assumptions as a given part of our world.*

We should be able to see that the religions of the world have all found ways—or had ways revealed to them—to relate the level where action and power are a must to the world of "the spirit," the transcendent. The reality of "the religious element" has always taken shape in an unmistakably real world of concrete power.

In the ancient city, we find the togetherness of religious cult and war. In the example of Alexander, we see the novelty of a new configuration of a universal worldly and a divine universal weal. We see in Egypt the continual assertion and confirmation of socio-politico-religious coherency.

Looking at this once again now, let us immediately turn to the biblical language of *God's righteousness*. That righteousness cannot be provided by even the highest human court. It is and remains *God's* righteousness; and yet, it is to be practiced.

> "What are your endless sacrifices to me?" says Yahweh.
> "I am sick of burnt offerings of rams
> and the fat of calves.
> I take no pleasure in the blood
> of bulls and lambs and goats.

> When you come
> and present yourselves before me,
> who has asked you
> to trample through my courts?
> Bring no more futile cereal offerings,
> the smoke from them fills me with disgust.
> New Moons, Sabbaths, Assemblies—
> I cannot endure solemnity
> combined with guilt.
> Your New Moons and your meetings
> I utterly detest;
> to me they are a burden
> I am tired of bearing.
> When you stretch out your hands
> I turn my eyes away.
> You may multiply your prayers,
> I shall not be listening.
> Your hands are covered in blood,
> wash, make yourselves clean.
> Take your wrong doing out of my sight.
> Cease doing evil. Learn to do good,
> search for justice, discipline the violent,
> be just to the orphan, plead for the widow.

These are the words of Isaiah.[6] And in the words of the prophet Micah:[7]

> "With what shall I enter
> Yahweh's presence
> and bow down before God All-high?
> Shall I enter with burnt offerings,
> with calves one year old?
> Will he be pleased with rams
> by the thousand,
> with ten thousand streams of oil?
> Shall I offer my eldest son

---

6. Isaiah 1:11–16 (NJB).
7. Micah 6: 6–8 (NJB); see also Psalm 51:16.

for my wrong-doing,
the child of my own body for my sin?
"You have already been told what is right
and what Yahweh wants of you.
Only this, to do what is right,
to love loyalty
and to walk humbly with your God."

Sophocles' *Antigone*

Our topic is the categorical imageries in each tradition that bind religion and power. Let us direct our attention to Greece. Besides Jerusalem, we look to Athens for what we regard as the cultural and religious roots of the Western world. Turning in particular to the classical Greek world that bears the signature of Sophocles, we will focus on one presentation of the juncture of religion and political power, as we come face to face with the *Antigone*.

The outline of events in the tragedy *Antigone* can be stated simply. When the play opens, Creon has become king of Thebes. Creon is the brother of Oedipus' wife, Iocaste; he accedes to the throne because of tragic events that have befallen the house of Oedipus. The latest calamity is that Oedipus' son Eteocles—who ruled the city—engaged in combat with his own brother, Polynices—who attacked the city—and they have killed each other. The siege has ended, and Creon, the new king, provides funeral rites for Eteocles but orders that outside the city, Polynices' body shall remain exposed, prey to vultures and roaming dogs. Antigone, one of the daughters of Oedipus, goes out and buries her brother's naked body. At Creon's order, her transgression is punished by death.

This ancient tragedy by Sophocles is arguably as modern as any play we have. We leave aside in this essay many issues of scholarly debate concerning Greek tragedy in general and Sophocles and his *Antigone* in particular. It has been suggested that the drama, first performed in 409 B.C., breathes the air of the Sophists, and no doubt it is possible to point out lines here and in other works of Sophocles that seem to contain a critique on divine activity in the world; traditionally accepted certainties appear to lose their footing. Indeed, a great scholar has opined almost disdainfully that Sophocles "is religious in the way a decent citizen is religious," and there may even be some truth to the suggestion that one can observe in Sophocles "a process in which a religious way of thinking is being demolished by generalizations concerning the divine."[8] Analysis of this sort, of which there is much, will not concern us here, except as a reminder that we should refrain from identifying Sophocles' poetic creation with general religious ideas that were held in ancient Greece.

Instead, we shall turn our full attention to the very vivid images of our problem of religion and power in particular scenes of *Antigone*: the dramatic confrontation between Antigone and Creon; the confrontation between Antigone and her sister Ismene—who "stands by" but does not get involved; Creon and the chorus of his councilmen, who echo the king and spend most of their time—but not all of it—consenting; Creon and the sentry who reports the illicit burial of Polynices. All of these scenes express without abstraction, without trappings, things which, deep inside, a modern person recognizes and knows.

In the first act of the play Antigone reveals to her sister Ismene her plan to cover Polynices' body with earth. She laments the denial of burial and mourning, the worst ignominy in Greek tradition, where a primary duty of each Greek was to bury and mourn the dead. With an additional tragic twist this great duty comes back at the end of the play, when Creon, seeing the wrongness of his decisions and frightened by the prophecies of the sage Tiresias, rushes his men out to rectify the errors. They go first to the dead Polynices to bury him properly with soil of his native place; then only, quite contrary to what would seem natural to us, they go to the deserted spot where Antigone was taken to meet her death—and arrive too late.

The sequence of the soldiers' efforts, honoring the dead Polynices before they attempt to save the life of Antigone, relates at once to the divine source of Antigone's action:

> Convicted of reverence—I shall be content
> To lie beside a brother whom I love.
> We have only a little time to please the living,
> But all eternity to love the dead.
> There I shall lie forever. Live, if you will;
> Live, and defy the holiest laws of heaven.[9]

---

8. See Nilsson, *Geschichte der griechischen Religion*, 1:758.

9. Sophocles, *The Theban Plays*, 128. All following excerpts from the *Antigone* are from this version, except where I have indicated otherwise.

Ismene, her sister, responds:

> I do not defy them; but I cannot act
> Against the State. I am not strong enough.

These words of Ismene give us the first glimpse in the play of the irresistible strength of the king's position. Admittedly, the translation I am quoting is rather free. The Greek text does not have the term "state." More literally, Ismene says that she is powerless to act against the citizens.[10] Yet the audience today would think, and quite rightly, of the state and its political power over us. Its rules are clear and straightforward; they appear eminently reasonable. Our outlook, our thoughts, are normally in tandem with the rules of the state and we feel that this is as it should be.

But at a certain moment the area of myth opens up. At the moment of crisis, it becomes as irresistible as the reason of the state. When King Creon decreed that the prince who defended Thebes would be honored in death but the prince who laid siege to the city had brought dishonor over himself, he was acting in harmony with the shared feelings of all the citizenry. What he could not have foreseen, what came to him as a great shock, was that Antigone, one of the offspring of Oedipus himself, would perform the act he forbade. Yet once that happened, what could the ruler do except remain consistent, as a strong king must?

In act 1, introducing the arrival of victorious Creon, the chorus of elders expresses the joy and relief felt in Thebes:

> . . .
>
> The Father of Heaven abhors the proud tongue's boasting
>
> . . .
>
> He heard the invader cry Victory over our ramparts
> And smote him with fire to the ground.
>
> . . .
>
> But see, the King comes here,
> Creon, the son of Menoeceus,
> Whom the gods have appointed for us
>
> . . .

The "Father of Heaven" of this modern translation is Zeus. It is he who protected Thebes, striking its enemies with his thunderbolt. It is he whom the citizens think of first when order is restored to the well-ordered

---

10. . . . τὸ δὲ βίᾳ πολιτῶν δρᾶν ἔφυν ἀμήχανος (lines 78–79).

city. And when King Creon speaks, we hear words that would be well received in any populace:

> No man who is his country's enemy
> Shall call himself my friend. Of this I am sure—
> Our country is our life; only when she
> Maintains her course, have we any friends at all.
> Such is my policy for our common weal.

Then Creon makes his proclamation concerning the sons of Oedipus, honorable burial and proper rites for the one, exposure for the other. He ends by saying,

> Now you know my thoughts, and I shall see to it
> That the unjust will never be honored as the just.
> But whoever is well disposed to this city I shall honor
> Alike in life and in death.[11]

And the chorus of Theban elders echoes:

> That is your view O Creon, Son of Menoeceus,
> Concerning friend and enemy of the city.
> It seems to us that it is in your power to apply each and every law
> To all of us who are alive, and also to the dead.[12]

We have an affirmation of Creon's decision. And yet, there seems to be a certain hesitancy to the words of the chorus; they are not a mere "echo" of the king's assertion of power. Wasn't there perhaps something arbitrary in what Creon did and said?

We might feel, with our habit of psychologizing, that the chorus seems to tell Creon: "*Personally* you can do as you please"; but that cannot be the poet's intention, for such a reading would be an anachronism. Why then does the chorus use language that is open to interpretation?

At this moment in the play, the chorus is extolling Creon in his royal function, and we know that in Greek tradition the decisions and acts of a king would always be aimed at preserving *nomos*, the established law, especially in the sense of "the right tradition." When the Theban elders say that the king in his royal function has the authority to decide over the living *and the dead*—do they not give the king an opportunity to protest

---

11. Lines 207–10 (my trans.).
12. Lines 211–14 (my trans.).

that their statement goes too far? Indeed this would have been perfectly possible, for in the climate of the time the king could have discussed matters with his counselors. Creon himself declares earlier in the play he has always held the view that a king should be willing to consult with his advisors.[13] Of course, it is hard to say to any king, even one tolerant of counsel, "you are wrong . . . you have overstepped your bounds." One can only provide an opening in the dialogue and hope the king will take it. I think this is what the elders in Thebes are doing. Which is to say, I think they are aware of the awesome clash that is occurring and the difficulty of choosing a way to act once the realm of the spirit makes its entrance into the realm of power.

The political realm inhabited by Creon is thrown into clearer relief through the presence of the sentry in the play. It is a minor role—but, like the roles of gravediggers and other clownesque figures in Shakespeare, invaluable as a bridge to the audience. The sentry watches over himself; he is intent on extending his life. His common sense is like a small mirror held up to the sense the king makes in his ruler's reasonings.

The sentry enters when Creon concludes his proclamation. His message is exceedingly simple: Polynices' body has been buried. Yet it takes him forever to get this information out, as it is couched in concerns for his own safety and endeavors to mollify the king. The sentry's fears are quite appropriate. Creon becomes enraged, and in a torrent of words assailing the evils of money—for as he perceives it, bribery must be involved in this sudden outrage—threatens the sentry's life if he does not find the culprit who buried Polynices. Then this exchange ensues between sentry and king:

> "May I say no more?"
> "No more; each word you say but stings me more."
> "Stings in your ears, sir, or your deeper feelings?"
> "Don't bandy words, fellow, about my feelings."
> "Though I offend your ears, sir, it is not I
> But he that's guilty that offends your soul."
> "Oh, born to argue, were you?"
> "Maybe so;
> But still not guilty of this business."
> "Doubly so, if you have sold your soul for money."

---

13. Sophocles, *The Theban Plays*, 131.

> "To think that thinking men should think so wrongly!"

Before the sentry exits, the audience is left in no uncertainty about his own "deepest" motivation. He wishes to preserve his life:

> Well, heaven send they find him. But whether or no,
> They'll not find me again, that's sure. Once free,
> Who never thought to see another day,
> I'll thank my lucky stars, and keep away.

But in fact he returns, and with him are two guards holding the prize he has found:

> We've got her. Here's the woman that did the deed.
> We've found her in the act of burying him. Where's the king?

And when the king reenters, the sentry, happy in his own change of fortune, becomes ever more garrulous, and we are allowed to see quite clearly the self-certain common sense that makes all of us in normal life so different from heroes:

> My lord, an oath's a very dangerous thing.
> Second thoughts may prove us liars. Not long since
> I swore I would not trust myself again
> To face your threats; you gave me a drubbing the first time.
> But there's no pleasure like an unexpected pleasure,
> Not by a long way. And so I've come again,
> Though against my solemn oath. And I've brought this lady,
> Who's been caught in setting that grave in order.
> And no casting lots for it this time—the prize is mine
> And no one else's. So take her; judge and convict her.
> I'm free, I hope, and quit of the horrible business.
> . . .
> I've never valued anyone else's life
> More than my own, and that's the honest truth.

That's the honest truth—of reasonable people, of reasonable kings, of reasonable states. The sentry embodies it unchangingly from the beginning to the end of the play. Creon will rise in some sense to the extraordinary occasion, sensing a fearful conflict between his political duty and the act Antigone has committed that now forces him to choose a response. But even his actions henceforth in the play cannot leave this realm of common political sense.

By contrast, the difference between both these figures and Antigone is absolute. The figure of Antigone is mythical. *That she is mythical is evidenced in the striking uncertainty she is aware of.* Where exactly is the authority for her action? She cannot tell.

It is typical of the authority of myths that the very question of their basis of authority either is omitted, or else is expressed with locutions that as "evidence" in the ordinary world of power and reason would not count at all.[14] (To be sure, the "uncertainty" is not a doubting attitude toward the dependability or value of the myth.) There is no standard form or style in which the issue is brought before us. However, as hearers of myth (or as readers who are still able to *listen*), we can have no doubt in noting it. The myth of creation best known in the West begins majestically: "In the beginning, God created the heavens and the earth." Equally well known are the words: "So God created man in his own image, in the image of God he created him; male and female he created them." No serious question asks what exactly the features were of that image in which humans were made. The stories convey their authority without having to offer proof. They seem to come "out of nowhere."

There are many ways in which myths can state their authority. *Sūtras* presenting the Buddha's teachings invariably begin with: "Thus I have heard." In a tradition thoroughly familiar with instruction of pupils by spiritual masters, no one is likely to wonder at those words. "I have heard" conveys authority in the teaching that is received.

In the initial conversation between Antigone and her sister Ismene, both women are aware, both know, that it is wrong to leave their brother unburied. This knowledge relates to the sacredness of family which they imbibed in their Greek culture. Ismene, although unwilling to transgress the laws of the state, also fears "to defy the holiest laws of heaven." As a matter of fact, even the chorus, the Theban elders and counselors of Creon, would not think of relinquishing those laws directly, and when the first reports reach them concerning the discovery that someone has strewn dry sand over the body of Polynices, they say to Creon:

> My lord, I fear—I feared it from the first—
> That this may prove to be an act of the gods.

---

14. I dealt with this matter in Bolle, *The Freedom of Man in Myth*, 56–63.

In principle, no one disagrees with Antigone. In some way, even the sentry agreed. But as the tragedy unfolds, none of this agreement suffices to cause anyone else to participate in the action that comes to life through Antigone.

It would be wrong to think that Sophocles intended to give us the trite wisdom that we must seek a happy balance between conflicting duties. At issue is the unavoidable encounter of forces dissimilar in nature. One prevails, although at a crushing price: Creon loses his son, who falls on his own sword; and Creon's wife dies, lacking the will to live. The other loses, but is the one remembered. The play is called *Antigone*, not *Creon*.

When the sentry brings her back, two guards lead Antigone into the circle of the stage.

> O gods! A wonder to see!
> Surely it cannot be—
> It is no other—Antigone!
> . . .
> Can she have recklessly disobeyed
> The order of our King?

Antigone confronts Creon. She admits her daring in flouting his order. That order, she says,

> . . . did not come from God. Justice
> That dwells with the gods below, knows no such law.
> I did not think your edicts strong enough
> To overrule the unalterable laws
> Of God and heaven—you being only a man.
> They are not of yesterday or today, but everlasting,
> Though where they came from, none of us can tell.

None of us can tell. This is the sign of myth, the model to be enacted, and the paradigm for which no substitute exists.

Creon, of course, tries to reason with Antigone. He explains—as if it needed explaining—that a distinction had to be made between the good and the bad. Only one brother was good. Antigone objects:

> Even so, we have a duty to the dead.

And Creon retorts:

> Not to give equal honor to good and bad.

Antigone has an answer of sorts—for she is in fact questioned on the source of the authority she obeys:

> Who knows? In the country of the dead that may be the law.

In this final exchange, Antigone also says:

> I have grown up to share in love, not in hate.[15]

The king, of course, has the last word:

> Go down, then, and love, if you have to,
> Them who are there [in the netherworld].
> No woman will rule [here] while I am alive.

It is not possible to explain the confrontation between Antigone and Creon in the terms of our scholarship or fashions. One could hardly make Creon's final scorn at the thought of woman's rule into the cornerstone of the tragedy. The conflict is too encompassing and surely not a skirmish between the sexes. (And too many references in the play point to Antigone's "stubbornness" as typical of Oedipus' line.) Nor could we be satisfied to invoke the learned distinction between the Indo-European, Olympic gods, and the preexisting gods "from below," the Chthonic deities. Nor can we sum up the play in any "moral," even though at one point the chorus reflects on the everlasting law that "for mortals greatly to live is greatly to suffer."[16]

We have to realize that the conflict is mythical in proportion. In fact, the myth consists in this *conflict* between power and spirit. Furthermore, once the myth is lived by Antigone, it cannot leave the ordinary world unaffected. Haemon, Creon's son and Antigone's beloved, in his words with his father, whom he wants to honor but has to oppose, says this to the worldly ruler:

> Do not foster just this one idea within yourself![17]

It would merely be a feeble suggestion—if it were not backed up, as in this case, and in Antigone's, *by the willingness to act accordingly.* The heroine never doubts that the gods safeguard the eternal law she obeys. But even this fact is insignificant next to the actual life with or

---

15. This and the next three lines quoted are my own translation.
16. Sophocles, *The Theban Plays*, 143.
17. Line 705 (my trans.). Watling has, "Let not your first thought be your only thought" (145).

participation in the myth. In the case of *Antigone*, the play, it is the *performance*, the "acting out" that matters most.

Categorical Imagery

Antigone is myth presented without idealizations. The myth remains inexhaustible. Do we not see ourselves in the *Antigone*? We see disconcertingly clearly that the predicament of our own time is not going to be solved.

As different as our world is from Greece in its golden age, we become aware of a kinship through Sophocles' play. We are aware of an extraordinarily precise attention on our part towards this play, as if we saw through a telescope. And of course, we have a telescoped view of the *Antigone*; we pick out the conflict of spirit and political power because it is the root problem of our modern world. (How peculiar this problem can seem will become striking when we turn to Hinduism and Buddhism!) No doubt we exaggerate in some way when we see so sharply the conflict of spirit and politics in the play. And nevertheless, we can claim to be right, because somehow what we choose to see is really there.

Because we recognize this ancient drama as our own, we see once more what it means to say that religion is not necessarily a pleasant thing. The old scholarly wisdom that held that myths function to preserve the status quo and to make society run smoothly seems like a dream. Probably all myths we listen to in earnest rest more on "uncertainty" and on conflict to be lived than on agreements and solutions reached.

Yes, for us, "church" and "state" became separated. Indeed, the mythic model our religion bequeathed to us has compelled us to adopt the separation. But all the same we are left with some mystery. Our image of the "strange togetherness" of spirit and power binds us. In its particulars, it differs from other cultures. In its power to orient us, it is the same. We are *in* our myth, as much as the ancient farmer of Egypt was in his.

Sophocles presents a paradigm, a mythic problem that can be stated but not solved. It can only be enacted. When the myth is enacted it changes the world.

7

Brahmanism:
The Balance of All and Everything

Brahmanism is of striking mental subtlety and penetration. The world is not opposed by transcendent or divine reality. The world is a manifestation—not an opposition—of the supreme.

Brahmanism, as a systematization of Vedic tradition, begins on Indian soil around 1000 B.C., after the Aryan invasions. "Brahmanism" is not a name a religion gave to itself. Outside observers assigned it—just as they did in speaking of "Hinduism," the word for the entire religious stream encompassing the religion of the Vedas, Brahmanism, and "later Hinduism" as it has run its course to the present day. Brahmanism is a *process* rather than a coherent, defined religion such as Islam or Judaism. It has no founder, and we cannot specify the time of its origin. At most we can say that it weakened after the appearance of Buddhism around the fourth century B.C., and again when the devotional, *bhakti* forms of religion appeared around the fifth to seventh centuries A.D., but it was never to be eclipsed and indeed it would utterly reassert itself in various religious, symbolic expressions. The consolidation of the *varṇa* or class system of India is among its lasting achievements. The historical process is one of an elite that gains sway over a whole subcontinent. Brahmanism proceeded by what we might call a process of *absorption*. In a sense, it never encountered anything new. It took what it saw and absorbed it and made it a manifestation of itself. Did a king give some brahmins the right to some land in a newly conquered village? The brahmins ask the villagers: who is the temple deity? And then the brahmins say, Oh, Viṣṇu! And the deity becomes Viṣṇu (without for that reason necessarily losing its original name). For the whole world is an emanation of the essence the brahmins thoroughly know.

The Brahmanic Texts

The example of Hinduism, even when we restrict ourselves to the early period, which we usually call "Brahmanism," places us before a very special case. Not only are we well documented on Indian religious tradition in general, but also by comparison with other religions we are unusually well informed with respect to the manner in which the political constellation sees itself embedded in religious certainties. Socioreligious certainties abound in Hinduism; they relate to worldly power, and the very wielding of that power clearly presupposes them. The intricacy of the foundation on which the exercise of worldly power rests is altogether different from anything else we are familiar with and certainly from the state of affairs we know in the modern world.

It is useful to remember that our word "religion" has no precise equivalent in most traditions. "Hinduism" in the widest sense—ranging from the ancient Vedic texts through the process of centuries that we call Brahmanism to the later, broad stream of (younger) Hinduism with its multitude of devotional, yogic, and cultic forms, and with its sacred sites everywhere (a geography crisscrossed by pilgrims)—uses the term *dharma*. *Dharma* has been explained as "religion," but frequently also as "law," and occasionally as a plural signifying "customs" or "duties engrained in tradition." Those customs, whether from our point of view religious or juridical or political or social in signature, are all matters of *dharma*. The idea of a demarcation between spirituality and politics is absent. And finally, it is good to remember that in Hinduism the notion of "faith" or "believing" is absent. Sanskrit, the major language of Hindu tradition, though according to all traditional lore able to express everything, does not have a word for "faith." In this particular respect, Hinduism is like all pre-Christian and pre-Islamic traditions.

Sanskrit, the ancient and persistent vehicle of Indian culture, certainly never lacked precision; it is not as if the distinctions between spirituality and politics so familiar to us could not have been made in India. In fact, the preciseness in the vocabulary of the Indian world is astounding. However, our distinctions about religion and power would seem to be naïve confusion from a Hindu perspective. A "separation" of church and state? What senselessness to separate the doings of human life from the unmanifest, the divine, if our life with all its visible and articulated separations is but a form that is taken by the Supreme.

The opening scene of the *Bhagavadgītā*—where the despondent Arjuna speaks his lament—always appeals to Western readers. Arjuna seems to express their own predicament. He sees in his mind's eye the horrible battle he is duty-bound to enter into. Trapped in a web of "power politics," he drops his weapons; he aches for what we might rightfully call "pure *dharma*." Only that will release him from the burden of the slaughter about to ensue. When Kṛṣṇa begins to speak the divine words to Arjuna that make up the instruction of the text, the narrator says that Kṛṣṇa did so *prahasann iva*, that is literally: "as if laughing"! Such is the beginning of the *Bhagavadgītā*'s teachings, and there will always be a certain helpful admonishment in what we learn from authoritative Brahmanic texts about our subject of religion and politics. For the give and take between notions of spirit and notions of power is brought into a balance that we can only dream of, and the Brahmanic texts seem to laugh at our problematic essays on religion and sociopolitical systems.[1]

A Case from Ancient India: The *Rājasūya*

The ritual texts in the religion of the Veda and Brahmanism have been disputed more extensively and for a longer period of time than most other documents in religiohistorical scholarship. Every fashion in interpretation has been tried on them, through the rise of historical linguistics and nature mythology[2] to tireless philological efforts from the nineteenth century onward[3] to endeavors to explain religion in terms of hallucinogens.[4]

---

1. The splendid historian of religions Bruce Lincoln wrote a book on myth in which myths become programmatic, political documents. What makes all of Lincoln's works very worthwhile, however, in my understanding of them, is his fascination with *justice*. He does not hammer on the theme, but it seems to me that his treatment of *justice* is what makes his writings absorbing. See Lincoln, *Theorizing Myth*. See also Bolle, *The Enticement of Religion*, 305–6.

2. Especially in the many works by F. Max Müller and Adalbert Kuhn.

3. Among the well-known names are Aufrecht, Weber, W. Caland, and Sylvain Lévi. In this line of philology-*cum*-interpretational effort, Frits Staal must also be mentioned because of his mighty tomes, *Agni: The Vedic Ritual of the Fire Altar*. They are based not only on knowledge of the texts, but on observations of the ritual in Kerala. The second volume presents contributions by a number of specialists.

4. See Wasson, *Soma: Divine Mushroom of Immortality*. For a critical discussion of

Sometimes the texts have been at the mercy of theories that relegated the rituals of ancient India to categories of primitive concern with magic. The twentieth century saw a good deal of sober interpretive scholarship based on solid philology, and such a work is J. C. Heesterman's *The Ancient Indian Royal Consecration*.[5] That ceremony of consecration, the *rājasūya*, is of prime importance for our present essay.

The *rājasūya*, the royal consecration, was lengthy and complex. In an open field made sacred by prescribed actions, filled with sacrificial fire altars and structures erected for the occasion, the king, his family, the brahmin priests, and others enacted a series of ceremonies that stretched out over more than a year's time. (A fairground atmosphere must have prevailed during the *rājasūya*. The site was a hub of royal power and invited money and goods. The scene and the mood are familiar even today at Indian religious festivals. There are storytellers and sellers of wares, and all manner of commerce and entertainment; perhaps people from the hill tribes, who look different from everyone else, have come down to watch.) The *rājasūya* ceremonies themselves are exceedingly diverse and of a textual attention to all and everything that is remarkable. It seems to me that in looking at the *rājasūya* we are in a position to see the outlines of an astonishingly original way of dealing with spirituality and worldly power.

The epilogue of Heesterman's book offers straightforward conclusions about the *rājasūya*, often supported by good arguments, yet leaves many matters unresolved. This is not unusual. Compared with other major religious traditions, Hinduism is "dense" to scholars. Most learned accounts evoke many more questions than they answer. So it is with Heesterman's work, despite the excellence of its textual presentation and annotation, and yet, by contrast with most efforts, Heesterman's treatise has built a gateway into a complex ancient ritual and enables us to see with some clarity where our problems of understanding lie.

One of the book's conclusions, quite convincingly drawn and documented, is irrefutable. Heesterman shows that we must reject a sociopolitical-ceremonial explanation; the very complex series of acts in

---

the book, see Brough, "Soma and *Amanita Muscaria*."

5. Heesterman, *The Ancient Indian Royal Consecration*. For a quick survey of the *rājasūya*, see Gonda, *Die Religionen Indiens*, 162–68. For the best available work on Indian ritual, see Krick, *Das Ritual der Feuergründung*. Renou and Filliozat, *L'Inde Classique*, 2:357–58 lists and summarizes the *rājasūya* among the various royal rituals, all of which are explained principally as magical means to enhance political power.

the *rājasūya* is definitely not a coronation festivity of the sort any Constantine, Wilhelm, or Louis would have enjoyed once in a lifetime. This point needed to be made in order to refute one of the most widespread uncritical assumptions concerning the *rājasūya*. The *rājasūya* is not like a ceremony from our own familiar history, dressed up in more exotic ways.

The ancient royal consecration, we are told, does not bestow royal power on a king once and for all. Heesterman says, "Its character can be best understood when compared with the yearly festivals known in Hinduism as *utsava* . . . by means of which the powers active in the universe are regenerated."[6] For the sake of brevity, but not altogether inaccurately, we may call this description "Frazerian," after the great Scottish scholar Sir James Frazer (1854–1941), whose memory is linked to his habit of positing the idea of fertility as the principal theme in religious traditions. Of course, Heesterman is no adherent of "primitivism," the collective name Georges Dumézil (1898–1986) disdainfully attached to theories such as Frazer's, which all begin by assuming a low state of mind in peoples of a "prescientific" and hence "primitive" world.

In the words Heesterman wrote concerning a regeneration of powers in the cosmos, there is no condescension. Moreover, Heesterman does not use the most typically Frazerian terms "fertility" or "magic" or "prescientific" at all. And I would not argue that there is no element resembling what Heesterman calls "regeneration" in the elaborate royal consecration. Yet I feel uneasy, for the ultimate suggestion that "powers active in the universe" are "regenerated" does not follow from a cautious search of the evidence. It is impossible to translate our modern cosmic powers or regeneration back into the Sanskrit texts; they do not use such expressions. Heesterman's conclusion follows upon certain assertions, the first of which occurs in his introduction. There at the outset we read what the world of Vedic India supposedly amounted to:

> A few words may be added here about the conception the Vedic ritualist had of his world. To the Vedic thinker the whole universe was constantly moving between two poles—of birth and death, integration and disintegration, ascension and descent—which by their interaction occasion the cyclical rhythm of the cosmos. In this world of floating forms there are no hard and fast lines; conceptually different entities and notions change with bewildering ease.[7]

6. Heesterman, *The Ancient Indian Royal Consecration*, 222.
7. Ibid., 6.

Certainly, it is possible that things we would like to call "integration and disintegration" or "cyclical rhythm of the cosmos" may have relevance as universal human concerns. But we should realize that they are great abstractions; they do not actually help us with a particular ritual in ancient India. What are we doing when we describe the *rājasūya* as a cosmic regeneration? These assertions with their "universal" sound can so easily become reductionistic. How is one to be universal in a way that is really fair to all the particulars? The question is truly fascinating at this point, because Hinduism found its own great way to do just that!

Heesterman does not make exaggerated claims for his interpretations. But he does imply that essentially the *rājasūya* is to be understood as a cosmic regeneration process. I wish to stress once more that this leaves matters unresolved. There is the possible inference of a precursor ceremony—a rite without the king's participation? Or including the king, but without an enthronement? A comparable celebration would be the new year *akitu* festival in ancient Babylon. In Babylon, the king was central in the ceremonies, and the feast was an annual event. But Heesterman does not mention the *akitu* festival and abstains from comparison. Furthermore, he does not deal with questions of when or how an annual event could have turned into the event of long, long duration we have in the texts. To do that, one would have to develop theories to account for all sorts of changes and accretions. Doing that, one unavoidably slides away from the necessary focus on the documents and back into a mental world of *our* making and our patterns of thought.

The particulars of the textual evidence of the great ceremony enlighten us much more than any general thesis. And the great merit of Professor Heesterman is that he presents us with the telling evidence of what happened. *This* is important, for it is incumbent upon us to see the human sense in the texts, without creating an artifice of concepts between the people of the texts and ourselves.

The Ritual Events

According to the documents we have, the enthronement of the king is preceded by an entire year of ritual ceremonies. Then come the great sacrificial procedures of the coronation itself; then follows yet another long period—another year in most of our sources—filled with many initiatory ceremonies and other rituals, concluding with still another inauguration of the king.

What are we to think, then? Our documents demand that we look at what is most apparent: this early Brahmanic religious vision carefully cultivates a forest of symbols.[8] By means of compilations of symbolisms, multitudinous relationships are ritually evoked, and all of them must be brought to bear on the investiture of the king. No single relation is paramount or stands apart from the others.

The first fourteen days, the preparation for the entire period set aside for the *rājasūya*, begins with a *soma* festival of five days and a series of *iṣṭis* (bloodless, cereal offerings): the *soma* offerings are expressly meant to purify the sacrificer (the king) and enable him to become divine, and the *iṣṭis* to prepare, to "sanctify" the year. Not only the royal sacrificer, but also time itself is transformed, reborn. It is more accurate to speak of the renewal of time than of an exhaustion and renewal of the cosmos. The renewal of time is a great preoccupation of Indian religion. In Brahmanism the time for the ritual must be made special, just like the sacrificer.

Dakṣiṇās are part of each ceremony in the long span of the feast's duration; they are the required gifts to the priestly brahmins, which together with the offerings to the gods are the gist of sacrificial life. On and on it goes, with sacrifices, and gifts, and always priests and priestly functions, and over and over the issue is not *just* this or that group or person, but all of temporal duration and the world.

The royal sacrificer becomes divine, of course, but it is of crucial importance to realize that the same "divinization" befalls every sacrificer in each sacrifice. At the occasion of the *rājasūya*, every participant would understand this simple fact.

There is a part of the proceedings that deals explicitly with the king and that turns around deities who presides in the ordinary household rituals and relate to the general, not specifically royal matters of conception and birth.[9] Here, the king, while emphatically presented in his royal function, is the ordinary sacrificer who is entitled to perform the sacrifice because he qualifies according to the standards set for such occasions, beginning with a perfect, *married* state. Hence his wife, the first queen (she is called "first" because there may well be other wives), has a special role to play, and an offering is to be made in her dwelling; this offering (*havis*,

---

8. I am using an image the eminent anthropologist Victor Turner employed to title one of his books: *The Forest of Symbols: Aspects of Ndembu Ritual.*

9. Gonda, *Die Religionen Indiens*, 1:164.

a burnt offering) is brought to no one less than Aditi, the great goddess, mother of the gods, and Aditi, says the text, "is the Earth." The language of the symbolism is too direct to require elaborate explanations; it is obvious that without the earth, the ruler could not rule, and, in exactly the same breath, without a wife, the man could not sacrifice, for he would not be complete—and of course, neither would he be complete as king. The married state is one of the many ordinary, natural relationships that meet the function of the ruler at every turn and make possible that rulership.

The king receives the anointment proper not merely from a brahmin priest, as if the latter were, so to speak, "the church" conferring its blessing, but at the hands of several priests and representatives of the *varṇas*, that is, all the "classes" making up what we would call society. (Our abstract word "society" does not have an equally abstract equivalent in Sanskrit; the word used is the compound *trivarṇa*, "the three classes," "the three estates.")

Another part of the ritual, not without its humor, has a text that confuses the name of the king with that of his son (or the expected son) and only then places them in the right order. Ritually the error must be made; ritually it must be set right. Thus the text clearly insists on another relationship. The king cannot be fully king unless after him a son will reign.

Each relationship in the rituals demonstrates a derived power, and to the extent power rests in the ruler, he nevertheless owes it to the relatives, relations, and givers who have made that power real.

After the king is anointed, he takes part in a game of dice—according to many scholars, a game that is played to establish the order and coherency of the world. (This is the sort of purpose that makes scholars very happy; they can point out a meaning in the motley proceedings.) Heesterman mentions the importance of games of dice that are "often connected with the passing of the old into the new year."[10] The king's opponents in the match are a brahmin, a *kṣatriya*, and a *vaiśya*, hence a member of the priestly class, the warrior class (the nobility), and the "third estate," or goods-producing class; these three together represent all his subjects collectively. As the ritual ordains it, although he plays against the whole of society, the king wins the game. At the end of the match, one of his opponents addresses the king: "Spend freely (*utsṛja*), O you who possess the full extent of life!" Whereupon the king replies: "I spend

---

10. Heesterman *The Ancient Indian Royal Consecration*, 153.

freely for the *brahman*, the *kṣatriya*, and the *vaiśya*. Virtuous conduct (*dharma*) should be the rule observed in my realm!"[11]

The game of dice is introduced with a ceremony in which priests beat the king on his back with sticks. The sticks the priests use for this purpose are sacrificially pure, and here most Sanskritists follow Frazer again, in this case for his explanation of ceremonial beatings: i.e. they are meant to stimulate fertility. (So according to Gonda.)[12] But in most of Frazer's examples, not men, but women undergo the ordeal. And since the text, furthermore, speaks of nothing that can be interpreted in terms of stimulating fertility, it would stand to reason to see this ceremony in analogy to other "relational" scenes we have witnessed. The brahmins beating the king not simply with sticks but with sacrificially purified sticks present a reminder that a higher order exists. Ultimately that higher order, although in itself not exerting worldly power, is in control. (I would say that the game of dice has to do with the obvious condition that in principle the king can lose the game. Although the ritual allows him to win, the circumstance the king is placed in is after all a game of chance.)

By now we must realize that trying to make sense of the extraordinary episodes, each different, in the long *rājasūya* festival by means of one causal explanation that satisfies our own reason would be a dastardly enterprise. Each of the relationships provided by the episodes, the first queen, the crown prince, the representatives of the three estates, and so on, points in a different direction. They are meaningful yet do not add up to a "system" of which we can indicate the center.

Spiritual Certainty

An image that seems to fit the whole is rather that of a forest growth. And this is what I would like once more to suggest. Only one statement of a more or less political-scientific nature seems sensible, although we must not take it in the framework of our democracy-habituated thought. The royal ceremony displays *relationships* from beginning to end, and everything appears to be designed, within this "wild growth," to prevent the king from becoming an absolute power. Of course there is no suggestion in the ancient Indian tradition of our ideas of fundamental rights, majority rule, and so forth. Instead, we find hierarchic relationships that

---

11. I follow the rendering given in Krick, *Das Ritual der Feuergründung*, 95.
12. Gonda, *Die Religionen Indiens* 1:166.

move to and fro in the ritual, and transactions with the divine world invoked without question. As in every tradition, "power" by itself is not the basis for the way power is bestowed and legitimized. At the same time, in comparison to other traditions, the Indian case seems unique in its extraordinarily precise attention for the to-and-fro movement felt and expressed in relationships.

All Indian texts—not only the ritualistic literature—like to employ as synonyms for the king terms that imply his rulership over the entire earth (*rājādhirāja*, "king over kings," *adhirāja*, "supreme king," *mahīpati*, "earth-lord"). It might seem almost like an echo of Alexander's rule. However, with the exception of Aśoka's empire, the territories ruled by Indian kings could not begin to compare in size with those of the Macedonian. Utter rulership was not to be defined in units of land. This is impressed upon us by the ritual texts with their dimension of spiritual certainty. It is not by coincidence that the term *cakravartin*, "world-emperor," was invoked as a title for the Buddha, whose rule of course was unrelated to territorial expanse.

The sense of the ritual consecration is not located in political utility, no matter its value as what we would call "propaganda" (that is, the impression made by the ceremonies on many people). The relationships we saw touch another string. The king, in order to be truly king, must be placed in relation to his wife, his son, the priests, as well as the other members of society, all of whom have their role in the royal ritual transactions. The activity of the king in ruling is an expression of this unity. And the myriad relationships that allow him his power of course bind and curb his selfish cravings. With the possible exception of Aśoka (whom we shall discuss in the next essay), India never had kings of the power-mad type.

Here we do not have the confrontation between spirituality and power that was found in Israel, or the neglect of kingship on the part of the religious community which, as we shall see, characterizes Buddhism (together with its unapologetic enjoyment of protection by kings), or the identification of law and spirit of the type central to Islamic history. What we do have instead is indeed a forest, a purposeful forest with a perfect ecological system in which no growth uproots another or takes over the whole. In the case of Hindu India, the priority of religious creativity does not ever present itself as a subject of controversy, and does not seem to have developed *in response* to something else. We have not the least suggestion that some historical political turmoil forced India to conceive and enforce such "ecological" measures. And we must conclude that the source and authority of such institutions as the *rājasūya* cannot be attributed to a single founder. There is no trace of a figure like Moses, Jesus, Muhammad, or Confucius to explain the Hindu state of affairs. Indeed, it seems as if "it just grew that way."

An observation in this key, nevertheless, does not do complete justice to the perfect balance we have observed. It we had nothing more to say, we might not really have improved very much on the supposition of an early annual fertility rite around which gradually all sorts of elaboration accumulated. We need to remember the wisdom of Gerardus van der Leeuw that every religion is a religion of salvation. In one way or another, all religious activity transcends explanation of the world and even preservation of the world. The "religious creativity" that we associate with India should not be taken lightly. It brings a weal that is not provided on the everyday plane.

A ritual such as the *rājasūya* of course rests on the authority of the Vedic texts, which is probably unlike that of any other authoritative scripture. According to Hindu tradition, Vedic authority is absolute and everlasting. It does not cease at the world's conflagration. It continues and sounds forth again when the next world is born. This authority (although in its articulation later than the Vedic texts) underlies what is done in the ritual. The balance of all there is in society and governance does not rest in a social contract or even in a covenant between man and God, but in that spiritual certainty that was before everything and will outlast it.

Such authority, such absolute certainty is basic to Hindu teachings. The high articulateness of Indian texts, with their habit of spelling out absolutely everything—all of the writings of the *dharmaśāstra*, the science of law and conduct, and the Purāṇas—reflects this everlasting certainty. Indian texts can indeed have a flavor of "knowing it all." Anchored in the religious tradition, such notions of authority indubitably foster a special sense of virtue. There is an air of supreme self-confidence about many Hindus that is probably related to this feature of their religion. It is not a vice! But indeed, Hindu intellectuals and functionaries sometimes strike non-Hindus as rather conceited. (Each religion fosters its own virtues. The Hindu "conceitedness" is comparable to the "righteous anger" many a Western intellectual or politician displays or is expected to display at certain occasions. From a Hindu point of view no anger can be virtuous.)

A further remark: the vision of a "forest," a balanced system of incomparable value, should not lead us to any romantic sensation of discovering in the East the longed-for cure to our political and religious malady. One could not attempt the Indian model in our modern world of senseless tyrannies and confused democracies. One must confront what is found in India without sinking into fantasy.

Not by chance did the History of Religions as a discipline arise largely as a result of the discovery of Indian civilization. It happened during the Romantic era, and many of the great Romantics were affected and inspired by the wisdom of the "Orient." These reactions have not run their course yet. Early in the twentieth century a Dutch parodist known by his pseudonym Charivarius[13] mused on the appeal of Indian swamis with this doggerel:

> *Al die vreemde zieletroosters*
> *Zijn zo heerlijk, heerlijk oosters.*
>
> (All those foreign consolers of souls
> Are so deliciously, deliciously Oriental.)

Historians of religions dealing with India have a special obligation to counter the suspicion that they romanticize.

Ananda Coomaraswamy: Politics as Part of a Total Unity

The Hindu texts themselves demand an extraordinary concentration. It is relatively easy to point out the inadequacy of pet ideas that have governed our theories of explanation. But, once we have decided not to rely on ideas that distort the thought and practice of Hindu tradition, we still have the greatest task before us.

With respect to this crucial assignment one name stands out: Ananda K. Coomaraswamy, author of the remarkable treatise *Spiritual Authority and Temporal Power in the Indian Theory of Government*.[14] It seems impossible to me to formulate an inquiry into the foundation of Indian political thought without paying tribute to Coomaraswamy. Indeed, our conclusions to this essay cannot be anything else than a reflection on his words—even if in the end we cannot subscribe to all he said.

Coomaraswamy is well known to students of Indian art. However, I owe the reader the admission that Sanskritists and historians generally

---

13. "Charivarius" was Gerard Nolst Trenité (1870–1946), best known for his witty contributions to the periodical *De Groene Amsterdammer*.

14. Coomaraswamy, *Spiritual Authority and Temporal Power*.

ignore Coomaraswamy. And their hesitance to accept him is explainable. Coomaraswamy did not make a secret of his devotion to the *philosophia perennis*, and he held this "everlasting philosophy" to be the font of all scholarly explanation deserving the name. Coomaraswamy is convinced that his *philosophia perennis*, mainly derived in its explicit terms from Plato, reaches worldwide. Side by side with his beloved Hindu and Buddhist texts (which in his conviction should be seen as elaborating on the same fundamental, perennial themes), he quotes ancient Greek oracles and the pre-Socratics, the biblical texts, the church fathers, Dante. As he strews his arguments with offerings from so many cultures and ages, it becomes no wonder that his pronouncements on Indian religion and politics can arouse the specialist's ire.

Historians of religions who attach value to the *general* and *comparative* history of religions may recognize the problem. We too are often confronted with the attitude that a true general knowledge is impossible and that anyone claiming a worthwhile understanding of several subjects or traditions must be something of a charlatan. Such convictions are not often followed up with reasons. Hence ignoring works such as those of Coomaraswamy is an easy way out.

Coomaraswamy's perennial philosophy appears to find some support in India's heritage. We have said that there always was in Brahmanism a supreme unity that somehow was put within reach. As well, there was an explicitness, an attentiveness to everything, a mentioning of everything by name. One of the most famous hymns in the *Ṛgveda* (X.90) has to do with the creation of the world. It is the *Puruṣasūkta*, the song about the *puruṣa*. The *puruṣa* is the sacrificial victim whom the gods used in the sacrifice they performed at the root of the world. (The *puruṣa* in later texts is identified with Viṣṇu.) His mouth becomes the brahmin, his arms the warrior, his thighs the *vaiśya*, his feet the *śūdra*. At this great primordial sacrifice, not only does the world come into being, but also at the same time all the ingredients of the sacrifices that people are to perform are born. The very hymns, the *mantras* of the Vedas, become manifest. The lived-in world, and the Supreme, and the central activity of the sacrifice are all part of a unity *that can be expressed*.

On the level of our own common experience, college graduates are sent into the world as "educated" people. Whatever this means, it certainly involves the assumption that in principle they can arrive at defensible thoughts and perform defensible actions vis-à-vis the entirety of the world, the whole of mankind. In the modern world in which no part is separate from the whole, political power everywhere has its meaning in a total unity. What does this unity consist of? No Linnaeus has arisen to mention all its parts by name and define its wholeness. Yet one cannot shun it. If one does, none of one's political actions really make sense. We pay tribute to this unity; we know we must take it into account; but we do not know how to act in accordance with it. Today as I write these lines, we cannot act in one coherent way with respect to the nations and peoples of the world. We take for granted the possibility of a balance achieved through the wielding of power, but how is that accomplished? Only in India at one time was it all spelled out. The fascination of the Indian material is that it presents an ultimate source of good governance that is constantly within human reach.

Coomaraswamy begins his *Spiritual Authority and Temporal Power in the Indian Theory of Government* by quoting the ancient Indian wedding formula: "I am That, thou art This, I am Sky, thou art Earth." And he states that in these words "the whole of Indian political theory is implied and subsumed."[15]

Coomaraswamy goes on to remind us that one of the older Brāhmaṇa texts (*Aitareyabrāhmaṇa* 8.27) has the *purohita*, the brahmin priest, addressing these same words of the wedding formula to the king. The *Sitz im Leben*—as biblical scholars would call the setting in which something occurs and belongs—is a *ritual* in which the nature of the king's function and dominion is at issue. This is the sort of evidence we are not allowed to ignore. The king, Coomaraswamy says, takes on the feminine role. The priest's role is masculine, not only for this ritual occasion, Coomaraswamy says, but in the very reality that is the ground on which worldly life is enacted. The principles of spiritual leadership (*brahman*) and worldly governance (*kṣatra*) must be unified. Thus, ritually, "the marriage of the Sacerdotium (*brahman*) and the Regnum (*kṣatra*)" takes place.[16]

In Brahmanism nothing suggests that the monarch is divine. (One could not say this with respect to all of Hinduism; everyone dealing with Indian religion knows about South Indian kings who are drawn closely towards divinity. Yet even there, nothing of the earlier, Brahmanic tradition is ever given up. Myths and symbols simply *multiply*. And even in South India, there is never a king comparable to an Egyptian pharaoh or an Inca ruler.)[17] Ritual texts of the *rājasūya* refer to the king emphatically as an

---

15. Ibid., 1.
16. Ibid., 2.
17. See especially the splendid book by Harman, *The Sacred Marriage of a Hindu*

ordinary, human sacrificer (*yajamāna*). At the same time, the hierarchic nature of the Indian world is abundantly documented even in the earliest texts. Coomaraswamy discusses features of kingship and features of the king personally that make him different from other people. On the king prosperity truly depends. (This does not mean that in some infantile manner Hindus held "beliefs" concerning rulers who caused sunshine and rainfall at the appropriate times for agriculture, et cetera.) Coomaraswamy translates and quotes from a passage in the *Śatapathabrāhmaṇa* in order to elucidate ritual formulas addressed to the king in the *rājasūya* (9.3.3.11). The whole passage in an older translation by Julius Eggeling runs as follows:

> And when he [the *adhvaryu*, brahmin priest] says, "This is thy realm; a supporter and sustainer art thou for the friend; for sustenance, for rain, for the lordship of creatures—thee!" this is to say, "This is thy kingdom; thou art consecrated (anointed)! Thou art thy friend's supporter and sustainer: for our sustenance art thou, for rain unto us art thou, for our lordship of creatures art thou!" They thereby entreat him, "For all this art thou unto us: for all this have we consecrated thee!" And therefore people thus entreat a human king who has been consecrated.[18]

The explanation the *Śatapathabrāhmaṇa* passage gives of the priestly formula should not be misunderstood. The lines beginning "for our sustenance art thou . . ." do not say that the king *is* our sustenance, and *is* rain, or that the king *causes* rain to fall. Eggeling's translation with "for" is a literal translation of the Sanskrit dative of purpose; the king is said to be there *for the sake of* our sustenance, and likewise for *the sake of* rain. In other words, well-being is brought about through the kingship, and we cannot experience well-being without the king.

For the most part, Coomaraswamy's translation of these lines is not very different, except at the end, where Coomaraswamy renders the Sanskrit text: "For our bread (*ūrje*) art thou, for rain unto us art thou, for paternity of offspring [*prajānām . . . ādhipatyāya*] . . . for all this have we aspersed [*abhyasicāmahi*, the literal translation of what Eggeling rendered as "consecrated"] thee."[19] The king is said to be there not only for

---

Goddess. As to the preservation of the ancient ritual theme of limiting the concentration of power, see Shulman, *Tamil Temple Myths*, 192–211.

18. Eggeling, trans., *The Sathapatha-Brahmana*, 219–20.
19. Coomaraswamy, *Spiritual Authority and Temporal Power*, 68.

the sake of our food and the needed rain but also *for the sake of children we will have.*

Once again, it is important to realize that we should not think of these words as magical formulas mixed in with the ritual *mantras*, as if the intention of the texts were to manipulate the future. I think that we should notice the truly spiritual dimension to kingship that has bearing on the ordinary existence of all the king's subjects. The usefulness of the king does not merely lie in his use of power; it is not simply his use of the army to protect the city or the state. The *spirituality* of the king is of immediate, practical use for all. Without a properly ordained kingship, life is not livable.

Part of the reason it has been difficult for Western scholars to discern this meaning which is present in texts of traditional India is not the obscurity of the texts, but the nature of our own mindset. I think the compilers of the Brāhmaṇa texts, were they able to see us, would express disbelief that anyone could be so bewildered as to consider a separation between religion and politics *real*.[20]

Another essential matter quite foreign for our "mindset" but indubitably present in the documents is this: the texts express that each human being and the entire society with its governance have their cornerstone in the performance of sacrifice. This ancient Indian theory of government exists in the experience of sacrificial procedures. The *Bhagavadgītā*, though composed in a time when Vedic sacrifices were no longer common, still expresses itself in sacrificial terms:

> Enjoying the food of immortality left over
> > from sacrifice, they [those who know sacrifice]
> > > go to the eternal godhead [*brahman*].
>
> A man who does not sacrifice
> > has no part in this world. How could he enter the other?[21]

---

20. Juergensmeyer, *The New Cold War?* should be mentioned here; it touches occasionally on such separations. The book is admirable for its attempt to shed light on modern problems of religion and politics.

21. Bolle, trans., *The Bhagavadgītā*, 59 (4:31). The lasting impact of sacrificial tradition is not unknown to the West. After the destruction of the temple in Jerusalem, the synagogue continued in its *sacrifice of prayers*. In the Christian church, the sacrifice of the mass witnesses to the enduring significance of sacrifice.

Coomaraswamy: Remarks of Caution

We have sounded a note of warning against romanticizing India. Heesterman, who led us into the *rājasūya*, could not be accused of romanticizing. Having turned to Coomaraswamy, and allowed ourselves to be guided by him, can we be sure that he is not unduly romantic?

Here is Coomaraswamy speaking about spiritual initiation and the ritual consecration of the king:

> The man is no longer this man So-and-so, but dissolved in himSelf. The outer man has been "crowned and mitred above himself" (Dante, *Purgatorio* XXVII.182). It is precisely such a crowning and mitering that is ritually enacted in the *rājasūya*: the King's divinity is not "his own," not "this man's" who sits upon the throne, but that of the principle that overrules him and of which he is, not the reality, but the living image, instrument and puppet...
>
> As the individual is assimilated to the Self, the woman to the man, so is the Regnum to the Sacerdotium: the consorts are unanimous, so that what the one enjoins the other performs. The individual is no longer enslaved by his own desires....[22]

Have we passed over into great abstractions? We noted before that Coomaraswamy wrote: "the whole of Indian political theory is implied and subsumed" in the ancient Indian wedding formula. Professor J. Gonda, a cautious and scrupulous scholar of ancient Indian texts, also believed that the wedding formula can help us interpret the *rājasūya* ceremonies. However, Gonda does not speak about matters in the same way. Gonda wrote that the *brahman*, the supreme, divine principle—at the same time the principle represented by the brahmins on earth—is "the firm ground" on which kingship rests,[23] and he pointed out that a number of times the two—in the person of king and brahmin—are united, and can indeed be said to become one. At a certain moment during the ritual, upon completion of the consecration, the king is addressed as "brahmin."[24] And according to some authorities, the royal sacrificer should drink from the sacrificial *soma* goblet in the company of ten brahmins.[25] This tradition underlines the wedding-like union between

---

22. Coomaraswamy, *Spiritual Authority and Temporal Power*, 84.
23. Gonda, *Die Religionen Indiens*, 1:164.
24. Ibid., 1:166.
25. Ibid., 1:167.

the king and the brahmin; normally, such participation on the part of a *kṣatriya* (the king is a *kṣatriya*) is not permitted.

There is indeed a "wedding" of sorts, yet Coomaraswamy's conviction cannot be acceded to—especially because the evidence he summons (here and throughout his book) goes far beyond the Indian world.[26] As wonderful as the writings of Ananda Coomaraswamy certainly are, the historian of religions cannot accept anyone's transformation of a particular tradition into a confirmation of what we must suggest are "great abstractions," "universal assumptions," and even "pet ideas".

Coomaraswamy's great merit in historical interpretation is that he showed the ancient Indian coherence of spirit and power more vividly than anyone else. This meant a giant stride forward. It countered lingering tendencies to explain the ancient rituals as early stages of a mental evolution.

Is the Indian model universal? Coomaraswamy's answer is yes. It is not difficult to see that this model was the key ingredient for his *philosophia perennis*. One of Coomaraswamy's most widely known books is called *Hinduism and Buddhism*.[27] As in the case of *Spiritual Authority and Temporal Power, Hinduism and Buddhism* gives us a central vision of ancient India—and, in so doing, causes Hinduism and Buddhism to become essentially the same.

But historians of religions cannot gloss over differences that show themselves in the historical record. Many Hindu texts condemn Buddhism outright. And there is this reason for caution with Coomaraswamy's presentation: it arises from his very mastery in showing the Hindu central vision. By enfolding all of human tradition into the articulations of Vedism-Brahmanism-Hinduism, he does indeed show us India's spiritual core; what he shows is precisely how this great spirituality sees itself. It is Hinduism's way of bringing out its claim to universal validity.

This final step by Coomaraswamy is not possible for the historian of religions. The historian of religions realizes that even when this ultimate core is reached and understood, there still remain religious structures that differ from each other. The normal course of the world in which we do our interpreting springs from those differences. We see that politics and religion are not related to each other in the same way everywhere.

---

26. See Coomaraswamy, *Spiritual Authority and Temporal Power*, especially 1–2.
27. Coomaraswamy, *Hinduism and Buddhism*.

This is a cardinal issue. Without such differences the very urge to understand would have no cause to exist.

In conclusion—does it need to be repeated?—we do not envisage ancient Indian texts such as those of the *rājasūya* as a model for our own political life or our religious life. It is, however, of incalculable value that we have treasures such as those Indian documents to show us the sense religiopolitical traditions other than our own can make. If from time to time they lead us to dreaming, we can only gain by the experience, and deepen our ability to understand human beings different from ourselves.

8

Buddhism

Buddhism and Kingship

Like the majority of Indian texts, the Buddhist texts do not insist on anything resembling the divinity of kings.[1] And there are cases where they give a truly scathing picture of kingship.

The historian Balkrishna G. Gokhale made a compilation of statements in Buddhist sources that heap criticism on kings; that critique is extensively documented in the Pāli texts.[2] Royal power, they reiterate, can be as devastating as fire or flood. It harms and it robs. No matter how much they have, no matter how opulent, kings will incessantly seek more wealth, more territory. They cannot tolerate views that differ from their own, and their "wayward wrath" leads to death and displacement for their subjects; many there are who have had to flee into the wilds or to monasteries merely to stay alive.[3]

The lists of miseries linked to kingship sound remarkably modern. It is almost as if Amnesty International or the UN High Commissioner for Refugees were speaking to us. Yet the context of the Buddhist litany is fundamentally different from that of biblical religion, for Buddhist tradition has been fundamentally different. On the whole, Buddhism had little to say to kings, unlike Brahmanism and Hinduism and very unlike Israel. Buddhism cultivated the protection of powerful rulers for its monasteries and for the teachings themselves. The patronage of kings was of supreme

---

1. We noted some variations in the previous essay.
2. Gokhale, "Early Buddhist Kingship."
3. Ibid., 16.

importance for Buddhism from its earliest days on; our major sources simply take this for granted.[4]

Professor Gokhale has offered the suggestion that the Buddha himself may have accepted the institution of kingship only with reluctance. But there is no convincing argument to be made attributing any sort of opinion on the institution of kingship to the Buddha personally. Documents of ancient cultures, whether they tell us of the Buddha, Moses, or Jesus Christ, do not make the slightest attempt to provide a psychological portrait.

The *Jātaka* stories, first collected in Pāli, have always been popular in South and Southeast Asia. No doubt they reflect real historical developments when they tell of kings and the acts of kings in India. These stories recount the legendary scenes of the soothsayers predicting to the future Buddha's father—himself a princely ruler—that his son would be either a Buddha or a *cakravartin*, a "universal monarch." It is true that the concept of a "universal monarch" or world emperor was still relatively recent when the birth stories were redacted (perhaps the first century B.C.), but kingship properly so called, not merely a tribal chieftainship of a rather "democratic" character but a central power in governing and judging, in the hands of one person, was quite common at the time of the Buddha, and certainly not an institution one was at liberty to reject. To reject it, if conceivable, would also have made no practical sense for the growing community of monks around the Buddha, the *saṅgha*, sustained as it was by royal and wealthy protection in a world of competing monastic orders.

There is, moreover, an inner reason in Buddhism that would preclude the idea of a personal reluctance toward kingship. One of the characteristics of the monk's discipline is the attempt to overcome desire and selfishness: it is the essence of the monk's existence to meditate on these as giving rise to the phenomenal world. And though these features, desire and selfishness, are the very things that made kingship so reprehensible, they are for Buddhist teachings the normal state of affairs in human life. To fight them as if they were to be conquered on the level of social or political institutions would have been nonsensical. This does not mean that the Buddhist monk is in any way inhuman. It simply means that like all human beings he must orient himself by the models given in his religion. One can see on the canvas of history that Buddhism's central force, its daring clarity, its ongoing analytical assessment of all phenomena, could

---

4. See the detailed and splendid work by Orzech, *Politics and Transcendent Wisdom*.

not provide a pattern for engagement with worldly rule. We should not apply clichés here about Buddhism being unconcerned with politics, history, rules in society. Buddhism did not ignore these things, but it sensed and expressed them in its own ways.

Early Buddhist tradition attributes a simple and striking assertion to Ajātaśatru (ca. 493–462 B.C.), the son and successor of King Bimbisāra, who had been the Buddha's great royal patron and friend. Ajātaśatru said to the assembly of monks at the legendary First Council, "Yours is the authority of the spirit as mine is of power."[5] The documents do not present this statement in a vacuum. There is a setting and a context, a "feel" in the texts that gives us the knowledge that the monks disapproved of that king. His portrayal has a quality we could almost call satanic. There are in Buddhism no explicit treatises on political morality, but in its way the tradition conveys the consensus of the monks that there is something quite wrong with this suggestion made by the king. The monks inform us that Ajātaśatru had killed his own father, Bimbisāra, the friend and protector of the Buddha, and usurped the throne.[6] Ajātaśatru embodied the craving for unrivaled power. Because of their discipline of meditation and the analysis of phenomena given in their teaching and mental training, the monks would have seen, too, that Ajātaśatru's claim was senseless. Much earlier, when the Buddha personally carried on discussions with his monks—and of course, still earlier, in the time of the Upaniṣads—the ideas of thinkers on the side of the religious institution were immeasurably more carefully worked out and profound than those of an Ajātaśatru.

Reasons of religious significance are never as easy to proclaim or to explain as Ajātaśatru's proposition or any "reason of state." Perfect separation is indeed easy to call for, but in the examples collected by Gokhale of a very elaborate Buddhist criticism, sharper than mere vituperation, in the form of precisely formulated descriptions and analyses of habitually misused royal power, not stated but easy to infer is the knowledge that perfect separation makes for perfect absolute, unrestrained, and terrible worldly power.

The basic analysis in our own tradition has fostered the imperative we now refer to as "separation of church and state." It is interesting to note that among us today are many who—as simplistic in their way as an Ajātaśatru—have no idea that our sense of some necessary separation

---

5. Gokhale in "Early Buddhist Kingship," quotes on page 22 from *The Samanta pāsādikā, commentary on Dīghanikāya*, I, 10; *Mahāvagga* V, i.

6. Lamotte, *Le Bouddhisme Indien*, 13.

came not from the side of the state but from within the church, and was intended to prevent distortion of the religious heritage.[7] This ignorance may be found on both the "left" and "right."

Aśoka

In a discussion of Buddhism and politics the case of Aśoka must be mentioned. Aśoka is the legendary emperor who united most of India under his rule. Until fairly recent times he was the only one to have accomplished this unification to such an extent. He reigned from ca. 267 B.C. until his death in 232 B.C. Presumably he was a Buddhist. He has certainly stimulated the imagination of historians with his pillars and his inscriptions that speak of the *dharma* that guided him and that he deemed the worthiest goal for his subjects and for all people. Aśoka is such a towering figure in Indian historiography that in the twentieth century independent India chose as its seal his emblem, the sculpted lion capital which stood atop a pillar. Was not this greatest ruler of India, sovereign over a vast empire, and at the same time, according to most interpreters of the historical record, a notable Buddhist, truly a perfect king, greater than the great Christian emperor Constantine? The quality of Constantine's adherence to Christianity may not be altogether impervious to scholarly doubt, but admiring scholars have seen in Aśoka a truly spiritual monarch.

The quest for the real Aśoka is revealing, not just because it shows us a powerful king operating against the backdrop of Indian Buddhism, but also because it shows us weaknesses in historical study that affect not only historians of religions, but all of us who like to think we have some understanding of the world.

In doing their work many historians have followed the lead of Rudolf Otto, not necessarily by reading him carefully but as if driven by instinct. They have focused on phenomena that seemed to present themselves incontrovertibly as meriting the epithets "holy" and "sacred." Following this habit, I am afraid, they may have missed a good deal in the historical record, including much that is revelatory of religions. They might have done well to reflect more closely on the relationship and conflict between

---

7. For an understanding of our notion of separation between church and state, see McLoughlin, *Isaac Backus*, 13. See also Sanders, *Protestant Concepts of Church and State*, especially chapter 4, entitled "Separationism: Defenders of the Wall."

spirituality and power, and to foster some suspicion when any historical "fact" presented itself as the perfect merging of the two.

Emperor Aśoka published the depth of his experience and wisdom by means of his edicts, chiseled into pillars and into rock at sundry places throughout his empire, particularly near its boundaries. These edicts reached not only the world that was within Aśoka's grasp; they have spoken across the ages, and because of them, historians admire Aśoka as a king who embraced religion and was transformed.

But should we pause here and reconsider, especially having looked at so many problematic relationships between religion and power? Could it be that Aśoka engaged in self-advertising—even if he did not do it as crudely as Darius and other kings? It is true that he sorrowed over Kalinga, the land of his major conquest. He himself said so (and in this regard we should note the not insignificant factor that for historians it is a welcome relief to have such personal inscriptions, written at the time, and not to need rely on later documents that are the residue of oral tradition). Aśoka declared, after his military conquest of Kalinga, that he had seen the blood and the tears, and he did not want to cause such misery ever again. The celebrated thirteenth Rock Edict contains the lines:

> When the king, Beloved of the Gods, and of Gracious Mien, had been consecrated eight years, Kalinga was conquered, 150,000 people were deported, 100,000 were killed, and many times that number died. But after the conquest of Kalinga, the Beloved of the Gods began to follow Righteousness (Dharma), to love Righteousness, and to give instruction in Righteousness. Now the Beloved of the Gods regrets the conquest of Kalinga, for when an independent country is conquered people are killed, they die, or are deported, and that the Beloved of the Gods finds very painful and grievous. And this he finds even more grievous—that all the inhabitants—brahmans, ascetics, and other sectarians, and householders who are obedient to superiors, parents, and elders, who treat friends, acquaintances, companions, relatives, slaves, and servants with respect, and are firm in their faith—all suffer violence, murder, and separation from their loved ones. Even those who are fortunate enough not to have lost those near and dear to them are afflicted at the misfortunes of friends, acquaintances, companions, and relatives. The participation of all men in common suffering is grievous to the Beloved of the Gods. Moreover, there is no land, except that of the Greeks, where groups of brahmans and ascetics are not found, or where men are not members of one sect or another.

So now, even if the number of those killed and captured in the conquest of Kalinga had been a hundred or a thousand times less, it would be grievous to the Beloved of the Gods.[8]

Scholars tend to agree that Aśoka was truly a Buddhist, even though his inscriptions, including the ones describing his endeavors to spread *dharma* through the entire world, do not exhibit all the characteristics of Buddhist teachings of the period.[9] It is most probable that he was a Buddhist officially.[10] We can be certain from the inscriptions that he knew about Buddhism and was concerned with its preservation.[11] That he was indeed the paramount royal patron of Buddhism in history is beyond dispute.[12] Lamotte is probably right in ascribing to Aśoka himself a clear distinction between his own *dharma*, comprising whatever he could do in his task as a sovereign lord for the good of all creatures, and the Buddhist Law as such; the latter is mentioned by its own specific name *saddharma*, the Good Law or the "real religion" of the Buddha, only in one edict (the one at Bhabhra).[13] "Beloved of the Gods" is Aśoka's favorite self-denomination in the inscriptions and makes it appear that he wanted to appeal to all inhabitants of his realms, and not just the Buddhists in particular.

The delight of historians in the edicts is fully understandable, for early India is not rich in precisely datable documents, and even more to the point, Aśoka has after all conveyed himself to us directly. The widespread enthusiasm, however, goes well beyond a joy in dates and first-person documents. Some specialists have expressed very strong feelings about Aśoka and have seen in him the embodiment of their own highest ideals of sovereignty. Paul Masson-Oursel wrote:

> His fight against sufferings of all kinds bears the stamp of Buddhism and Jainism, but the determination to establish a universal order, regulated in its smallest details, for the safeguarding of all interests for which the king assumes responsibility is the purpose of a "King of Kings."

8. De Bary, *Sources of Indian Tradition*, 142.

9. Renou and Filliozat, *L'Inde Classique*, 2:498.

10. See especially the Maski Rock Edict in Nikam and McKeon, *The Edicts of Aśoka*, 66, where Aśoka refers to himself as a "lay disciple" (*upāsaka*) of the Buddha "for more than two and a half years."

11. Ibid., especially 66–69.

12. Bareau, *Die Religionen Indiens*, 20.

13. Lamotte, *Le Bouddhisme Indien*, 249.

> ...
>
> Just as a wide-awake government provides for the policing, financial affairs, and general economics of the country, so there are officials to enforce the reign of moral law as well as of the purely legal.
>
> ...
>
> His attitude is that of a Great King in whose imperialism no distinction is admitted between spiritual and temporal.[14]

This glorious portrayal of Aśoka does not quite stroke with the thirteenth Rock Edict, his most famous inscription. Its text, describing the king's grief over the misery he has caused to Kalinga, immediately goes on as follows:

> The Beloved of the Gods will forgive as far as he can, and he even conciliates the forest tribes of his dominions; but he warns them that there is power even in the remorse of the Beloved of the Gods, and he tells them to reform, lest they be killed.[15]

In telling the hill tribes to "reform," as the translation has it, what is Aśoka actually saying? Do not raid the valleys I have so painstakingly conquered; kindly remain in the hills and starve to death. Historians need to give up romanticizing, and also cease being only technical and linguistic, and *think about the realities* that surrounded their documents. As for the people of the hill tribes, killing was the treatment they had received for centuries from rulers over the settled populations in the rich valleys, out of which they had always removed the first inhabitants—who from then on became "hill tribes."

The historian Fritz Kern devoted a book to Aśoka whose eye-catching subtitle is *Kaiser und Missionar*, "Emperor and Missionary." He compares Aśoka with great rulers of all ages, including Akbar, Marcus Aurelius, and Constantine, and draws into the comparison even Saint Paul, who was, as Kern reminds his readers, second in significance after the founder of a religion.

> Aśoka is the earliest ruler in world history who devoted himself fully and completely to the service of a religion of salvation, and this fact alone allows us to locate him properly in history.[16]

14. Masson-Oursel, *Ancient India and Indian Civilization*, 38, 39, 40.
15. De Bary, ed., *Sources of Indian Tradition*, 1:142.
16. Kern, *Aśoka: Kaiser und Missionar*, 109.

Might it be that these sympathetic images of Aśoka are more culturally conditioned than we realize? Is it altogether by chance that Masson-Oursel, the Frenchman, admires "a universal order, regulated in its smallest details"? The French penchant for centralization in government is proverbial. The same writer is drawn to a vision of Aśoka's success in solving the distinction between politics and religion. There is rationality for you! And would it be only coincidence that Kern, the writer in German, sees a supreme achievement in the emperor's devotion to a transcendental system of salvation? This does gloss over the reality of the hill tribes, who stood in the way not so much of transcendental systems as of a source of revenue for the great king.

Ananda K. Coomaraswamy, our guide in the previous essay and eminent writer on Hinduism and Buddhism, expresses himself most articulately, with deference toward the texts, but I feel that his own great esteem for Aśoka is also culturally conditioned and ultimately misplaced. On the last page of his treatise *Spiritual Authority and Temporal Power in the Indian Theory of Government*, he locates in Aśoka the exemplar of the perfect king. According to the theory of authoritative Indian texts, the king should have perfected control of himself ("allying himself with the Self against himself");[17] only then can he hope to exert control over others. Coomaraswamy writes:

> It is clear from the great king Asoka's Thirteenth Edict that he had understood the real meaning of "victory"; for after recounting his political victories and expressing his deep regret for them, because of the suffering inflicted on the conquered, he continues (line 7), "And this is the foremost Victory, the Victory of the Dharma," while (line 10, 11) he enjoins upon his successors to "regard as 'Victory' the Victory of the Dharma, which avails for this world and the other."[18]

In my opinion, this is a spiritualization of the legendary sovereign that goes exceedingly far. I do not think it is possible to get around the problem that arises between the *meaning* of Brahmanic enthronement texts, or Buddhist monastic discipline, and the actual decisions made in political life by an aggressive king in the exercise of his power, least of all by telescoping one into the other. This, I think, is what Coomaraswamy

---

17. Coomaraswamy, *Spiritual Authority and Temporal Power*, 86.
18. Ibid., 87.

does in his desire to see Aśoka as the actual, living expression of the documents.

Aśoka may really have been sorry for what he did to Kalinga. On this point we owe him our sympathy, and we wish the humble heroism of his spirit of public confession on many another ruler. But, apart from his painfully ordinary policy toward the hill tribes, we must also note nothing indicates Aśoka wished to let go of Kalinga after so publicly regretting his conquest, or searched for its original rulers or the owners of the fertile valleys, or set anything in motion to return the deportees. Kalinga must have been approximately what on the modern map of India is the state of Orissa. It presented great wealth to Aśoka, and hence was an imperial affair, not an item for the meditating devotee's contemplation.

There needs to be skepticism in the face of the wonderful images of Aśoka that scholars have drawn for us. Excuses on behalf of Aśoka even on a mundane level will not really work. Returning conquered territories was not a custom at the time? Of course not. It has never become a custom. But then, what of Aśoka's regrets? The conquest could not have taken a day or a week. Clearly Aśoka had plenty of occasion to witness or at least to receive reports of killings, deportations, and other miseries. And then, at the end, would it have been unroyal to add to his long and amazing inscriptions a word of regret that now he was unable to undo any of the harm he brought over Kalinga?

Caṇḍāśoka

Even though our questions about a number of historical details are not likely to be answered, we do have more documentation than what the inscriptions provide. It is documentation historians do not eagerly reach for, but it was available long before the edicts were deciphered. That other documentation comes from what are often referred to as Buddhist "legends."[19] The attitude of many an excellent scholar, I believe, can actually inhibit our understanding here. Typically, Jules Bloch, to whom we owe a most accurate text edition of Aśoka's inscriptions, introduces his assessment of the Buddhist narratives with the following words:

---

19. Major documentation of the legends can be found in Przyluski, *La Légende de l'empereur Açoka*, and in Strong, *The Legend of King Aśoka*. The latter work is a truly splendid and complete accomplishment. It should be required reading for anyone who has taken note only of the inscriptions by Aśoka himself.

The Greeks do not mention Bindusāra's son and successor, Aśoka. What India tells us of him does not amount to more than a tapestry of legends and miracles, into which, in distorted form, some probable or possible events disappear.[20]

He might as well have added: what else can you expect from religious documents? Yet ought these same worthy scholars trust Aśoka's inscriptions as far as they do? My professor Joachim Wach taught that true biographies may occasionally be found, but as to true autobiographies: they do not exist. It is an observation we might keep in mind.

I do not think there is any good reason to dismiss the Buddhist "legends." With our historical problem concerning the relation between politics and religion we have very good reasons to take note of them.

Earlier we cited a statement from Ajātaśatru, the ruler who murdered his father, Bimbisāra, and said to the monks at the first Buddhist Council, "Yours is the authority of the spirit as mine is of power." This record is legendary. But who will dismiss its historical truthfulness?

With respect to Aśoka, the Singhalese chronicle that is devoted to him provides some details of the great emperor's life. Aśoka was one of a hundred and one sons born to the sixteen queens in Bindusāra's household. The crown prince was not Aśoka, but Sumana (known as Susima in the Sanskrit sources). In this large family only one brother, Tissa (Vītaśoka in the Sanskrit sources), was born from the same mother as Aśoka. While still young, Aśoka served as viceroy in Avanti, and he also married a merchant's daughter, who bore him a son and a daughter. As soon as the news of his father's death reached him, Aśoka set out for the capital, Pāṭaliputra, established his power over the city, and ascended the throne. He killed all his brothers, with the exception only of his full brother Tissa. This massacre ensured his supremacy and also gave him the epithet Caṇḍāśoka, cruel Aśoka.[21]

It is not reasonable to dismiss the historical value of the Buddhist sources. There are several of them, and in the North and in the South they agree in the general portrayal of Aśoka's cruelty, if not its particulars.

20. Bloch, *Les inscriptions d'Aśoka*, 15. Note also the words of Basham in *The Wonder That Was India*, 57: "The Aśoka of the Buddhist legends is, in the words of a nineteenth-century authority, 'half monster and half idiot,' his humanity and practical benevolence overlaid by the accretion of monkish legends of later centuries; but the king of the rock and the pillar inscriptions comes alive, a real man, and a man far ahead of his times."

21. Lamotte, *Le Bouddhisme Indien*, 272–73.

Even if much of the legendary material is incorrect on many points, it still adds intelligibility to "facts" in the inscriptions that otherwise would remain obscure, not only to our religious or historical, but also to our ordinary, human imagination—a faculty we cannot do without in grasping what happened.

We have already observed that for all his regret over Kalinga, Aśoka did not record any plan to vacate that acquisition to his empire, or any sorrow over not being able to do so. In his Buddhism—if Buddhism it was—he still was not different from other kings and emperors. We have more to reflect on. We know from the inscriptions that Aśoka took very special measures to guarantee the effectiveness of his rule—and it does not seem advisable to share Masson-Oursel's enthusiasm for the centralization of administrative authority that ensued. Aśoka created a staff of high administrators to supervise what went on in every region of the empire; these functionaries were especially charged to investigate how well royal instructions were being adhered to. We read that the purpose of all this was the well-being of Aśoka's subjects. But the administrators were to monitor obedience of the populace to the rules of the state. These rules are considered as *dharma* in the sense of "positive law," without further ado.

I am not interested in detracting *ad absurdum* from the picture enthused historians have given of the great ruler. Indeed, there are many statements in the inscriptions that one can hardly read except as truly meaning the moral and religious things they say. Rock Edict XII exhorts all people to be tolerant, and indeed *honor* religious traditions other than their own.[22] Among its many other arresting precepts is the following:

> A man must say to himself, "Ferocity, cruelty, anger, arrogance, and jealousy lead to sin; I must not let myself be ruined by these passions." He should make a clear distinction between actions, saying, "This action is directed to my good in this world and that other to my good in the world to come."[23]

I am willing to assume that all Aśoka's pronouncements, including the ones he may have made without having them engraved on rocks for the world to read, are well meant. But I still have my problem with royal appointees charged to supervise obedience to *dharma*. Especially

---

22. Nikam and McKeon, trans. and eds., *The Edicts of Aśoka*, 51; de Bary, ed., *Sources of Indian Tradition*, 1:151.

23. Pillar Edict iii, in Nikam and McKeon, trans. and eds., *The Edicts of Aśoka*, 48.

when their duty is defined further as concerning "all sects," my suspicions are not allayed. I think we are entitled to suggest that in Aśoka's empire occasionally people must have been struck with terror at an announcement of the impending arrival of a delegation of those officials bearing the great title *dharmamahāmātras*. We might not be far off the mark by understanding this title as "high supervisors and judges of *dharma*." One can scarcely imagine anything that would be outside the scope of their jurisdiction.

Should we speak here of a "secret police"? This would be an anachronism, for many things had to happen before that sort of organization could emerge in the modern era. And furthermore, what is conveyed with the word *dharma* has no equivalent in the modern world, for it embraces both what we call "religious" and "secular." Yet, something within us recoils from this use of the power of the state to enforce an emperor's concept of religion.

The Sense in Other Structures

At the root of our religious traditions certain virtually unalterable lines are drawn. If we are incapable at this point of feeling unbridled enthusiasm for Aśoka, it is not because of some scholarly reappraisal alone, but because our instincts follow our own age-old structures. We understand the opposition of Nathan to David. Such a conflict, we feel, is basic.

Yet it is at just such a point as this that we must push aside the curtain around ourselves, around our own structures, which are the foundation for our judgments, and see the *sense* of other structures. Historically, Buddhism has many experiences of royal patrons protecting the religion. We should not apply an "instinct" born of our own religious conditionings to try to understand what this state of affairs really consisted of. (We might remember that we do not even know with any certainty what precisely caused Constantine to protect Christianity.) Structurally, the contrast given between a Nathan and a David is our basic imagery. This contrast makes us sense an opposition in all political events in history. For Buddhism, however, the crucial issue is the reality of "liberation," *nirvāṇa*, toward which the Buddhist monk reaches out. All other things are at best endowed with a degree of reality, and a good deal of Buddhist discussion through the ages has carried on its debates on those degrees (the theory of the *skandhas*). This makes for a very different relation between politics and religion. But it makes *sense*.

What constitutes Buddhism's orientation to the world's problems of power and spirit is indicated by pointing to the meditational activity of the monk or layman, whose inner discipline is fostered within that very world that everyone misunderstands "by nature," or, quite literally, because one is born. To set up an opposition between the worldly ruler and the monk would serve neither the world nor the spiritual goal.

Structure of Buddhism

Of the world's great religious traditions Buddhism seems to be the most "appealing" for many educated Westerners. We do not need to belabor the point that such affinities are not necessarily very profound; religion is not a matter one may determine by taste.

Many Westerners who praise Buddhism do so because they deem it more spiritual than their own traditions. As to their knowledge of Buddhism, the same Westerners are as a rule dependent on sources that have little or nothing to say on the question of how Buddhism relates to politics. These are also people who take the separation of church and state to be a natural model, not realizing that it owes its origin to the biblical heritage. Misunderstandings! And we need constantly to clear away misunderstandings as we try to approach our subject.

From the beginning, the monastic cultivation of the meditation-borne way toward *nirvāṇa* depended upon protection by laymen, more specifically the wealthy and powerful. Clichés about not biting the hand that feeds you could not begin to explain this relationship. As with the biblical case, the fundamental structures are spiritual. We recall the political and juridical quality of the crucial biblical terms. Buddhism has no equivalent for "judgment." Biblical religion has no equivalent for *nirvāṇa*.

The Buddhist teachings are throughout an endeavor to fight the odds, with the odds being all the normal facts of existence. From the earliest instruction on the first Noble Truth, the realization that all that exists is unpleasant, to the Zen teachers and their call for watchfulness in all conditions, especially when *satori* seems certain, this fight goes on.

The popular suggestion that one religious tradition is more spiritual, more mentally refined, another more materially obsessed, does not go to the heart of the matter. In each case, there is always some conflict between two extremes that remain extremes; neither can ever annihilate the other. The difference between religions consists in the manner the conflict is sensed and expressed.

For Buddhism, the manifestations of existence are to be guarded against watchfully by the monk or layman in meditation. Buddhism's structure in seeking the goal of *nirvāṇa* allowed it to enjoy the protection of rulers who were paradigms of the unpleasant world. That world is to be confronted with alertness, certainly not with indignation. The vigilance needed for clear recognition of the two constitutive extremes of existence has been preserved throughout all forms of Buddhism, even on the highest levels of meditation.

Around 1700, the Zen teacher Takasui said,

> Zen practicioners must accept the fact that while in meditation they are likely to suffer one or more of the three maladies: *kon*, *san*, and *chin*. *Kon* is sleepiness and *san* instability, both of which are too well known for comment. *Chin*, on the other hand, is a grave malady and always leads to unhappy results. It is a state in which one is free from sleepiness and instability, and all mentalization ceases. One feels gay, immaculate; one can go on in zazen for hours on end. One has a feeling that all things are equal, neither existent nor non-existent, right nor wrong. Those possessed by *chin* regard it as satori—a most dangerous delusion. If you were to remain in this state, you would go far astray. At such times, in fact, you must have the greatest doubt.[24]

The watchfulness that is necessary for the meditating monk is something different from the spiritual judgment of the biblical prophet. In each case, the underlying orientation of the religion creates the worldly relationship between spirit and power. Buddhist ideas concerning kingship or political power in general—especially when fully understood as carried by selfishness—have deep roots. But what the monk or serious Buddhist is asked to overcome—desire, lust, greed—one does not try to eliminate from the world or the city or state.

The uniqueness of Buddhist symbolism in this area cannot be touched by means of stereotypes such as: Buddhists did not consider the world real; nor by the variant that history has no significance for Buddhists.[25] The problem with this type of negative observation is that

---

24. Stryk and Ikemoto, comp. and trans. *Zen: Poems*, 71.

25. This line of thought (the absence of history for Buddhism) occurs from time to time in the work of Edward Conze. (See especially his admirable book reviews collected in Conze, *Further Buddhist Studies*.) Suggesting that Buddhists do not regard the world as real, or that the idea of history as real is foreign to them, is as misleading

it does not disclose anything of what is essentially Buddhist; it merely gratifies our need for categories and bolsters our confidence in the labels we attach. With respect to the link maintained in Buddhism between the two extremes of the religious goal and the world generated by greed and desire where sovereigns rule, it is related to the fact that the monks *must meditate on the appearances of the world*; there is no way for them to say, "let us separate the spiritual from the world."

Keeping in mind, then, that the situation in which Buddhism placed its kings did make its own particular sense in relating spirit and worldly power, we can probably say that it does somehow look as if for Buddhism kingship remained an unresolved problem. This is how Buddhism looks from a Christian, Islamic, or Jewish perspective. It is also how it appears from a Hindu-Brahmanic point of view. The difference from Brahmanism is especially revealing because Buddhism inherited its religious vocabulary from Brahmanism, and nevertheless the Hindu and Buddhist documents and histories are radically different.

Aśoka was the renowned king who—in ways that are not altogether clear to us—took up the cause of Buddhism, assuming in his sovereign power the supervision of *dharma* in his realm. No Hindu king, to my knowledge, ever tried anything like it. This use of one central authority to guarantee the law and the religion would make no sense from the point of view of Hinduism, which has so many different groups, all with their authority anchored in the tradition. To get a flavor of Buddhism in contrast to Hinduism, we may bear in mind that in India Buddhism never developed mechanisms for dealing with the ordinary stuff of life—weddings, funerals, and the like. Those matters continued to be handled by brahmins during the thousand years when Buddhism presented a challenge to Brahmanism in India. Buddhism had no channel for that Brahmanic openness toward the everyday reality of the world.

Although Hindus have not made criticism of others a habit, it is not difficult for us to imagine that the "perfect balance" of the Brahmanic view of rulership could be translated into a condemnation of the Buddhist example (as well as of most forms of government in the modern world). From a Hindu perspective, Buddhism looks completely unrealistic in its lack of concrete relations to the world we are in. The *brahman*, "the highest principle," "the absolute" of which the Brāhmaṇas and many

---

as the argument that Judaism, Christianity, and Islam rest on materialism because they hold to the doctrine of creation.

other Hindu texts speak is not only the goal of religious practice; at the same time it is clearly the origin and basis of this world.

An interesting glimpse of what is "missing" and what is present in Buddhism with regard to politics comes from a major Buddhist text, composed by the great Buddhist philosopher-monk Nāgārjuna (second century A.D.). Nāgārjuna is among the most magnificent thinkers the world has known. He addressed one of his treatises explicitly to a king. It is titled *Ratnāvalī, The Garland of Gems*. To our amazement perhaps, what Nāgārjuna has to say about kingship is scant and barely to the point. The text repeatedly uses the vocative "O King!" or "Great King!" yet it is nothing other than a summary of Nāgārjuna's Mahāyāna teachings, occasionally refuting other schools, and presenting to the addressee (who may have been a Sātavāhana king of Andhra) as the proper destination of his career the entry into monastic life (4.400). The fourth chapter (which ends with this advice) is the most explicit about royal duties. This is how it begins:

> If useful but unpleasant words
> Are hard to speak to someone else,
> What could I, a monk, say to a king
> Who is lord of the great earth?
>
> But because of my affection for you
> And through compassion for all beings,
> I tell you without hesitation
> That which is useful but unpleasant. (4.302–303)[26]

Observe that these words would set up in the Western reader an expectation that the text is about to criticize the king. But what follows is general moral advice; there is nothing Nāgārjuna tells the king to do for his own personal well-being that he would not also advise to anyone else. And it is impossible not to notice the "commercial" for the *saṅgha*. It comes unobtrusively after an elaboration on the good Buddhist theme of the fleeting nature of all things, including the health and wealth of kings.

> Therefore while in good health create now
> Centres of doctrine with all your wealth,

---

26. Translation in Hopkins and Rimpoche, trans. and eds., *The Precious Garland*, 62. See also Tucci, "The Ratnāvalī of Nāgārjuna." This presents text and translation of the first chapter.

> For you are living amidst the causes
> Of death like a lamp standing in a breeze.
>
> Also other centres of doctrine
> Established by the previous king,
> All the temples and so forth,
> Should be sustained as before.
>
> Please have them attended by those
> Who harm no others, keep their vows,
> Are virtuous, truthful, kind to visitors,
> Patient, non-combative and always industrious. (4.317–319)[27]

After this follows more advice, concerning aid of the sick and disabled, best appointments to civil and military posts, the need to punish criminals compassionately, to abstain from torture, and so on. There is no special emphasis on the extraordinary responsibilities and duties that come with the paramount power invested in kingship, and there is nothing on the possible abuse of such power. On the whole, Nāgārjuna's announced "unpleasantness" amounts to little more than the ordinary Buddhist precepts given to laymen, each of whom would be reminded of "living amidst the causes of death."

(The civilizing significance of religion is evident; it stands out in the recommendations on the punishment of lawbreakers. In this context, it is interesting to notice that a few centuries after Nāgārjuna's time, Chinese Buddhist monks Faxian and later Xuanzang, and their companions on their pilgrimages to India, arriving at Pāṭaliputra were shown the "hell of Aśoka." This was a prison Aśoka had constructed and equipped with the worst instruments of torture. The design of the prison was said to be inspired by the image of Yama's hell, and hence was justifiable within the tradition as a stimulus for good conduct. But Faxian's account emphasizes that Aśoka had the prison built immediately upon his enthronement, hence before his conversion. The text leaves no doubt that Buddhism curbs cruelty and promotes gentleness. Aśoka had appointed the cruelest man available as warden of his prison, but that same man becomes instrumental in the conversion of the king.[28])

---

27. Hopkins and Rimpoche, trans. and eds., *The Precious Garland*, 64–65.
28. Ibid.

Nāgārjuna's words do not have the "bite" of Nathan's speech before King David, or, for that matter, Calvin's dedication to King Francis in the *Preface* to the *Institutes*, or Hildegard von Bingen's reprimands addressed to the dignitaries of her day.[29]

On the other hand, Nāgārjuna certainly never takes a servile attitude toward the king, and there is really something superb about the way he confronts the king as he would any other person. Borrowing from our vocabulary, we might say that Nāgārjuna and the king are "equal": he, and the king, and every creature "living amidst the causes of death like a lamp standing in the breeze." Here we can see a type of equality different from the forms we are familiar with. Each notion of equality is created by structures central in the dominant religious tradition.

(An earlier discussion between a Buddhist monk and a king took place in the second century B.C. in Bactria, in northwest India; the dialogue is quite important among the texts of early Buddhism and widely known. The monk was Nāgasena, and the ruler the Greek king Milinda [Menander].[30] Nāgasena shows himself aware of the risk in disagreeing with kings, yet the dialogue never goes to any issue of spirit and power in confrontation. It is significant that this text, by contrast with the Mahāyāna writings of Nāgārjuna, belongs to the Theravāda tradition. This major division in Buddhism makes no difference with respect to our topic.)

Among the many mythical themes that Buddhism carried on from Brahmanism is one concerning the Uttarakurus, a tribe to be found somewhere in the North and characterized by a perfect existence—in Brahmanic myth, without a king to rule over them; the Brahmanic texts make clear that the absence of a king is the Uttarakurus' characteristic feature.[31] Buddhism knows of the existence of the Uttarakurus in inexhaustible bliss, but there the sameness ends. And the Buddhist modification of the story highlights Buddhism's meditation-borne view of worldly power. By contrast, the earlier, Brahmanic tradition made the issue of royal power and its limits central. We see this clearly in a Brahmanic document, the *Aitareyabrāhmaṇa*.

29. Hildegard von Bingen's concern for political matters flows from her spiritual life, as shown by North, "Mysticism and Prophetism in Hildegard von Bingen and in Ramanuja." See especially ibid., 47–51; and ibid., chapter 3.

30. Davids, trans., *The Questions of King Milinda*.

31. For a list of textual references, though limited to cosmographic texts, see Kirfel, *Die Kosmographie der Inder*, 11, 18, 19, 183, 184, 188.

The *Aitareyabrāhmaṇa* comments on the *rājasūya*, the royal consecration we discussed in the last essay, and makes use of the story of the Uttarakurus in a commentary dealing with a part of the ritual known as the *mahābhiṣeka*, the "Great Anointing." With this anointing, the gods made Indra a universal king; hence the ritual is also known as "the great anointing of Indra." The text goes on to list a number of kings who were anointed likewise. In every case a sage taught the new king the real power of the ritual. As a result, the king became empowered and conquered the earth. Each time, the text repeats: "Therefore he [each king concerned] went round the earth completely, conquering on every side..." Then, the end of the narration adds a dramatic twist, whereby the issue of power—and its possible misuse—is made to stand out. The last conqueror to receive the teachings is in fact not entitled to kingship ("... Jānaṃtapi, though not a king ...") and the sage who initiated him finds to his dismay what tresspass he has brought about: Atyarāti Jānaṃtapi wants to conquer the Uttarakurus. Only wrongly conveyed and misappropriated power could lead to such overstepping. Jānaṃtapi's proposal amounts to a total upheaval of what *dharma*—proper custom, tradition—prescribes:

> Bṛhaduktha [a priestly, Vedic poet] proclaimed [="taught," not "administered"] this great anointing of Indra to Durmukha, the Pāñcāla. Therefore Durmukha Pāñcāla, being a king, by this knowledge went round the earth completely ["by this knowledge" is an addition to what was said of the preceding kings], conquering on every side. Vāsiṣṭha Sātyahavya [a sage in the line of Vāsiṣṭha, the Vedic seer] proclaimed this great consecration of Indra to Atyarāti Jānaṃtapi. Therefore Jānaṃtapi, *though not a king* [my italics] through his knowledge went round the earth completely, conquering on every side. Vāsiṣṭha Sātyahavya said: "Thou hast conquered entirely the earth on every side: do thou make me great." Then said Atyarāti Jānaṃtapi: "When I conquer, O Brahman, the Uttara Kurus, then thou wouldst be king on the earth, and I should be thy general." Vāsiṣṭha Sātyahavya replied: "That is a place of the gods; no mortal man may conquer it. Thou hast been false to me..."[32]

The story ends badly for Atyarāti Jānaṃtapi. He loses his strength, and is slain by another king. The moral lesson is explicit in the text: a man deals falsely with a brahmin when he would become overweening in his

---

32. Keith, *Rigveda Brahmanas*, 336–38. I changed the word order in the translation slightly for the sake of clarity.

kingship. In this narrative the realm of the Uttarakurus is called "a place of the gods." Jānaṃtapi's desire to conquer it clearly brings out his transgression of the limits set for worldly power. Thus the Hindu text shows its concern for politics; the religious structure of Bramanism visibly curbs it, emphatically bringing to our attention that real, legitimate worldly power cannot exist if it does not accept and affirm the priority of the divine purpose. The Uttarakurus are used by the text to bring home this point.

No such concerns arise when the same Uttarakurus of the *Aitareyabrāhmaṇa* occur in a Buddhist *Mahāyānasūtra*, the *Akṣobhyavyūha*.[33]

Here the realm of the Uttarakurus functions solely as an analogy to a Buddha-realm of fulfillment for devotees who have gained sufficient merit.

We read what the Buddha says to his disciple Sāriputra:

> Sāriputra, the food at the disposal of the inhabitants of this Buddha-realm has colors, fragrances, and tastes that do not differ from those of the gods. It is like the inhabitants of . . . Uttarakuru who have one single king; this universe [known as] Abhirati [=delight] . . . is completely equal to it: only the Tathāgata Akṣobhya is here regarded as the king of the *dharma*. It is as with the thirty-three *gods* [=the Vedic deities], when Śakra [=Indra] was enthroned, he unfolds his thought, and then the gods come to receive his instruction. And just as the thirty-three gods honor Śakra, these people all serve the Tathāgata.
>
> This, Sāriputra, is how you should know the splendor of the qualities of Akṣobhya's Buddha-realm.
>
> Sāriputra, the minds of the beings in this realm (of the Buddha) are free from indolence. Why? This is likewise thanks to the force of the original vow of the Tathāgata Akṣobhya.[34]

This "heavenly" realm, for which the text uses the Uttarakurus to bring the image home to the listener, does not provoke issues of a necessary balance of the type we saw in the *rājasūya* ceremony, nor of the necessity to set a limit to power, as emphasized in the *Aitareyabrāhmaṇa*. The fact that the *Akṣobhyavyūha* must be ranked among the sūtras of early Mahāyāna Buddhism adds to its significance for our purpose. It cannot

---

33. The *Akṣobhyavyū*ha has been translated and provided with an elaborate introduction and notes in Dantinne, *La splendeur de l'Inébranlable*. The passage that follows bears Dantinne's heading: "The Absolute Sovereignty of Akṣobhya."

34. Ibid., 197–98 (my trans.).

be considered a "systematic" text; it is far from doctrinally thought out.³⁵ Obviously not intent on eliminating contradictions, not the work of logicians, it is likely to be more reliable when it comes to traditional mythic details, and to give us a flavor of Buddhism as *lived*.

Now a note of caution. It is true that Buddhism has tended to leave issues of power very much on their own. Yet there are notable exceptions. We may refer to the long and tumultuous history of Southeast Asia, where in many instances the intermingling of Hinduism and Buddhism is in evidence. In Cambodia and elsewhere, kingship and religion were intricately interwoven, and in temple art the realms of "the holy" and "here and now" were often identified.³⁶ The phenomenon of Buddhist monks burning themselves to death during America's engagement in Vietnam remained an incomprehensible puzzle for the White House; a "prophetic" concern of Buddhism for worldly rule does follow its own line of history.³⁷ Also, the general inclination of Buddhism to leave imperial rulers untouched, even allowing them to take on the role of defender of the good *dharma*, can cross over from being an acquiescence in politics into being a very consequential merging of religion and politics. This happened in Japan in the modern era.

Tokugawa Ieyasu's Edict

As a transition to a discussion of Buddhism and politics and religion and politics in general in modern times, I would like to look at a document from seventeenth-century Japan. In some way it echoes Aśoka's political assurance of speech concerning spiritual matters. It does not contradict Ajātaśatru's peculiar utterances either.

Christian traders, especially Portuguese traders, and missionaries had entered Japan, and Christianity had made converts among the

---

35. See Dantinne, *La splendeur de l'Inébranlable*, introduction, 39–40.

36. The most remarkable case of a blending of spiritual and political power is that of Tibet. I regret that the format of our essay does not permit its inclusion. An excellent work dealing with the subject is Snellgrove, *Indo-Tibetan Buddhism* (2 vols.). See especially in Snellgrove, "The Combination of Religion and Politics," 2:470–526. Lest one think that such complexities are limited to northern Buddhism, see the book by Holt, *Avalokiteśvara in the Buddhist Traditions of Sri Lanka*; see also the critical review of this work by Obeyesekere, "Avalokiteśvara's Aliases and Guises."

37. The classic work on this history is Coedès, *The Indianized States of Southeast Asia*.

Japanese. Then, in 1614, the ruling Tokugawa Shogun, Ieyasu, issued an edict directed against the religious intrusion by foreigners. Although a large-scale persecution of Christians did not come about until later, after Ieyasu's death in 1616,[38] the wording of the edict leaves no doubt as to the right the ruler assumed in speaking on behalf of the Buddhist tradition and urging certain actions to protect it.

> The party of Christians has come to Japan, not only by sending ships of its merchant marine to trade goods, but also attempting to spread an evil law, to subvert the Good Law in order to overturn the government and to take possession of the country. That is the seed of disaster and must be destroyed. Japan is the land of the gods and Buddhas; it honors the gods and worships the Buddhas. The principles of benevolence and justice are considered of supreme significance, and the law of good and evil is secured so as to expose evildoers, wherever they are found, to the five penalties, in accordance with the severity of their crime: branding; splitting of the nose; cutting off the feet; castration; and the death penalty . . . An excessive accumulation of evil should not go free; the punishment will be meted out by crucifixion or burning at the stake, for this is the way to encourage the good and chastise evil. Although one may entertain the wish to suppress evil, it accumulates easily; although one may wish to make progress in the good, it is nevertheless difficult to persevere; hence it is incumbent to be watchful. This is how it is in the present life. And as to the hereafter, not even all Buddhas together, past, present and future ones, can save from the accusations of the king of hell, nor is the line of our ancestors able to help us. Fear and tremble! The Bater [=*patres*, the Catholic priests] party is opposed to this order of things . . .[39]

To be sure, the Shogun does not invoke only Buddhist sources in support of his pronouncements. Japan was not a nation of just one religion;[40] Confucianism was strong, and the edict mentions Confucius by name as an authority. What cannot fail to strike us, however, is that the text allows no space for the question of whether a worldly ruler is entitled to speak on behalf of the right law, the *saddharma*. No Buddhist asked the Shogun to do so, but also, no Buddhist tried to stop the Shogun from speaking on behalf of the totality of the religion. The words of the Sho-

---

38. Sansom, *Japan: A Short Cultural History*, 425.
39. Chantepie de la Saussaye, *Textbuch zur Religionsgeschichte*, 78.
40. See Tsunoda, et al., eds., *Sources of Japanese Tradition*, 331–35.

gun's edict are aimed at Christians literally. He is speaking to them when he says "fear and tremble!" No Buddhist raised a question about this. The Shogun has taken upon himself to speak on behalf of religion, and the manner in which he does so rolls his rulership and the religion into one.

Buddhism within a Worldwide Discourse

A splendid book, *Of Heretics and Martyrs in Meiji Japan: Buddhism and Its Persecution*, by James Edward Ketelaar, commences by narrating events that began in 1854 with a government order to collect the bells of temples so they might be "refashioned into cannon and rifles."[41]

For some of us such an anecdote can bring back memories. Personally, I remember a similar order by German authorities requisitioning church bells in Holland during the Second World War. It was not a command in a fairy tale. It drove home for those who heard it an awareness concerning the involved relations between power and "something higher." This awareness was as confused as it was profound. It was a thoroughly modern awareness.

Professor Ketelaar's book describes the persecutions of Buddhists in Meiji Japan, and how, in developments that followed, Buddhism came to see itself as the great Asian spirituality, and indeed the genius of Japan. The book owes a good deal of its fascination to the resemblance we can discover between conflicts in Japan and Europe. We are forced to recognize that "the problem of religion and power" has become universal in the sense that it can no longer be viewed understandably within one religion alone. The closer we come to the present, the more our problem begins to resemble a single creature with many arms.

In the nineteenth century a profound transformation affected both Buddhism and Christianity. An international shift of view concerning religion occurred in Christendom—perhaps first in Germany and England—and very soon thereafter in Japan. A convenient date at the beginning period of this shift is August 15, 1811. On that day, Colonel Joseph Boden, founder of the Boden Chair of Sanskrit at the University of Oxford, signed his will. Boden stipulated that "the special object of his munificent bequest was to promote the translation of the Scriptures into Sanskrit" so as "to enable his countrymen to proceed in the conversion of

---

41. Ketelaar, *Of Heretics and Martyrs*, 3.

the natives of India to the Christian religion."[42] Boden's testament seemed to take for granted that somehow religion equals civilization. (More particularly, Christianity will civilize the uncivilized.) The matter of whether religion and civilization should be distinguished, or how they might be distinguished, was not raised. The two seemed very close, if not the same. The ensuing intellectual history of the nineteenth century made them the same.

By 1893, the World's Parliament of Religions, held in Chicago at the occasion of the Columbian World Exposition, was a conspicuous expression of the new age. A conversation among representatives of the world's great traditions took place for the first time and caused a stir internationally. What is seldom realized is that this event could hardly have come about were it not for a change that had crept unobserved into the climate of thought. Certain political events in the East as well as the West had a great deal to do with the change of mood that animated the organizing committee and the participants.

All over Europe in the second half of the nineteenth century so-called school struggles occurred. Debates raged over matters involving schools and religion—for example, the question of whether church-related schools should be subsidized by the governments. In the course of debates within the parliamentary system, self-consciously secular voices grew loud and clear. They included not only those of the "liberal" parties—representing the rising industrial and commercial classes—but also the growing socialist parties, as both had their own reservations with respect to the old, established religious institutions and their influence.

At the same time, voices rose with proposals for "scientific" professorships in the universities for the study of religion. Fiery clashes took place over this issue. The new professorships would address not only the biblical texts and Christianity, but also the religions of the ancient world, and modern religions outside the Christian orbit. Of course, such changes amounted to a revolution in the accepted order. Yet by and large they came. Since the time of Erasmus and Spinoza, study of the biblical texts themselves had reflected the influence of contemporary critical methods. More significantly, the world outside of Christianity could not be ignored by nations that had developed colonies in Asia, Africa, and America. These conditions no doubt prepared the ground for the parliamentary victories. The first chair in the history of religions was

---

42. Monier-Williams, preface to *A Sanskrit-English Dictionary*, ix.

established in Geneva in 1873. In 1876, the three state universities of the Netherlands (Leiden, Utrecht, and Groningen) and the city university of Amsterdam were each granted their chair in the same field. The Collège de France followed in 1879, the Sorbonne in 1885 (with several chairs), Brussels in 1884.[43] What seemed to be a battle for "open-mindedness" appeared to have been won.

In assessing what was taking place, we need to look at the mood of that time, and, above all, the evolutionistic assumptions that ruled supreme. The work of Nathan Söderblom (1866–1931) presents an eloquent example of this model of thinking which dominated the period. Söderblom was a devout man, a theologian, an early advocate of the modern ecumenical movement, professor of the history of religions in Uppsala (1901–1912), in Leipzig (1912–1914), and archbishop of the Swedish church from 1914 until his death. In 1930 he received the Nobel Peace Prize, in recognition not only of his ecumenical efforts but also for his work reconciling adversaries from the World War. Professor Charles J. Adams describes Söderblom's central idea as follows: "He held that revelation is dynamic, not confined to the words of the Bible but also to be seen in nature, history, and genius."[44] Söderblom titled his major work *Das Werden des Gottesglaubens*,[45] literally "the becoming of the faith in God." The dynamic nature of revelation, so it seemed to him, was graspable in its historical development, and the book attempts to show this with a remarkable vision of religious traditions and facts all over the world. Characteristically, Söderblom's Gifford Lectures, interrupted by his death and published posthumously, introduced the term "continued revelation."[46] He held that this continuing revelation in a variety of forms, attested in the history of all traditions, had its fullest manifestation in Christianity.

With scholars such as Söderblom within Christianity and the newly "secular" voices without, we cannot fail, in hindsight, to see that in some way both "religious" and "secular" thinking were now moving along the same path. (Many a traditional believer saw no value in the learned expositions of "modernists" such as Söderblom. The political debates that

43. Eliade, *The Sacred and the Profane*, 217.
44. Adams, in his article on Söderblom in *The Encyclopedia of Religion*, 2nd ed.
45. Söderblom, *Das Werden des Gottesglaubens*.
46. "Continued Revelation" is the title of the concluding chapter of *The Living God: Basic Forms of Personal Religion*, Söderblom's Gifford Lectures delivered at the University of Edinburgh in the year 1931.

were flaring up, the doubts about new historical and relativistic views of religion, all were linked to a general objection that continued below the surface.)

It is difficult today to recapture the simplistic evolutionistic view of history and religion that was at the core of Söderblom's work and the work of many scholars at the time. The first edition of the great encyclopedia of religions *Die Religion in Geschichte und Gegenwart* was published between 1909 and 1913. Its many contributors can for the most part be said to have been in agreement on the dedication to historical inquiry as the royal road to an understanding of religious phenomena and to have shared in the ideas of Söderblom. A broad and "objective," cultural understanding had come to take precedence over single religious adherence and over the importance of traditional theologies.

John Henry Barrows (1847–1902) was the principal organizer and chairman of the World's Parliament of Religions at the World Exposition of 1893. His thoughts seem like blunt exaggerations of Nathan Söderblom's historicizing theologizings:

> We believe that Christianity is to supplant all other religions because it contains all the truth in them and much besides . . . Though light has no fellowship with darkness, light does have fellowship with twilight. God has not left himself without witness, and those who have the full light of the cross should bear brotherly hearts towards all who grope in a dimmer illumination.[47]

Barrows' ideas were in the same stream as those of prominent scholars in Europe. Religion and civilization had been, as it were, rolled into one. The uneasiness with this intellectual practice that did exist remained no more than a murmur in the background.

Compared to the state of affairs in the West, events in late nineteenth-century Japan were a great deal more tumultuous. Professor Ketelaar's book recounts how rebellious elements—from the government's point of view—became martyrs—from the point of view of many a Buddhist. Individuals were arrested, flogged, or hanged, or they perished in prison under brutal conditions. As in the West, the national system of education was an issue of fierce contention. However, much more directly than in Europe, the struggle was characterized by vehemence further intensified

---

47. Ketelaar, *Of Heretics and Martyrs*, 139.

by a zeal for the essence of the national culture.⁴⁸ Moreover, what made the Japanese case different was direct governmental interference in religious rituals. The influence of Shinto tradition was officially strengthened at the expense of Buddhist rites, beginning with imperial funeral ceremonies. (Funeral ceremonies have always been of exceptional significance in Japan.) Government officials were well aware of what they were doing, for they were experts on cultic matters. Professor Ketelaar repeatedly speaks of the ideology employed by officials of the Meiji era.⁴⁹ Apparently, ideology as our notion has it (by definition imbued with politics) became fused completely with religion. And when orders came down to Buddhist temples to change themselves into Shinto shrines, there was no mechanism to resist such orders directly.⁵⁰ No commonly shared tradition allowed a line to be drawn between "church" and "state."

Of course, Buddhism did not perish under the onslaught by the state. In all its many groups and sects, Japanese Buddhism remained the major tradition and it renewed itself. In many of the renewal efforts, however, as in the struggles that led up to them, the major stakes were felt to be: the central spirituality of Asia, the central spirituality of Japan. Nationalism and religion were felt to be intertwined. As early as 1868—three years before the "anti-Buddhist storm" would die down—some Buddhists attempted to form an Organization of United Buddhist Sects; the first two points of the new organization's platform were "the inseparability of the Kingly Law and the Buddhist Law" and "the critique and expulsion of Chistianity."⁵¹

In Japan, as in Europe, "religious" and "secular" thinking were undergoing transformations. And as in Europe, the same climate, the same forces, affected all sides in the turmoil. Many a government official in Japan had come to look upon Buddhism, the single most important institutional religious tradition, as an obstacle to the development that was desired in the modern era; the order to recast temple bells into weaponry pinpoints the conflict. At the same time, while Japan faced military threats from Russia and the United States, it was largely due to Germany that the "modern era" filtered into Japan. Japanese students and scholars

48. Ibid., 86.

49. Ibid., especially 44.

50. A very informative work on the subject is Ebersole, *Ritual Poetry and the Politics of Death in Early Japan*.

51. For vivid descriptions of such orders and of Buddhist circumventions, see Ketelaar, *Of Heretics and Martyrs*, 74.

who studied in Germany were exposed to that identification of religion and civilizing (read: political) power as envisioned by Christians with missionary aspirations. If the religion of Europe could be empowered with such far-reaching force, could not Buddhism, a religion that had spread across numerous boundaries, become its Asian equivalent—if not its superior? The national feelings of Japan allowed this idea to take a course analogous to the idea of religious evolution in history that German and other Western scholars had developed. Among the countries of Asia, Japan had "obviously" known the highest development of Buddhism, and it was the task of Japanese Buddhists to show the world how much Japan had to offer for the future.

The similarity of progressions in nineteenth-century Christianity and Buddhism—fraught in ways that are so obvious now and could not have been evident at the time—has much to do with that confused entanglement of history and evolution. The Parliament of Religions at Chicago turned into one of the more peculiar spectacles: Christians, Buddhists, Hindus, and others all making the case for the ultimate spiritual and civilizing validity of their religion. This universalistic and evolutionistic view of religion, of civilization, presented itself at the time as a kind of modernization. In reality, it was making religion into an absolute in a way it had never been before. The new intellectual climate allowed a telescoping of religion and power into one entity, with no breathing space between them. This rivets our attention today because it holds up the mirror to some of our own portrayals of political power and its "ultimate" legitimization. We are thoroughly familiar with political leaders who believe they are doing God's work.

The unseen religious shift of the nineteenth century is at the heart of Professor Ketelaar's work on the Buddhists of Japan. The atrocities of the twentieth century had their prelude in these ideological shifts, which helped allow the rise of Fascism and National Socialism. The "regrouping"—no, let us call it what it is—the *ideologizing* of Christians in Europe and in America had very much to do with the groundwork for terrible events throughout the whole world. We repeat: when evolution—the thing Darwin investigated, in which laws of nature are established—and history—that science in which people inquire into causes, and moreover into meanings and purposes of human acts—are telescoped into one another, religion turns into ideology. History is transformed into something whose meaning has been pared down to its force to support power structures—and we imagine it as coming close to "laws of nature." The spiritual component of the twins, spirit and power, has then collapsed.

I do not want to propose a postmortem witchhunt on nineteenth-century scholars in Germany, Japan, Italy, England, America. Granted that many Christians and Buddhists submitted to the spirit of the age without a struggle; granted that many accepted it in their scholarly, historical work of interpreting religion, and granted also that many simply withdrew into their study and did not speak up until the wars came to an end and everything was safe again. Nevertheless, there were Japanese scholars who did marvelous work on the history and meaning of Buddhism, Germans who did marvelous work on the history and meaning of Christianity. Not every scholar who can be ranked with the *religionsgeschichtliche Schule* (the "History of Religions School") early on in the twentieth century, and who lived long enough, became a Nazi. Neither did every learned Japanese who had taken part in the intellectual reinvigoration of Buddhism become dedicated to the state in the 1930s and 1940s.

Without ever dealing with events relating directly to the Second World War, Professor Ketelaar touches the heart of the problem: the extreme difficulty of relocating the real religious tradition once the confusion of history and evolution has brought about its worst results.[52] In some ways Zen Buddhism with its paramount lucidity—and its penchant for surprises—might seem to have held the greatest potential to "stand up" for the Buddhist tradition in the onslaught of talk about righteous war efforts. However, Zen Buddhism is not organized with the purpose of filling a prophetic role. The constantly watchful, critical Zen Buddhist can nevertheless ignore the political process, and, perhaps unintentionally, become a bystander, an instance of collaboration through inaction. The alternative is to become an active defender, interpreter, and instructor of the religious authority that matters.

What our imagined Zen Buddhist could have done is not fiction. Moreover, the alternative at hand had its exact parallels within the Hitler era in Europe. When we consider the overwhelming horror of times like those, the horror that prevails today in many parts of our world, we may be tempted to conclude that trying to figure out the real relations between religion and politics is an irrelevant exercise. We might be led so far as to suggest that with respect to this problem all religion is the same in the

---

52. Ibid., 73, and also ibid., 219–20.

end. But thoughts like this are not worthwhile, and leave us in a state of do-nothingness—where we may ourselves become inactive collaborators with any evil, blindly self-important regime.

A more proper conclusion is that the critical study of religions is absolutely vital now that the problem of religion and politics has become an international affair; it is right to say that human fates depend on our understanding. Reviewing the events in Germany and Japan in the last century, considering their relation to what intellectuals did in the century before that, we may feel enlivened and ready to assume the modicum of courage serious intellectual endeavor requires. Every religion, Buddhism, Christianity, or any other, needs responsible intellectuals to address it. The potential of any religion to be turned inside out for the sake of an egomaniacal power continues to exist. Intellectual scrutiny of religion is of central significance. It is all the more urgent in the intellectual void that opens up beneath the modern university—the void that has been ever widening since the end of the nineteenth century.

9

The Monotheism of Islam

The "Threat" of Islam

We have not tried in this series of essays so much to present a chronological account of things as to give the best order in which to understand them justly. Before we turn in the next essay to the problem of ourselves as religious beings, it is time to concentrate on the great religious tradition that has always touched a raw nerve in the "Christianity-affected" West.

Islam is part of the family to which Judaism and Christianity belong. It is one of the "Abrahamic" religions. And today it is second only after Christianity in the approximate number of its adherents in the world. Everyone is aware of the political importance of Islam.[1] We are aware that Islam exhibits a most striking conjunction of religion and politics. Nowadays there is a commonplace belief that Islam fosters a special, a unique, fanaticism. Actually, this idea is old in the West. The perception has typically involved the sense of a "threat" from the Muslim world.[2] We

---

1. A work frequently invoked in this context is Huntington, *The Clash of Civilizations.*

2. See Esposito's sober *The Islamic Threat* and *Unholy War*. For an excellent analysis of politics and religion in Islam and Hinduism in the ongoing conflicts between Pakistan and India, see Larson, "Nuclearization in the South Asian Region." The multifarious revivals of Islamic self-awareness in recent years may not seem religious to some Western observers, but belittling that awareness as fanaticism or simply terrorism is a grave error and a tragedy perhaps of gigantic scope. Like Christianity under Soviet oppression, like all religions, Islam too gains in strength under duress.

have often posited some alien fanaticism on the part of Muslims. However, I believe we have been unaware of the real roots of our scorn.

Islam and "the Christian world" are neighbors who many times have been at each other's throats. This mutual history does not prepare the ground for an undisturbed attitude such as we can assume in broaching Buddhism or Hinduism. Relations between Islam and Christianity have seen recurring skirmishes, open war, and vehement philosophical and theological antagonisms.

Western chroniclers gloried over Charles Martel's rout of the Muslim army in 732, and poets wept over the legendary hero Roland doing battle with the Saracens at Roncesvalles in 778. (In fact, there were no Muslims left to fight there at the time, but poetic and popular memory could re-create Basques in a minor encounter into Moors.)

The force of the Muslim warriors is clear from the fact that only two decades before they faced Charles Martel in France, the first Muslims had entered the south of Spain, under the leadership of Tariq. Centuries later the West was delighted by the victory that finally drove the Moors out of Spain. This happened the same year Columbus set foot in the New World. By then, Muslim civilization had reached a very high level of expression on the Iberian Peninsula.

The era of the Crusades stretched from the eleventh to the fourteenth centuries. Incited by the Church, European Christians entered the Near East in raid after raid to wrest back the "holy land"—the place of Jesus' birth, death, and resurrection—from the possession of Islamic rulers.

Muslim advances in Europe would continue for a long period of time. Osman (1258–1326), the leader of the Seljuk nation in Asia Minor, founded the dynasty that brought about the downfall of Byzantium; it was a later successor, Sultan Mehmet, who conquered Constantinople in 1453. The power of the Ottoman Turks, and hence Islam, came to extend over a large part of Eastern Europe: the seat of the Eastern Church moved from Constantinople to Moscow.

In 1529, a year that saw intense activity by Martin Luther, Turkish armies entering the heart of Europe came close to capturing Vienna. Luther's well-known statements summarized in the cry "rather Turkish than papist!" predate that event considerably and were uttered in his zeal against the Church of Rome.[3] The significance of Luther's words, for us, is that they show the unquestioned persuasion that Muslims were *pagans*,

---

3. Luther's own treatise *Vom Krieg wider den Türcken* (About the War against the Turks) makes this quite clear.

complete outsiders to the kingdom of God. The Ottoman Turks provided a perfect imagery for Luther in his fulminating against the corruptions of the Church. (We should note that for their part, the Muslims called themselves "believers," as they have always done, and all others "infidels," and would sometimes call the Christians "polytheists" on account of their doctrine of a trinity.)

The course of Islamic expansion eastward changed the face of Asia. Many in India embraced Islam. When India emerged from the colonial era and became independent in the twentieth century, the new nation of Pakistan with its Muslim majority—which formerly had been part of the Indian realm—was formed in strife and bloodshed. Early Pakistan included also what is now Bangladesh, another region predominantly Muslim. Indonesia is in fact the largest Muslim nation on earth. And at the present time, about one-fifth of Islam's adherents live within what was once the Soviet Union. All of missionary history attests to the sheer impossibility of converting Muslims to Christianity throughout these wide regions. The Soviet Union under Stalin deported Muslim Chechens to a distant place, and post-Soviet Russia has used its army to suppress the nation of Chechnya and has reached no just accord with these "rebels"—or "terrorists." A historian cannot help but reflect that in communist times and postcommunist times alike the typical anti-Islamic feelings continue to wreak havoc.

Discrimination

Although much excellent material exists to present us with a fair account of Islamic tradition,[4] unwillingness to understand Islam has generally been the rule. And I think the explanation for Western antagonism is so near that it escapes scrutiny: Islam is a very close relative.[5]

---

4. See for example Hourani, *A History of the Arab Peoples*; Hodgson, *The Venture of Islam*; Boullata, *Trends and Issues in Contemporary Arab Thought*; Cook, *Muhammad*; Lewis, *The Political Language of Islam*; Esposito, *Islam: the Straight Path*; Esposito, *Islam in Asia*. Primary documents are available in Kritzeck, *Anthology of Islamic Literature*; and McNeill and Waldman, *The Islamic World*. Useful also is Glassé, *The Concise Encyclopedia of Islam*.

5. It is useful to take in the words spoken by George W. Bush and Osama bin Laden. See especially appendices B and C in Lincoln's *Holy Terrors*. These are statements by men who are absolutely sure they have seen each other's wickedness; they are uttered by men formed in traditions that are closely related.

Without a doubt, the negative feeling toward the Islamic, Middle Eastern world that characterizes the West has its most profound source in the religious familial relationship between Christianity and Islam. Islam is a mirror in which we see ourselves: be it as we were, as we are, or as a part that is now hidden in us longs to be. What is especially problematic here is that so many educated Westerners are ignorant of their own religious heritage—the very heritage that continues to inform their thought and speech. Hence that which they share with Islam is only dim in their minds, and the causes of their reactions escape them. (An effort to gain insight into this problem vis-à-vis Islam should also shed light on anti-Semitism.)[6]

Our lack of understanding of our own tradition may be examined a bit by considering a particular foolishness that is regularly invoked among us: the all-encompassing "*Judeo-Christianity.*"

Let us note that no one speaks of "Judeo-Islamo-Christianity," although this would be a more accurately formulated synthesis. For reasons of chronology, we might improve the expression further by speaking of "Judeo-Christiano-Islam." However, our love for the whole of our tradition works more selectively than that.

The popular use of the term "Judeo-Christian" is a post Second World War phenomenon. Until then, there were no "Judeo-Christians" among us. In fact there never was a time in which there were any such beings (except in the day of the earliest Christians, because they were Jews; for them the term is perfectly accurate). All that we had were Jews and Christians. Only when the Jews had been decimated at Hitler's order did the world develop not only the neutral recognition of a "Judeo-Christian" tradition, but even of "Judeo-Christians." I see in this not a deep understanding or a profound reconciliation but merely another abstraction that has come to function as reality—to the detriment of the reality in which people exist and recognize themselves.

It is essential to see with respect to the neutral "Judeo-Christian tradition" that its only mode is as an abstraction. It is shorthand to refer to the fact that there is a coherency between the Old and New Testaments, and the development of Judaism and Christianity that followed. (Let it be noted that the Eastern Orthodox churches, in whose midst pogroms occurred more persistently than anywhere else, have paid more attention

---

6. For a moment I am taking the term *anti-Semitism* in its wrong sense that has come to stay—as a synonym for "anti-Jewishness." The simple fact often ignored when the term is used is that the Arabs are as Semitic as the Jews. *Semitic* is a linguistic term.

to the Old Testament, both in their liturgy and teachings, than other Christian denominations.)

This neutral broad-mindedness is symptomatic of the uninformed rationalism that often prevails among us in matters of religion. As this rationalism has no basis in any serious religious understanding, it is merely a stance, a groundless affair. In a simple way, it appeals to our easy goodwill. But it is useless.

Problems of discrimination, racism, and persecution invariably *hide* themselves; the most telling symbolism of the Ku Klux Klan is not the burning cross but the robes and masks with which its members *hide* themselves. There is a problem of discrimination at work underneath the veneer of the rational when we condemn Islamic "fundamentalism"—or try to denounce our own religious heritage, as we shall momentarily observe a most intelligent and well-intentioned Westerner doing.

In the midst of an American political campaign, a respected writer attempts to expose the underlying cause of great wrongs in the nation and the world. To provide a remedy, we should elect the proper president, the writer argues. But even if we cannot get the president we prefer, the basic evil must be addressed. And what is this fundamental cause of all misery? It is named in the title of the essay: "The Great Unmentionable: Monotheism and its Discontents." Here follows a crucial passage:

> Now to the root of the matter. The great unmentionable evil at the center of our culture is monotheism. From a barbaric Bronze Age text known as the Old Testament, three antihuman religions have evolved—Judaism, Christianity and Islam. These are sky-god religions. They are, literally, patriarchal—God is the omnipotent father—hence the loathing of women for 2,000 years in those countries afflicted by the sky-god and his earthly male delegates. The sky-god is a jealous god, of course. He requires total obedience from everyone on earth, as he is in place not just for one tribe but for all creation. Those who would reject him must be converted or killed for their own good. Ultimately, totalitarianism is the only sort of politics that can truly serve the sky-god's purpose.[7]

We may be sympathetic to the political conclusions toward which this essay guides its readers. Nevertheless, our purpose here is to examine the discriminatory tendencies in ourselves that would lead us to

---

7. Vidal, "The Great Unmentionable," 54.

misunderstand Islam, and in that context we have to question the vehement outburst against monotheism.

To begin with, the author has remembered his anthropology so imprecisely. It is inaccurate to call the religions that developed on the basis of the Old Testament "sky-god religions." That term is accurate only for much earlier traditions. The author of the essay meant to say "storm-god religions." A god like Yahweh typifies the deity who in the midst of deities rose up to the highest place only in the course of time. Such a deity is not primarily related to the sky, but to the weather—more particularly storm and lightning. Allah belongs to the same family, as does, to some extent and much earlier, Marduk in ancient Mesopotamia. (The fact that gods of this type are leaders in war might actually have supported the author's argument.)

Were our author to write about nuclear power plants and confuse "fission" with "fusion" or misspeak other specifics, he would be thought unqualified to express himself on the subject. But writing about religion, he goes on his merry way. He blames the development of modern totalitarianism on the self-righteous vengefulness of monotheism: "Those who would reject him [the skygod-ruler] must be converted or killed . . ." In essence, he argues, there are two factions on the scene:

> The party of man would like to re-establish a representative government firmly based on the Bill of Rights. The party of God will have none of this. It wants to establish, through legal prohibitions and enforced taboos, a sky-god totalitarian state. The United States ultimately as prison . . . with the sky-godders as the cops, answerable only to God, who may have just sent us his Only Son [some candidate for the presidency], as warden.[8]

But the concept of a formation of religious dictatorship painted here simply is not applicable to the religious world of biblical Israel—no matter how often each of us may have heard it invoked as an argument in discussion. That *concept* is part of *our* world. What is unfortunate is that displays of ignorance such as this are not rare, but flare up across the board, in Christian, non-Christian, and anti-Christian circles. And moreover it would be a mistake to see these outbursts merely as random scapegoating and blame-fixing. Rather, displays of this sort in our time are the product of an imperialistic Christian ideology, as it was standardized in the nineteenth century, imagining itself as guardian over

---

8. Ibid., 57.

the globe. *This particular Christian ideology* is the precise model of our author's uncritical self-reliance and self-overestimation.

The lack of any actual foundation and the absence of any desire to find one is striking in the popularization during the nineteenth century of ideas about the superiority of the white race. One thinks of the shared compounds of many a Christian missionary with the colonial government's local administrator in Africa, Asia, or Australia. The superiority of the Church and the Western political forms was never questioned. It is not necessary to "explain" this conviction of superiority by the works of Gobineau or any other racist theorist. It is a heritage shared by the descendants of Adam Smith and of Karl Marx, of Hegel, and of Schleiermacher.

Why the widespread, self-righteous anger the West has long directed towards Islam? It is simply because Islam is the most visible stand-in-the-way to our unexamined ideologies and urges. Islam was and remains an expanding religion. It caused and it causes great frustration for Christians as well as their "secularized" brethren. This frustration renders us blind to human experience, poisoning our human imagination and compassion. We are cast in that mold when we blame Islam—or monotheism—for our problems.

The inaccuracy of bypassing the singular significance of *Islam's* monotheism is also worth noting. Not only the good left-wing author who blames the "high godders" for everything abysmal in our world, but most modern educated Westerners imagine that "monotheism" refers to a clearly identifiable reality in the world of religion, one that can be called upon to draw a single line of demarcation. At bottom, the issue is the same one we have seen elsewhere in the interpretation of religious facts. It is the confusion between a label attached to something from without, and the living fiber of the subject we want to understand.

The issue of monotheism demands our special attention so that it may guide us into the subject of Islam and politics.

Monotheism and Prophecy

With special emphasis, we should state that Muslims are monotheists. Of course, a disciplined historical imagination will realize that the early followers of Muhammad, if questioned about their religious adherence, would not have said, "we are monotheists." In fact, no adherent of any religion could be expected to respond with anything so neutral and general.

Instead, a Muslim would at once respond that he was a Muslim. But any person questioned, even in earliest Islam, on further discussion would affirm that he had in common with Jew and Christian a faith in one god, and indeed, he was a monotheist. At that imagined early exchange, intellectual history is in the making. This was the seventh century, the century in which Muhammad established his religion, and memorized the holy book, the Qur'an, as it was dictated to him by God. The Qur'an was first written down by people to whom Muhammad recited it.

Before the days of Muhammad the notion of "monotheism" would not have been easy to introduce into an ordinary exchange of ideas. The oneness of the god of the Jews, the same one god of the Christians, had not been an urgent subject in common discussion. A great novelty in the religion of Muhammad was the change it brought into this situation. The unity or plurality of the divine was not in itself a new topic; the Greeks and the Indians discussed it many centuries earlier, and Christian theologians had found occasion to refer to it in a world of classical culture and myth. But it remained in some manner an abstract problem. It was not tied directly to actual religious experience (as perhaps it must have been in the time of Moses and Aaron in ancient Israel).

With the birth of Islam monotheism truly enters the scene. Furthermore, as Wilfred Cantwell Smith has pointed out, monotheism as an idea is in harmony with the strong Islamic awareness of the concept of "religion," each religion being a coherent tradition of practice and thought, and each to some extent conceived of as an option.[9] Islam sees itself as "a religion" in a very special way; it is the essential religion that was already present in each of the "book religions."

> People of the Book! Why do you dispute
> concerning Abraham? The Torah was not sent down,
> neither the gospel, save after him.
> What, have you no reason?
>
> Ha, you are the ones who dispute on what you know;
> why then dispute you touching a matter
> of which you know nothing? God knows very well,
> while you know nothing.
>
> No; Abraham in truth was not a Jew,
> neither a Christian; but he was a Muslim

---

9. Smith, *The Meaning and End of Religion*, 81.

and one of pure faith; certainly he was never one of the polytheists.[10]

When at the age of forty Muhammad begins to organize his community, a precision, a consciousness, a way of thinking comes into view that neither Jews nor Christians had developed or could appreciate. Until this very day it seems to many Jews and Christians (as well as to more "secularized" speakers of their language) as if Muhammad somehow merely imitated them, by having a revelation from God and a holy scripture, as well as a community of the faithful that could lay claim to recognition everywhere—his *umma*, his "nation."

But in the notion of monotheism as handled by Muslims the novelty of a new order becomes evident. *Monotheism* becomes the truth of all the prophets, of Abraham and of Jesus, to be confirmed at the end of the prophetic line by Muhammad, called "seal of the prophets." Muhammad and his followers invoked an all-encompassing divine jurisdiction incorporating whatever Judaism or Christianity could speak of. In linking together the prophetic line through monotheism, Islam brought monotheism to the fore with a mighty prophetic clarity, and henceforth monotheism became a decisive spiritual tool, from its first use in the Qur'an speaking to the traditional tribal polytheists of Arabia. It was immediately effective among peoples who shared the Arabic language, similar patterns of life, and notions concerning gods and spirits, and who were all to some extent affected by the complex of ancient Near Eastern religious legacies and impressed by the palpable importance of Judaism and Christianity in their midst.[11]

Historically, Muhammad's monotheism can be said to affirm his nature as founder of a religion with a clearly attested universal claim. More philosophically speaking, he purified the notion of "God" of any "ethnosociological" tone and restored to it a true theological and metaphysical force, far more self-consciously and obviously so than Moses or Jesus Christ; in fact, Muhammad was fully aware of returning to the God of Abraham. God had not dictated the New Testament to Jesus Christ, and even the relation between God and the "books of Moses" was a matter of rabbinical discussion of some complexity, unlike the unambiguous relation between Allah and the Qur'an.

---

10. Qur'an 3.58–60, in Arberry, trans., *The Holy Koran*, 93.
11. See the lengthy description by Hodgson, "The World before Islam."

Of course, it is not erroneous to continue calling Judaism and Christianity "monotheistic," but for neither one did the concept carry the weight that it took on for Muslims. Monotheism became a basic part of each of Islam's powerful statements and institutions.

The Christian resentment of Muhammad is rooted in his claim to prophecy. All the great nineteenth-century Western scholars of the biblical texts followed the mode that was already set by influential thinkers in the Romantic Movement; among these were the philosopher Hegel and the theologian Schleiermacher, who both equated "Israelite" with "Jew" and equated Judaism with legalism—an early and incomplete form of religion made complete in Christianity. Prophecy came to be understood as the element of lasting significance in the biblical texts, receiving its perfect expression in Protestantism, and this topic of scholarly concern became a certainty with which textbooks were written. A new popular tradition originated, in the century in which public education became the rule. This view of "the prophetic" as belonging properly to the churches would have its consequences. In Hegel's all-encompassing theories Islam did not play a role of much significance. Hegel had inherited the general Western distaste for Islam. He dismissed it as a "fanatic religiosity" in his lectures of 1824.[12] It is the standard misconception. Thus a tradition that took prophecy fully seriously in the sense of the word of God, revealed literally and heard and acted upon by the community, aroused disdain in another people who had staked their own claim in "the prophetic."

Perhaps there has always been resentment, too, of the inner coherency that characterizes Islam. Islam sees itself as the conclusion of the whole earlier tradition, but this time the unity of God is not clouded in mysteries as difficult to the experience of the believer as they are to the intellect. In Islam, religious experience, morality, and worldly power are inseparable; dilemmas of religion versus power do not exist from the perspective of most Islamic documents. God is one, the Almighty, whose power and compassion are over all. God asks only submission to God. Theocracy is the model of proper governing, far more straightforwardly and directly than elsewhere. All power to rule is from God, and outside the Islamic world as well no government can be exerted without His consent. As a result very much of Islamic theology turns to discussions of law.

12. Hodgson, ed., *Lectures on the Philosophy of Religion*, 71.

Many texts in the Qur'an can be read as commentary on the one term *Islam*, the very name of the religion. Islam is "complete submission" to God. The term "Muslim" comes from the same stem: a Muslim, one who submits completely (as the Qur'an says in 3.17), one whose religion is Islam. In Islam, we do not find the predicaments arising from a God who changes his mind, nor the mystifying abstruseness of the Christian "history of salvation." Nor is anyone led to rack his brain over who constitute the true believers and who do not. Always, the Qur'an reiterates that Allah knows the believer and the unbeliever. Each puzzle that might begin to emerge becomes subject to the almighty unity of God Himself.

> The unbelievers say: "This man [Muhammad] is a skilled enchanter." Yet your Lord is Allah, who in six days created the heavens and the earth and then ascended His throne, ordaining all things. None has power to intercede for you save him who has received His sanction. Such is Allah, your Lord: therefore, serve Him. Will you not take heed?[13]
>
> ...
>
> Do men think that once they say: "We are believers," they will be left alone and not be tried with affliction?
> We have put to the proof those who have gone before them. Allah knows those who are truthful and those who are lying.
> Or do the evildoers think that they will escape Our punishment? How ill they judge!
> He that hopes to meet his Lord must know that Allah's appointed hour is sure to come. He alone hears all and knows all.[14]

One *sūra* gives man a rhetorical question to recite: "Say: Should I seek any but Allah for my God, when He is the Lord of all things?"

The text of the Qur'an becomes clear for us if we know what "awe" is and can listen as if for the first time.

Authority

Many of us have reached the wisdom that neither a nation's system of government nor the "ultimate" foundations on which that system rests can be imposed upon another nation. We would not dream, for example, that the United States could will its government and its laws upon

---

13. Dawood, trans., *The Koran* (Sūra 10), 63.
14. Ibid., (Sūra 29), 191.

countries of Latin America, as "Christian" a part of the hemisphere as itself. The entire complex tradition woven together from Hobbes, Grotius, Hume, Jefferson, Hamilton, Lincoln, and a host of other influences: what a stupendous illusion it would be to imagine that the particular religious blend of Israel and Hellas on which our government rests could be instituted elsewhere at our behest.

But in this general wisdom, we are forced to see ourselves contradicted by one system. Islam exported its political and religious structures, its notions about authority—and we of the West are forced to look upon great successes of this one model of authority and power.

We are mistaken in our commonly held impression that this force is newly arisen. From the beginning Islam abundantly manifested its concern for the world in which men exist, rule, and are ruled. It is interesting that Western media, and often Western scholarship, appear surprised by such religious vigor and attempt to "explain" it. Perhaps there is some envy here. We see a tradition that seems to prevail in pristine form. Is this not what many among us would want for our own tradition? To be dominant, unquestioned, coherent.

What has given Islam such success? I believe the answer to this question lies in the particular structures of Islamic monotheism. There is a paradigm in Islam that allows it to "convert" and convince, and gives it its authority. The history of answers about God's power and rule and concerns for their management in human existence is consistent in Islamic tradition. It is different from the biblical contrast between God's judgment and man's plans as displayed in the image of Nathan and David. Instead of the hide-and-seek of church and state in their mutual relations, we have in Islam a model that is present at the start. Islam speaks with great clarity on the basic issue of God's power and human consensus.

Absolute Power and Consensus: "Ruler over the Faithful"

The prophethood of Muhammad, as recorded in the Qur'an and in the tradition of his deeds and pronouncements (the *Hadīth*), spoke on moral, legal, social, and political issues directly. Pronouncements in the Qur'an, presented as the word transmitted directly by God, never demanded a preliminary search for a "hermeneutic" with the urgency the biblical texts required.

This is not to say that the interpretation carried on by Muslims was literalistic in the sense in which Christian Fundamentalists came to practice their exegesis in the nineteenth century. The intellectual environment that prevailed in early Islamic text interpretation and that in which Christian Fundamentalism was born are altogether different.[15] As we observed while discussing secularization processes, the intellectual concerns of biologists and other scientists irritated and alarmed certain Western Protestant congregations and triggered the formation of Fundamentalism. In contrast, the world in which Islam developed its method of interpreting authoritative texts was intellectually marked by questions of a much more conspicuously religious type. These questions were not asked by physics and biology but by experts in the discourse of Talmudic problems and among Christian theologians. In response to that climate, Qur'an and *Hadīth* spoke a clear language.

Discussions and struggles ensued after Muhammad's death, but no faction in the intellectual realm of Islam ever cast doubt on the reality of prophecy and the reality of God's revelation.

> This book is not to be doubted. It is a guide to the righteous, who have faith in the unseen and are steadfast in prayer; who bestow in charity a part of what We give them; who trust what has been revealed to you [Muhammad] and to others before you, and firmly believe in the life to come. These are rightly guided by the Lord; these shall surely triumph.[16]

Certainly, the schools of law that developed found matters to dispute, beginning with those rules within which interpretation could proceed to decide the authenticity of utterances and customs attributed to the prophet, but *sharīʿa* (Islamic law: lit. "path") had been completed by the end of the ninth century; it is valid uniformly for the entire Islamic

---

15. Especially instructive for an understanding of what is erroneously called "Islamic fundamentalism" is Esposito's *The Islamic Threat: Myth or Reality?* With respect to the specific misapprehension that Islamic "fundamentalists" are militant and politically reactionary, see the general survey by Voll, "Fundamentalism in the Sunni Arab World." Voll points to the vast majority of "fundamentalists" involved not in militant acts but in social services such as medical service and education. In this context, it is interesting to bring to mind the Islamic equivalent of the Red Cross. Obviously, no Muslim would care for a cross, which for the Swiss, who developed this very important medical organization for times of war, was an obvious sign; but in the Islamic world the Red Crescent is the equivalent. It is a detail, but an eloquent one. See the important book by Benthall and Bellion-Jourdan, *The Charitable Crescent*.

16. Dawood's translation of the *sūra* known as "The Cow," 324.

world. Notwithstanding minor variations in the four surviving schools of law, *shari'a* is striking in the absence of great disagreement on most questions that arose in the course of time. Controversy in Islamic law has remained relatively rare—in sharp contrast to the pattern in Christian theological schools of thought.

The singular harmony in Islam is a theme that must not be ignored, as it typifies the religion. Perhaps we can best understand it by noting that the absolute power of Allah is accompanied by the brotherhood of the believers.[17] If we try to explain the great appeal of Islam on every continent, in every age, it would seem to lie here, in this twin vision of God's omnipotence together with His appeal to men as brothers. It is abundantly clear in America in the Nation of Islam (and should be clear to readers of *The Autobiography of Malcolm X*).[18] In 1976 the Islamic Council of Europe published a statement that addressed itself to the contemporary world. In it we read:

> The religion of Islam embodies the final and most complete Word of God ...
>
> It stands for the harmonization of the human will with the Divine Will ...
>
> ... the unity of the Creator has as its corollary the oneness of His Creation. Distinctions of race, colour, caste, wealth and power disappear; man's creation with fellow man assumes total equality by virtue of the common Creator.
>
> Islam is not a religion in the Western understanding of the word. It is a faith and a way of life, a religion and a social order, a doctrine and a code of conduct, a set of values and principles and a social movement to realize them in history.[19]

These words are not a newfound missionary gimmick. They reverberate with the traditional concerns of Islam.

In the civilization the Arabs established from inner Asia to Spain, and, on an even broader scale, the new faith that spread through Africa and South and Southeast Asia and America, the variety of preexisting

---

17. A famous and authoritative text on the subject is al-Ghazālī (1058–1111), *On the Duties of Brotherhood*. This text is a section of the great work by al-Ghazālī, *The Quickening of Religious Knowledge*.

18. X, *The Autobiography of Malcolm X*.

19. Republished in Foy, *The Religious Quest*, 530–32, 534.

cultures was enormous. Islam did not bring about or try to bring about homogeneity in these places. In this respect, Islam was like Hinduism.

The harmony that seems to exist nevertheless in each Islamic place between absolute power and general consensus leads one to ask: what is it in Islam that allows it to take its characteristic form in so many differing cultures? With respect to Hinduism, we would think in the first place of a language: Sanskrit. Sanskrit belonged to one people, but it became the vehicle by which religion and art and social reality took shape over an entire subcontinent and elsewhere in the world as well. Likewise with Islam, a language comes to mind: Arabic, the language of Muhammad and the Qur'an. The principal art of Arabia had always been the art of the word, the spoken word; the poetry of the Qur'an was a tool that shaped the new religion in Arabia. Nevertheless, although the moment of revelation is in Arabic, and Arabic retains its hold, Islam did not spread by the force of Arabic. Islam was spread by the efforts of Turkish-speaking peoples and by various Iranian speakers, and a host of Indian Muslims and speakers of a variety of languages in Southeast Asia and the Indonesian archipelago. (Islam was aided in all this by its commercial trading, which for the first time effectively linked the Mediterranean with the Indian Ocean.)[20] Whereas Hinduism typically *renamed* what it encountered, Islam found local ways of establishing its institutions and a multitude of expressions that became its own, in literature, systems of law, of schooling, theology, and spirituality.

We might say Hinduism assumed that if you scratched the surface, you found *Hinduism*. Islam assumed pure paganism. But it said all that mattered was to recognize Allah. As long as the community was in the right relationship to Allah, it could remain the community. The local forms Islam brought forth everywhere testify to the *symbolic* juncture within Islam of a great central power and the unanimity of the community.

Like Christianity, Islam is a confessional religion. Islam expanded carrying a creed and persuading people of its truth—a creed much less mystifying than the creeds of the Church: "There is no god but God and Muhammad is His Prophet." Unlike Hinduism, Islam spread not by renaming local cult places and local cultic customs in its "sacred" language, but by *conversion*.

There is more worth mentioning. Unlike Christianity, Islam converted not by seeking to save individual souls but by emphasizing the

---

20. See Hourani, *A History of the Arab Peoples*, 5.

entire community. This stance is given, as we have just said, in the symbolism of the religion. Of course, Islam, like Christianity, converts *people*, yet it rarely seems to have dealt with strictly individual conversions of the type so familiar to Christians. And due to the importance it placed on consensus, and authority *as related to* the community, Islam always tended to reinforce the community even in the process of converting it.

Conversion to Islam has been a disturbing matter to think about for many Christians and their "secular" cousins. Often we have spoken of jihad and the notion of "holy war" as if jihad had been the instrument that caused multitudes to accept the new faith. In this respect, scholarly works by Western authors have become more accurate. The recorded process shows a very different picture. The spread of Islamic faith, even in its earliest centuries, through imperial power over large territories in North Africa, Spain, Iran, and India, had little to do with anything resembling forced conversions. And Muslim rulers recognized religions that remained independent—albeit in a secondary status. Zoroastrians, for example, were counted among the "book religions," and thereby assigned a secondary place that nonetheless brought them close to the Jews and Christians to whose history Islam related itself.

The ease with which people accepted Islam must not be forgotten. One returns once again to Islam's clarity with respect to the basic issue of God and His power. The appeal was especially strong for many faithful Christian laymen who were confused by controversies that were disputed and settled far above their heads. It was hard enough for Christian theologians to rebut the Muslim reproach of tritheism, and the arguments they used in this regard were difficult to follow.[21] Other Christian disputes, finally resolved with creeds and pronouncements, were vastly more complicated. A notorious series of disagreements occurred concerning the nature of Christ. At issue was his divine or human nature, or some argued, his nature at once divine *and* human. Many problems of doctrine and faith emanated from this question. Did Mary give birth to God or to the Christ? Was the body of Jesus Christ like ours or was it deified? Was it God Himself who suffered on the cross? And could there be a formula that might allow local churches to attach their own interpretations? Although the controversy arose in the fifth century, and hence predated the birth of Islam, it lingered and flared up for centuries.[22]

---

21. For a survey, see Pelikan, *The Spirit of Eastern Christendom (600–1700)*, 230–32.
22. Ibid., 39–49.

Regions where many had chosen the side of the monophysites (espousing the doctrine of "one nature" and acknowledging no duality of Christ's divine/human nature), who lost the principal debates, were among the first that Christianity lost to Islam. The general confusion caused by centuries of controversy certainly made the transition to Islam effortless for many, if not a downright relief. In the words of one church historian: "Christianity, weakened and divided by dogmatic struggle, in a situation where the subtle development of doctrine had left the faith of the people far behind, did not offer much resistance."[23]

Of course, the inhospitability of Christian doctrinal argument should not be taken as the prime reason for Islamic success in conversion. The key issue remains the persuasive force of Islam. Indeed, that is the feature that makes Islam unique in the history of the world's religions.

The Venture of Islam: Conscience and History in a World Civilization is a splendid three-volume work we owe to Marshall Hodgson, whose death in 1968 at the age of forty-six was a great misfortune to Islamic studies. Hodgson was an Islamicist with an extraordinary sense for the wider canvas of history in which Islam developed, and hence he was able to draw comparisons that illuminated Islam's uniqueness. The title of one of his chapters, "The Sharʿī Islamic Vision, c. 750–945" promises a presentation of the legal views developing from the middle of the eighth to the middle of the tenth century—a dull prospect for many a reader; however, anyone eager for an interpretive perspective that makes human sense is in for a delightful surprise. Hodgson was the humanist who fully realized that in order to be just to a culture one must not only explain that culture, but work simultaneously on our framework of understanding. Our present theme, the Islamic linkage between absolute power (as deriving from God) and consensus of the people, is much enlarged upon by Hodgson. In the chapter I have mentioned, Hodgson calls the first section: "The Islamic aspirations: universalistic, populistic spirituality."

Hodgson begins by reminding his readers of an inclination that characterizes confessional religions. They wish to make themselves felt in society, so that moral and social forms will conform to the religious truth. In this wider historical comparative context, Islam has had paramount success. Hodgson writes:

---

23. Bakhuizen van den Brink and Lindeboom, *Handboek der Kerkgeschiedenis*, 188.

In China, to take one extreme, any such wishes developing in the more markedly confessional traditions failed almost totally. The occasional triumphs of Buddhist or Taoist religionists against Confucian philosophy, in the centuries just before Muhammad, did not prevent the Confucian elite from regaining a dominating position in Chinese social life—though not without introducing into Confucianism itself a cosmic orientation colored by the confessional religious outlooks. In Europe, on the contrary, the Christians did succeed in eliminating the social power of the Platonist and Stoic philosophers, though their triumph was not completely unchallenged till the sixth century, shortly before Muhammad's time.[24]

But contrasted to Islam, this triumph of Christianity was far from total. In fact, Roman law continued to exist and to develop, even if a "Christian tone" was added. Plato, the Greco-Roman historians, and the epic literature of pagan Greece remained an essential part of Western learning and had great influence on the education of Christian Europe. In Islam the many components of civilization and erudition remained subordinate to the central authority deriving from Allah.

Hodgson examines the institutional forms Christianity took in the centuries under consideration and suggests some reasons for its failure to reach people as successfully as Islam. One factor involved in the contrast is the Christian development of monasticism. Islam did not create anything like it, nor any institution representing a supreme and distinct spiritual level from which the spirituality of the religion was nurtured. On the contrary, throughout its history Islam tended to lack interest in such separateness. Instead, in the face of the concentration of power—visible worldly, legal, or spiritual power—it preserved the voice of what Hodgson likes to call "the piety-minded Muslims."

Here we have an interesting and really consequential distinction. Sanctity—which must counterbalance the worldly side of power—resides not in a separate group of people who live differently, but in the whole community of the faithful. It is the power of Allah that allows a king or a dynasty to rule, yet the same omnipotent God remains with His faithful—whom only He knows. Their brotherhood, to the extent that they are true and faithful, will justly reflect God's word, even against the power set over them if the case demands it.

---

24. Hodgson, "The Shar'i Islamic Vision, c. 750–945," 315.

(A portion of Christian history that shows a resemblance to the Islamic model would perhaps be John Calvin's Geneva—which of course marks some deviation from the general pattern of Protestant Christianity. The endeavor of the faithful to experience the Church's faith as the channel through which God's rule over civil life would be made manifest is an obvious parallel to this constant concern found in the history of Islam.)

The history of the "piety-minded Muslims" begins with the history of Islam itself. Hodgson points to some "influences" that can allow our understanding to proceed without violating the inner reality of Muslim devotion. Pursuing the reality of "confessional" religions, he notes that in the eastern regions of the earliest Middle Eastern Islamic world, Mazdeism had many adherents. Mazdeans were descendents from the early Iranian religion of Zoroaster. Like the typically confessional religions, Mazdeism was quite conscious of the difference between itself and traditional religious cults. Among Mazdeans, and likewise among the Jews, there was:

> an explicit effort to build a code of personal and social life which should spring in every detail from the received principles of religion. All adherents should equally be subject to the all-embracing religious requirements, while being married and carrying on the ordinary work of the world.[25]

In other words, at the beginning of Islam's great expansion, certain models were present. Beside the Christian example, with its problems of doctrinal subtleties, and its double nature of a lay church and a higher, monastic spirituality, there was the more accommodating fiber in Jewish and Mazdean heritage linking religious life to the ordinary, lived-in reality of human existence.

If there was a "choice" to be made, obviously in its own structure Islam came to reject the Christian model as unworkable. In all likelihood, as Hodgson demonstrates, of the two others, Judaism and Mazdeism, the former was by far the more significant. "By the time of Muhammad, Judaism was very important numerically between Nile and Oxus, particularly in the towns of Iraq, where its most widely recognized chiefs came to reside."[26] As Islam did not organize itself in a manner that required a priesthood, the learned teachers characteristic of diaspora Judaism must have seemed an evident feature of religion.

25. Ibid., 316.
26. Ibid., 316–17.

Alongside such observations as these, we keep in mind that we are merely attempting to fathom what is given in our documents by employing the best framework we know how to bring to them. It is not that we "explain" Islam as a rejection of Christianity or as the recognition of Judaism as a model. The originality of the new religion does not disappear in the presence of historical strands, but rather shows itself in sharper outline. It does seem that the unique structure of Islam is nowhere as clear as in its own dialectic, visible throughout its history, between the power leading the community of the faithful and the voice of that community. In this respect Islam is related to Christianity yet exhibits its own forms and copes with problems in its own way.

Power and Consensus Enacted

Upon Muhammad's death, a relatively brief period began that saw four leaders whom most Muslims call the *Rāshidūn*, the "Rightly Guided."[27] In Sunnī Islam this period came to be regarded as normative. The first of the rulers was Abū Bakr. When Muhammad died, Abū Bakr spoke the marvelously simple words: "O men, if you worship Muhammad, Muhammad is dead; if you worship God, God is alive."[28] The great virtue the *umma*, the community of believers, came to associate with this earliest period no doubt reflects the will of the community to preserve, in addition to the virtue of the Rightly Guided, the devout directness of that early community's faith. In all likelihood it is not by chance that the term *sunna* can be rendered variously as "the trodden path," thereby including the customs of the pre-Islamic tribes, and as "the Sunna" in the sense of the example set by the Prophet, and hence law for the community's life.[29] (In the tradition of the Sunnites, the term eventually came to be used interchangeably with *Hadīth* and thus to denote "orthodoxy.")[30] Everything we see here suggests that there must be continuity in the community. The well-known fact that Muhammad rededicated what had been a pagan (and polytheistic) shrine, the Kaʿba, to Allah, points in the same direction.

The knowledge we have of the Prophet's life comes from traditions formed in the early Islamic community. As Professor Esposito sums it

---

27. Hourani, *A History of the Arab Peoples*, 25.
28. Ibid., 22.
29. Esposito, *Islam: The Straight Path*, 14.
30. Kramers, "De Islam," 370.

up, Muhammad "served as both religious and political head of Medina: the prophet of God, ruler, military commander, chief judge, lawgiver."[31] We know that occasionally God spoke through Muhammad of jihad in the sense of holy war conducted in God's name. Muhammad waged such wars in his lifetime. Of this spirituality and politics in one Professor Esposito says: "Those who wage war (*jihad*) for God engage in a religiopolitical act, a holy war."[32] Here the expression "religiopolitical" truly has meaning as one word. Muhammad's life blended spirit and power, wholly in line with many biblical texts.

The title given to the leader of the Muslim community after the Prophet was *Khalīfa*, "successor" or "deputy." Hereby it is important to realize that this successorship did not carry the prophetic function that had received its "seal" in Muhammad. The caliph, however, appointed by the community's leaders, did head the community, and hence did have a certain religious prestige, demonstrated in later history by his right to lead the Friday prayer meeting and the inclusion of his name in its prayers.[33] The express noninheritance of the prophetic function maintained the purity of God's revelation.

Abū Bakr ruled from 632 to 634. He had to wage war to bring back tribes in Arabia that had left the fold after Muhammad's death. Under the second caliph, ʿUmar (634–644), the territorial expansion of Islam beyond the early confines began in earnest. ʿUthman, the third caliph in this ideal period, ruled longest, from 644 to 656. The fourth and last of the Rightly Guided was ʿAlī, who ruled from 656 to 661.

ʿUmar was the first to be given the title *amīr al-muʾminīn*, "Ruler over the Faithful."[34] The name unmistakably expresses the Islamic joining of power and consensus. This junction of great symbolic significance is

31. Esposito, *Islam: The Straight Path*, 14.

32. Ibid., 16.

33. Ibid., 111. In Sufi ritual meetings, passages of the Qurʾan are chanted, as well as Divine names (a custom reminiscent of what occurs in Hinduism in the so-called *sahasranāman*, the recitations of "a thousand names"). In Islam those recitations of divine names are called *dhikr*. As a rule, a teacher (*shaykh*) is in charge. This is always someone who enjoys special respect. He is comparable to the guru in Hinduism. It seems of great importance to me to realize that social structures among human beings are usually recognizable because as human beings we are all familiar with basic social forms and relationships that can be recognized everywhere in forms of politeness paid to certain people, and, yes, also in reverence paid. And as human beings we borrow a great deal from each other, also in very obvious religious matters.

34. Kramers, "De Islam," 364.

neither a definition nor a dogma; its expression in history often reveals it as a *tension*. It is enacted rather than discussed, and hence we might call it an *integral* ritual part of Islam. Historically, but "ritually" and not accidentally, the inseparable linkage finds its expression. The tension appears very soon, at the end of the early "golden" age, during the reign of the last of the ideal caliphs, ʿAlī.

It is not difficult to see that with the growing realm under Islamic domination the caliph's position became more complex. It is also easy to understand that as a result the caliphate itself changed. ʿUthmān, the third caliph, gave members of his family important posts, and this was the major cause of his assassination in 656. It is illustrative of the growing empire that Egyptian soldiers in the Islamic army played an active part in the unrest his acts provoked.[35]

ʿAlī's reign brings radical change. The religious significance of events under his rule allows us to speak of a mythical ring—in the religiohistorical sense of carrying a lasting and ever-new truth. Like his predecessors, ʿAlī had to become embroiled in politics. The support he enjoyed in some circles at the beginning of his caliphate must have been quite strong, although his support was far from universal. ʿAlī was married to Fāṭimah, one of the daughters of Muhammad and his wife Khadīja. Fāṭimah bore ʿAlī two sons, al-Hasan and al-Husayn. The fact that Muhammad himself had no male offspring lent a unique fervor to those who set their hopes on ʿAlī's line. This line of Muhammad through ʿAlī has been the most influential element in the formation of Islamic renewal movements and of other groups and "sects" through the centuries. ʿAlī and his offspring were part of the Prophet's own family, and many favored the view that this familial relationship was the most perfect line of authority. The significant party formed around this opinion became known as the Shīʿa (Shīʿites, from *shīʿat ʿAlī*, party of ʿAlī). Different from the Sunnī (Sunnites, followers of the good Sunna of the Prophet), they did not recognize the first three caliphs as legitimate, holding that those three had usurped ʿAlī's right to lead at once upon Muhammad's death. The fact that indeed three caliphs were selected before ʿAlī could make his claim forcefully enough indicates that the older associates of Muhammad formed a powerful group. Soon after becoming caliph ʿAlī moved his residence from Medina to Kufa in Iraq.

---

35. Hourani, *A History of the Arab Peoples*, 25.

There followed a series of events in which two sides vied for control; the troubles under ʿAlī's rule transformed the caliphate into a hereditary position. Viewed from without, there was a struggle for power and then a political reorganization. However, the actual impact of what occurred on those who listened and memorized, who mourned the dead and rekindled hope, was infinitely more than this. The series of events fired the imagination. What Muhammad had said and meant, what the faith of the faithful really amounted to in the down-to-earth legal leadership of the *umma*, was all at stake.

The principal military activity in the short span of ʿAlī's rule was directed against the rebellious governor of Syria, Muʿāwiya, who belonged to the same clan as the previous caliph, ʿUthman, and had held his position since the days of ʿUmar, when Syria was conquered. Muʿāwiya opposed ʿAlī's claim to the caliphate. In the battle of Siffin in 647 ʿAlī came close to victory over Muʿāwiya, but then an unexpected twist in the history occurs—precisely in the manner in which myths typically move. Muʿāwiya had a suggestion to make. Why not allow judges to determine who was entitled to the caliphate? ʿAlī consented to this idea. So doing might strike a modern listener as noble, but ʿAlī's act was at odds with the right way to conduct a holy war. ʿAlī's consent itself seems to be made of the dramatic material of myth. A large part of his own army left him, not for "political reasons" in the sense we would attach, but because, as they declared, God alone could decide. This is why they had fought on ʿAlī's side. Those dissident soldiers who left ʿAlī became the core of the "Khārijites," which is the name for the general collectivity of various groups ever since who have been vociferous and militant actors on behalf of the faithful. They have formed a real force in many parts of the Islamic world, from that day to this arising in the name of the faithful against unworthy rulers. They associate themselves in a completely mythical fashion with the proper line of descent from ʿAlī. (Some resemblance exists in the way Christians in the Reformation saw themselves aligned with the early Church.)

The story of ʿAlī continues. The judges could not come to a clear decision, and the resulting situation was impossible. ʿAlī did not have their support; as a result, Muʿāwiya could not drop his claim. Muʿāwiya returned to Damascus, ʿAlī to Kufa in Iraq. The fourth caliph could not make his rule effective except in Iraq and Iran. Like ʿUthman, he was murdered. After his death the regions of his reign fell to Muʿāwiya. Thus

Muʿāwiya became the first caliph in the dynasty of Damascus: the dynasty of the Umayyads.

There was more from the line of ʿAlī. We cannot trace it here in detail, but ʿAlī's line can be said never to have come to an end in the ritual life of Islam. In 680, ʿAlī's son al-Husayn accepted the call to go to Iraq and lead a rebellion. He lost his life and thereby became the first martyr of Islam. Among Shīʿites of Iran his death is commemorated annually. On a more popular and festive scale, most Muslims in South and Southeast Asia celebrate the feast of "Hasan and Husayn." (In India the feast has taken on features of surrounding firewalking ceremonies of popular Hinduism.)

On all levels, the events surrounding ʿAlī had lasting results. The Shīʿites became a distinct part of Islam, a movement with its own subgroups, its own teachings, its own political aspirations; together the Shīʿites compose about one-tenth of Islam. But most significantly, the time when caliphs ruled with the certain support of the community ended with those mythically proportioned events. Although the term continued in use after ʿAlī, and the caliphate became hereditary, the faithful of the community have often opposed the wielders of power—both those calling themselves caliph and those, as in modern rule, without any pretension to the title. The life of the community has been decisive in determining what is customary, legal, right.

Fear of Theocracy

> The Prophet (God bless him and give him Peace!) said:
> –The believer is a mirror to the believer.
> By this he meant that one can see from the other what he cannot see from himself. Thus a man can profit from his brother by learning his own faults, whereas if left to himself he would lose this advantage, just as he can benefit from an ordinary mirror by becoming aware of the faults in his outward appearance.
> —al-Ghazālī[36]

The longstanding "problem" of Islam for the West is not merely the unpleasantness of an entity in the world that embodies a vigorous competitive political power. It is above all the West's horror at coming face-to-face

---

36. al-Ghazālī, *On the Duties of Brotherhood*, 54–55.

with a living expression of a unity and a more than merely political reality that it vainly searches for in itself.

American frustration with Islam has focused on Arabs, specifically on individuals such as Muammar al-Qaddafi in Libya, Saddam Hussein in Iraq, Osama bin Laden, and Yasir Arafat, until his death in 2004 the chief of the Palestine Liberation Organization. In all cases, the conscious focus of the problem is power, perceived in its most frightening form.

The focus of anti-Islamicism on one ethnic-linguistic group is a typical mechanism of discriminatory movements. Likewise the insistence on imminent threats. A narrow and precise focus obliterates the need to investigate the more abiding sources of one's worry.[37]

More than a century ago, in 1894, the French writer Bernard Lazare published a book on anti-Semitism, its history and its causes.[38] The term "anti-Semitism" had come into fashion, and Lazare was the first to point out its dubious, indeed treacherous character. On the first page of his book, he declared that its use was due only to the desire to suggest that hostility towards the Jews was of a philosophical scope truly worthy of attention: "to give it a philosophy and at the same time a reason that is more metaphysical than material."[39] The fitting term, however, is anti-Judaism.

Still on the first page, Lazare makes a suggestion that must only be understood within the argument of his entire book. Given the fact that the enemies of the Jews are to be found in the most diverse nations, under the most different circumstances and conditions, laws and customs, far apart in their views of things, or even ignorant of each other's existence, we must infer that something *exceptional* which "has always existed in Israel itself" has led the *general* world to create anti-Semitism.

This is at odds with ideas like those of Jean-Paul Sartre, which suggest that somehow the anti-Semite *makes* the Jew.[40] Sartre's analysis is one that most reasonable people today can take to very easily. Yet there is something about Sartre's presentation that I believe was effectively dispelled in Lazare. Sartre argues from a point of view that holds that all people are the same; until the anti-Semite creates them, "Jews" are the same as everybody else. Jews are not afforded particularity by Sartre. It is rather amazing that the name Moses doesn't occur once in Sartre's

---

37. This is the essential and central insight of Sartre, *Réflexions sur la question juive*; English translation, *Anti-Semite and Jew*.

38. Lazare, *L'antisémitisme, son histoire et ses causes*.

39. Ibid., 11.

40. See Sartre, *Réflexions sur la question juive*; or *Anti-Semite and Jew*.

book! There is, however, no need for rubbing in the issue. Those of us old enough to remember the German mass murders of Jews instinctively agreed; our friends who were killed were human beings like all of us. It is an obvious point—but the obviousness of the point is not what makes any one of us what we truly are.

Lazare's book invites us to *reflect* on the *idea* that all people are the same. This idea, I would assert, should not be mistaken for anything but a religious proposition of a most dictatorial nature. This idea has been with us in roughly its current form for several centuries; its application is visible in the modern state, which has become its guarantor. The state as we know it has among its appurtenances such items as the applicability to everyone of the state's law, and the imperative of all to have their part in the duties and obligations of the rationally organized community. Even states that do not give these items the inflections we prefer nevertheless center in the idea that all people are the same. Not so many years ago, the Soviet Union resisted the idea of special exit visas for Jews. The logic is not hard to grasp. Why should some special freedom be granted to one group that could not be granted to all? The willingness of the ancient Roman state to be accommodating and grant Jews the right to adhere to their own law can be seen as a remarkable sign of civilization. The ancient world could be much more accommodating than the world of abstract propositions we have been living in since the Enlightenment.

Lazare discusses the history of anti-Semitism largely in the context of the development of the state together with the expansion and dominance of Christianity. The starting point of his survey is the time when the earliest Christians were as Jewish as Jesus himself. Wherever the Jews moved within the Roman Empire, they did what they always did: clung to their own customs and laws, and hence to their own community. In this respect the Jews were *quite different* from other nations.[41] For the others, it did not constitute a problem to submit to the law of the world's conquerors; or at least, to separate their life as inhabitants of the empire, submitting to its laws, from their religious life. The Jews, however, insisted everywhere on a necessary exception in their case. The Jew was an *être insociable*, writes Lazare,[42] not a social being, and initially, the Christians were the same, and usually lived in Jewish settlements within

---

41. I do not want to give the impression that Bernard Lazare said all the things that I infer in this essay. At the same time, I see my conclusions as closely related to his.

42. Lazare, *L'antisémitisme, son histoire et ses causes*, 12.

the Roman Empire. Christianity first grew under the aegis and protection of the synagogue. But soon things changed.

Not only the despised Galileans, but others, real Gentiles, began to be converted, and these outsiders became part of the Christian sect in Jewish settlements. Strains began appearing. Problems of pollution, inevitable under the Law, had to be solved. Solutions the Christians proposed were felt to transgress the commandments and only worsened the quarrel. Problems of faith had always been discussed and interpreted, yet questions about the immutable law—including the blasphemy of recognizing someone as the son of God—became more and more pressing. The rest of the story is this: when Jerusalem is destroyed, and the Jewish diaspora begins in earnest, Judaism reconstitutes itself, and Christianity establishes itself, until it becomes the dominant religion in the empire.

Christians who leave the Jewish compound and its particularity are assimilated into the state, and then, far more than this, they come to control, to be, the state. Their own peculiarity becomes the generality. Henceforth the establishment of the Church and the establishment of the Empire go hand in hand. An entirely new sequence of events follows.

We cannot summarize Lazare's survey of the historical flux from the time of Rome to Lazare's own late nineteenth-century France. The wealth of detail he assembles makes the conclusion inescapable that theories, reasonable sociologies and philosophies, and other rational constructs by themselves cannot possibly explain the indulgence in anti-Jewish sentiments and actions that history records.

In the final pages of his book Bernard Lazare addresses himself to our world. He argues that the process leading to the modern state is a process of de-Christianization. The anticlericalism of Lazare's day helped greatly in speeding up the process. In this movement of anticlericalism some Jews—of course, a tiny segment of Judaism—had an active part. There were a far greater number of liberal, anticlerical Christians than Jews, numerically many more Christians than Jews tied together in their abandonment of their respective religious traditions. But those who regretted and resented the "loss" of the former state tended to blame one ethnic group for that loss.

Here Lazare put his finger on a modern phenomenon in the complex history of anti-Judaism. It is the feeling of uncertainty in oneself rendered as anxiety about the state, and is generally found to accompany racist expressions: *the Christian state is disintegrating!* And who is to blame? The Jews!

On his last page, Lazare declares: "*Le juif est le vivant témoignage de la disparition de cet état qui avait à sa base des principes théologiques, état dont les antisémites chrétiens rêvent la reconstitution.*"[43] ("The Jew is living witness to the disappearance of that state that had theological principles at its root; Christian anti-Semites dream of the reconstruction of that state.")

It is an insight Lazare brings to the fore and which holds to this day: in the area of ethnic antipathies, the (often imaginary) well-being of the state has remained the touchstone for the hatreds people indulge in.

There were those who accused Bernard Lazare of anti-Semitism. If it were our task to discuss the case of Lazare as a typical specimen of assimilated Jewry, I should spend time on that accusation. However, in the final analysis, this could never be the last word on Lazare. If Bernard Lazare did not love Judaism, he came to love Judaism; he was a Jew and came to belong to it. In his own life, and in the course of his friendship with Charles Péguy,[44] the particulars of Jewish existence that were the starting point of his book took on great value for him, especially that most particular of particularities, a studious concentration on Torah—Torah in the sense of the nucleus of the structure of Judaism, the wonderfully precise evidence of the direction given by God Himself and the guarantee of his involvement with his people.

We have discussed "brotherhood" and "theocracy" in Islam. These two cannot be separated in the religion. It seems to me that both, and especially the latter, historically have produced the anxiety and the irrational discriminatory feelings of the West towards Islam.

Many of us would smile at the notion of "theocracy." It conjures up the hand of God governing a nation. But if we formulate the idea somewhat differently, the smile goes away. It is possible to argue that what is spiritually real should be the point of orientation for politics. But what is meant by this? How can one direct oneself to the sacred and act politically in good faith? Perhaps one should, but . . . here uneasiness sets in. The very vocabulary to speak about such matters has been lost. Ours

---

43. Ibid., 177.

44. Lazare was close to the poet and essayist Charles Péguy, who endorsed and eulogized him in his essay "Notre jeunesse." Péguy strengthens me in my reading of Lazare. Yet another stimulus for my view of Lazare comes from Gershom Scholem in his essay "Jews and Germans." Scholem calls Péguy one "who had an insight into the Jewish condition rarely attained, let alone surpassed, by non-Jews" (p. 35).

is the misery of people who have no coherent instruction in their own religious tradition.

The thirst for a state, a community of strength, solidity, and inspiration that *seems to have existed* is not easily quenched. When mature religious understanding is lacking, the atrocities of racist wars and bloodshed multiply. Hitler's Germany acted upon that sentiment that Bernard Lazare detected as typical of modern anti-Semites. The modern world, as functioning in each modern nation, has not outgrown such insane drives.

From the perspective of the West's confusion, the reality of the Qur'an and the reality of the Torah are parallel phenomena. Religious envy is a deep disturbance. It is hard to bear when something obvious, profound, and true that we would like to be able to say ourselves is said by someone else. It can be aggravating to perceive (even dimly) the coherent, God-given existence of others. These are typically phenomena that occur between close relatives. Thus we have Christians (and their Christianity-affected brethren) who begrudge Judaism (the father) and Islam (the sibling) the light in their eyes.

The Islam-hater as much as the Judaism-hater imagines he sees before him the cause of his own misery, the destroyer of his own certainty. But blood is thicker than water on both sides. Relatives suffer inordinately from the disoriented soul of one of their kin who harms and uproots them, and they react in kind. They look upon what their kinsman does to them and—not surprisingly—see him and his helpers as enemies of God. No one in the West should feel amazed to hear Muslim voices speak of the enemies of God.

10

The Religious Structure of Modern Man

Religious Types

Historians of religions and anthropologists are able to speak of the structural type of religions in hunting cultures, in agricultural cultures, and in pastoral cultures (although it must be emphasized that none of these typologies provide the details of any specific civilization or religion, and typologies do not go beyond serving as useful and inevitable generalizations).

Knowing about the type of religion in archaic hunting cultures helps us to understand existential and religious experiences of peoples widely separated by geography—in Siberia, in Australia, in North America. The recognition of such a type lets us apprehend something concerning the seat of life that is conceived as present in the bones of the hunted game, the symbolism of a higher power that is lord or mistress of the animals, a cultic life that on the whole is not concerned with bloody sacrifices, and so on. (Again, it is understood that there are differences of great significance within the typology. Think only of the difference in hunted animals: rabbits or buffalo, or elephants, or, in early times, the mammoth. Or consider how far we are from neat boundaries. For instance, the hunter's symbols can very well continue long after the culture and economy of hunters has ceased to be central, as in the case of beautiful Artemis, the great huntress, in Greek myth.)

With the birth of agriculture in the Neolithic, and the spread of peasant civilizations, a new human type came into being. With this type there is a close connection between religious and economic features; the idea of "wealth" takes on enormous meaning. (In English usage, we still have the word "weal," which has much more than an economic connotation.) The source of wealth and well-being is the central deity, usually a goddess. As a rule, periodic, bloody sacrifices assume an important place; the "common weal" demands them. Grains can be stored, and in fear for failed harvests and in their concern for surplus, people learn to hoard. The conception and experience of time is uniquely marked by this new existence. With respect to peasant cultures in the ancient Near East, we possess detailed information—no matter how difficult to translate into our own modern tongues—about the subtle relations between death, life, and wealth.[1]

The origins of sheep- and cattle-herding societies may have predated agriculture in some regions, may have come later in others; that question cannot be settled by suggesting a general rule. However, it is certain that some great cultures of a pastoral signature take us well into "history." Peoples of a pastoral type invade the settlements and towns of peasants. Their most conspicuous feature is their militancy: a feature that stands out in their cultic life as well. Here we have the Indo-Europeans, Semites, Hamites, Mongols, and Aztecs—all invaders who finally settle in rich agricultural regions that had attained their level of wealth well before the arrival of the newcomers. Again, also in this "type," the variety of traditions is great, and yet, we are justified in using the one word "pastoral" as indicative not only of the means of production but of a type of man who is recognizable politically by an urge to build defensible states, and to conquer, and who is religiously often recognizable by rigid cultic processes. Among the principal deities we find martial figures such as Indra, Mars, Odin. Historically, the biblical "Lord of Hosts," hence the Christian God, and Islam's Allah, inherited features that belong to the same type.

Peoples who are of the same religious "type" generally can recognize each other's cultural expressions. Eliade pointed out repeatedly that peasant cultures everywhere show a homogeneity, similar features, a similar tenacity. A. K. Coomaraswamy suggested, quite convincingly, that it would have been perfectly possible in the Middle Ages for Hindus and Europeans to understand one another's symbolisms, for instance in the architecture of temples and cathedrals.[2] Nomadic hunting tribes in North America may not always have liked one another, but they were no

1. A classic work on these intricate relations is Kristensen, *Het leven uit de dood*.
2. See Coomaraswamy, "The Christian and Oriental, or True Philosophy of Art."

strangers to each other's motivations. Pastoral militants could participate in the same "game" of war, following more or less the same rules on opposite sides of the battle.

It is much more difficult for one type to recognize another. Encounters between pastoral and peasant cultures have probably never been without conflict. Likewise, peasant and hunter have confronted and misunderstood each other innumerable times, often with disastrous consequences. Such is the perennial opposition in India between Hindus in the fertile valleys and the hill tribes. It is also well known that the European farmers settling in North America were very far from comprehending the North American hunter, who appeared to them undependable, untruthful, devoid of a proper conception of time and sense of duty.

Ourselves

Could we identify our own religious orientation? Is it possible to recognize ourselves?

Asking a question like this, we enter the frame of mind Wallace Stevens spoke to in his poem "Recitation After Dinner."

These words are part of Stevens' reflections:

> ... the character
> Of tradition does not easily take form ...
> It is not a set of laws ...
> ... The commanding codes
> Are not tradition.
>
> ...
>
> The bronze of the wise man seated in repose
> Is not its form. Tradition is wise but not
> The figure of the wise man fixed in sense.
> The scholar is always distant in the space
> Around him and in that distance meditates
> Things still more distant. And tradition is near.
> It joins and does not separate ...[3]

---

3. Stevens, "Recitation after Dinner," 86–88.

Modern Religious Man

"Our" modernity may be said to begin in the Renaissance—even though historians differ in their preference for dates and happenings to delineate that new birth in the West. In the period of the Renaissance, a new orientation is born.

For the subject of this essay, we can make a good beginning by looking toward an illustrious figure, Giordano Bruno (ca. 1548–1600), who championed the theories of Copernicus and was condemned by the Inquisition and burned at the stake. Generations have delighted in referring to his case as evidence that religion is intolerant by nature. We would rather turn our thought to a statement Bruno makes in one of his treatises, the *Spaccio della bestia trionfante* (Expulsion of the Triumphant Beast), where he says, "God, considered absolutely, has nothing to do with us . . ."[4]

It seems to me that this one phrase shows us something of the birth of "modern man." The statement does not indicate that God has become irrelevant. On the contrary, it detects a problem which arouses intense scrutiny. God was certainly not irrelevant for Bruno—but Bruno had begun to wonder, what could God actually be? A person such as Giordano Bruno may have felt a type of human loneliness that was something new.

I fully realize that the assertion made by Bruno can be seen in several ways. Although it is certainly an expression of the growing distance that begins to be felt toward God in the late Medieval and Renaissance periods—a feature that should be obvious to historians of religions—we might generalize and consider it an instance of a worldwide religious experience that has been observed in any number of tribal mythologies. Scholars refer to the phenomenon of the *deus otiosus*, after the type of deity who upon creating the world withdraws into the sky and henceforward stays aloof from man.[5] However, historically and existentially—in the sense of what we may imagine, on the basis of our documents, the experiences and reactions of people to have been—the developing awareness in the Renaissance of the "absoluteness" or patent "remoteness" of God was significantly related to the growing rational order of things. The new notion of God has its place in the mathematical researches into astronomy of the period. Bruno's interests exemplify that. Hence we are dealing with

---

4. Yates, *Giordano Bruno and the Hermetic Tradition*, 269. The words come from an eighteenth-century translation. Yates presents it in its lengthy context.

5. Eliade, *Myth and Reality*, 96.

an item of the greatest interest in the history of science. (Historians of science are well aware that the "socioreligious" environment of scientific concepts is of vital importance in grasping their significance.) Giordano Bruno had learned much from Nicolas of Cusa, who was a Christian mystic, theologian, and devoted astronomer-mathematician. For Nicolas of Cusa these three modes of activity—mystical experience, theology, and astronomy—are interwoven at every point, and so they are for Bruno. The distance to God is a mathematical as well as an immediate religious problem. It is not as if only distance in astronomy were a matter of fact, and the distance to God allegorical. If they were two at all, and not really one, they are still inseparable. Thus we are reminded that the modern sciences and their methods did not come on the scene as something different, maintaining a pristine purity ever after. They were born in all the exertion and confusion that comes with the human endeavor at orientation.

I insist on this for the sake of our topic: what makes modern man different religiously? One answer that must be rejected out of hand is that the rise of science "did it." There was not a disappearance of one set of concerns and the rise of another; ideas about God were not eclipsed by the rise of a rational, scientific system. Neither was there a germinal separation between people who set store by science and others who clung to religion. Nothing of the sort—no matter how often depictions to the contrary are made—actually took place. Even though we can clearly see that the Renaissance brought something new, it was and remained a mixture of reason/religion and science/theology. Giordano Bruno's life, his conflicts and passions, witness loudly to this state of affairs. He studied in Naples, was a member of the Dominican order; he was accused of heresy by Catholics and also by Calvinists (whom he joined for a while in Geneva), was excommunicated also by Lutherans; he studied and lectured in various parts of Europe, probably making more enemies than friends. Just the same, in his day he must have been one of the most fascinating of men to hear—an expert on theology and astronomy, as well as on the theory of atoms and matters of magic.

The growth of rational investigation at the beginning of our modern world should be conceived in very broad, indeed all-embracing terms. The historian Crane Brinton's widely read book *The Shaping of Modern Thought* is one of the texts that somewhat distort matters when it speaks of "a cluster of ideas that adds up to the belief that the universe works the way a man's mind works when he thinks logically and objectively."[6] What stirred at the origin of our "modernity" was much more than a protocol for the Enlightenment of the eighteenth century, and it did not pave a route toward atheism. Many such interpretations give us a false idea of ourselves, and cause us to think that our religious questions are figments of the imagination. In the worst case, they cause us to repress the most vital epistemological issues throughout our scholarly and scientific researches. This means that they mislead us with respect to what it means "to know."

Mere mention of the great names associated with the birth of modern man should make clear that the most popular explanations of modernity are wholly inadequate: Francis Bacon; René Descartes; Benedict Spinoza; Copernicus; Tycho Brahe; Kepler; Galileo; Newton. Descartes is often given the place of honor when it comes to the beginning of "modern thought." And one item of textbook knowledge is worth recalling in this respect. In 1641, Descartes dedicated his *Méditations métaphysiques* "to the Dean and Doctors of the Sacred Faculty of Theology of Paris." This was four years after his pioneering *Discours de la Méthode*. And *Méditations métaphysiques* dealt not really with different material, except that here he wanted to make abundantly clear his opinion that philosophy was in fact the discipline that independently could strengthen the theological enterprise. Descartes lays out a clear conception of coherency in our knowledge, demonstrating a relationship between our philosophical and theological ways of knowing.

The idea of God persisted at the origin of modernity and at the same time underwent a change. Furthermore, in the growing rational order of the universe, as the idea of God acquired a new distance, an aspect appeared that was even more important than the way in which the *idea* of God persisted: a matter of *experience* that somehow accompanied the idea yet constituted something new.

This experiential change seems to me of supreme importance for identifying the characteristic religious quality of modern man that otherwise might escape us. The history of ideas by itself leaves an essential part of our understanding untouched and unformed. After all, we have come to understand far too much in terms of ideas alone. We have even come to understand our most crucial experiences as if they were only ideas. We invoke the help of experts in ideas and definitions in order to

---

6. Brinton, *The Shaping of Modern Thought*, 82.

figure out our experiences. It seems an irrational route that can only lead to a kind of insanity.

It may be said that the idea of God's existence and certainty became diminished by the rational ordering of the universe and everything in it. But from the beginning of our modern world, there is quite conspicuously a new and paradoxically parallel movement to the movement of rational clarity. It is the *inner* movement that occurs together with that outer movement which the historian of science Dijksterhuis called the *mechanization* of the world picture. We must call it an inner movement, because it serves to preserve the inner life of human beings.

John Calvin (1509-1564)—a man most maligned in our textbooks—is a powerful exponent of that concern for the inner life that grew parallel to the "rationalization" we celebrate so disproportionately as the gateway to the modern world. In an interpretation of the account of creation in Genesis, Calvin says, "since the most tolerable description given by the philosophers, that God is the soul of the world, is utterly vain and worthless, we require a more familiar knowledge of him, to prevent us from wavering in perpetual uncertainty. Therefore he has been pleased to give us a history of creation, on which the faith of the Church might rest."[7]

The *idea* of the revelatory value of the creation account is not new, of course, but what is striking in Calvin is his pastoral concern. His disdain for "the philosophers" underlines his pastoral care for his parishioners. Whatever does not edify the soul, whatever is pastorally questionable, is theologically useless; the purpose of the creation story is to give the faithful access to God. As we read and reread Calvin's lines, the story in Genesis becomes seen as a tender gift from God. Calvin finds in God the same concern for the inner life that stirred in himself. Calvin is without a doubt the most lucid, the most rational of Protestant theologians, but precisely in his lucidity the *inner*, pastoral concern becomes clear.

Let me go a step further. Let me say that the rationalization of the world has a *complement* rather than a mere parallel development in this inner concern that arises. In a variety of ways, this complementarity exists in Descartes, Newton, in all the great scientists and thinkers of those centuries that made us "modern." It exists obviously in Calvin, and obviously also in Leibniz (1646-1716), who was not merely engaged in the technique of calculus, but in personal thought on the infinity of

---

7. Calvin, *Institutes of the Christian Religion* 1.14 (p. 176).

God—and the latter explains his interest in the former, rather than the other way around.

I do not suggest that the discovery of the concern for the inner life as a component in early "modernity" is startling. It is well known that before the period of reformation begun by Luther, Calvin, and Zwingli is finished, movements of pietism make themselves felt and sometimes inspire great crowds. Indeed, we can observe that all ages have had their own combinations of reason and devotion.

I am not sure that the series of suggestions I have to offer will amount to a proof in full detail. And we are aware of the difficulty in describing our own age, and hence ourselves, with accuracy. And yet, I am more and more convinced that we can see something of a new type of religiosity in ourselves that sets us apart from other "types" as much as the traditional peasant, the hunter, the pastoral peoples are set apart. The concern for inner life is what is new and characteristic in modern *homo religiosus*.

We might note the ardor of expression which was produced by that inner concern. Leibniz's passion seems identical with his rational zeal, whether he writes about the reconciliation of churches (for which he exerted himself greatly) or mathematics. Ignatius of Loyola (1491–1556) was the most spirited leader of the Counter-Reformation. His religious zeal has been compared to that of his arch opponent, Calvin, and at the same time is grouped with that of many renowned mystics. All the mystics of the Renaissance are clear witnesses to the passionate concern for human inner life. There were Protestants, like Jakob Boehme (1575–1624), among this mainly Catholic group. It was a concern that crossed dogmatic lines.

Let us return to Calvin, who is not normally classified among the mystics. Because of his great influence as well as his incisive style, he may be a most trustworthy compass to the spirit of the time. Calvin was educated as a lawyer, and he makes his case on the side of our inner life almost like a prosecutor, denouncing the sterile uses of reason. "Cold and frivolous... are the speculations of those who employ themselves in disquisitions on the essence of God, when it would be more interesting to us to become acquainted with his character, and to know what is agreeable to his nature. For what end is answered by professing, with Epicurus, that there is a God, who, discarding all concerns about the world, indulges himself in perpetual inactivity? What benefit arises from the knowledge of a God with whom we have no concern?"[8]

No wonder that in the wake of Calvin's teachings, in the period of "Protestant scholasticism," most theologians veered away from "frivolous speculations" on the essence of God in and by Himself (His *aseitas*). Following Calvin and the other great Reformers, they emphasized God's *acts*. Using the scholastic vocabulary of the time, an anthologist of these later reformed theologians sums up their preoccupation with the saving activity of God: "The pronouncement that God is *actus purissimus* ["purest movement"] or *simplicissimus* . . . or God is *essentialiter actuasitas* ["in essence lively activity"] . . . is stereotypical in reformed theology."[9]

Purest movement; the simplest, not manifold, but unmixed, purest activity; essentially efficaciousness; all these stilted Latin expressions amount to an attempt to speak of God systematically and clearly in a new light. Above all, the theologians try not to lose sight of the fact that any knowledge of Him is predicated on His turning to man in the first place, His decision to save man, and the acts of salvation He performed. We perceive a certain difficulty in speaking of those things with the theologian's refined vocabulary. The first Christian theologian, Saint Paul, occasionally broke out in song and praise, but in the Latin scholastic vocabulary—not interrupted, but continued by the theologians of the Reformation—that model was hard to follow.

The concern for the inner life goes on unabated, in spite of such encumbrances. It has to, because it is the only avenue to understanding. It is not just the interest of a religious elite. No thinker at the dawn of our modern history would have conceived of dismissing it. It is visible across the board, in the tortuous Latin of theologians, in the mystics, and the scientific thinkers of the Renaissance and the Reformation.

The Modern State

As nations begin to be organized more and more rationally and efficiently, concern for the inner life gradually intensifies. And as the new organization of states progresses, with the application of rational principles on human existence more and more accepted, the endeavor to preserve the inner life of human beings takes on a special urgency. My thesis can easily

---

8. Ibid., 1.2 (p. 52).
9. Heppe, *Die Dogmatik der evangelisch, reformierten Kirche*, 43.

be stated: the connection and opposition of rationality and the urge to preserve human inner life which emerged in the seventeenth century has become constitutive of our existence—in fact of our religious experience.

It is startling that the word "society" occurs for the first time only in the sixteenth century. Even then, it has not yet acquired the meaning we attach to it. It merely meant "companionship." With this meaning it was directly derived from the Latin *socius*, companion. Our general, abstract meaning, summing up the aggregate of all people and their relationships, takes some two centuries to come about.

The common modern notion of "society" is an immediate reflex to the rationalization of the world. We have come to imagine, or rather, to accept as reality, that we can somehow form an adequate mental picture of large groups of humanity, groups that can even move or be steered in one direction or another. Compared to such rational, abstract certainty, the Medieval conception of "three estates," the triad of the nobility, the clergy, and the third estate, was indeed something real: an imagery of *organic* functions that depended on each other.

A manifestation and an emblem of the change that gradually came about is of course: bureaucracy. Bureaucracy embodies the concerted application of the human mind to organize human life. It is the written reflection of this mental process. With its *planning*, its *procedures*, its *hierarchy* of concerns, it is a *design* to cause the state and the society to operate as a unit.

The problem of bureaucracy and problems related to bureaucracy have been considered extensively by scholars, who have looked at the need of monarchs to govern efficiently, at the inevitable clerical encroachment in the rise of the banking system and the development of high capitalism, at the need for taxation structures to finance armies. Scholars have also applied themselves to the evil use of bureaucracies by absolute rulers, and the inability or unwillingness of people under such rule to be free.[10]

Bureaucracy is here to stay, as the multifarious expression of human reason in the modern world. At the same time, there is an undercurrent, or rather an endless number of currents that spring from the concern for

---

10. See Jacoby, *The Bureaucratization of the World*; Arendt, *The Origins of Totalitarianism*; and Arendt, *The Human Condition*; Rosenberg, *Bureaucracy, Aristocracy and Authocracy*; Seidenberg, *Post-Historic Man*; Fromm, *Escape from Freedom*; and Fromm, *Man for Himself*; Ortega y Gasset, *Revolt of the Masses*; Krummacher, *Die Kontroverse*; Bettelheim, *The Informed Heart*; Skinner, *Beyond Freedom and Dignity*; Bryson, et al., eds., *Freedom and Authority in Our Time*.

a nourishing of the inner life in the face of so much rationality constantly surrounding human existence.

Both movements, bureaucracy, and inner concern, had their predecessors, and they are not confined to the West, but their very close relationship in modern times is a new structure mainly of Western origin. An attempt to get closer to the image of modern religious man takes us outside the ordinary realm of the church historian or other specialist in religion. The inner experiences in our modern history are not just subspecies of mystical or devotional phenomena in Christian tradition, explainable within that tradition. They take their often surprising forms in reaction to sociopolitical events. Furthermore, the historical pressures that give rise to them are complex and do not allow for a simple exposition. One cannot say, for instance, that in modern times an urbanization process left less and less territory to which a religious inner life could withdraw (although this is no doubt a fact, even for traditional Indian sages for whom there is not as much forest left any more in which to practice their asceticism). The modern inner life is qualitatively different from what the ancients knew. And we can try to see what happened to make it so.

The eighteenth century witnessed the rise of bureaucracy in Prussia, and not everyone looked upon this as a laudable development. Among the voices raised in dissent was that of a brilliant young German, Wilhelm von Humboldt (1767–1835), who would become famous as a founder of the science of language. Humboldt declared in 1792, "I have tried to oppose the mania for governing and to tighten the limits of state action everywhere. Yes, I even went so far as to insist that such action be limited exclusively to ensuring the security of the individual."[11]

In spite of the favorable atmosphere in the late eighteenth century for individualism, expressed in the concern for the rights of man in the French and American revolutions and in the mood of the German Romantics, the work in which this statement occurred had no influence to speak of. Although one no less than Friedrich von Schiller endorsed it, only part of Humboldt's book was published; by the time it appeared in its entirety, posthumously in 1851,[12] the new form of administration had become accepted as an instrument of good government. Liberals who

---

11. Quoted in Jacoby, *The Bureaucratization of the World*, 84.

12. Humboldt, *Ideen zu einem Versuch die Grenzen der Wirksamkeit des Staates zu bestimmen*, which is translated in Burrow, *The Limits of State Action*.

had made the case for the individual man now filled important posts in the bureaucracy.[13]

The significance that is given to the individual by the Danish philosopher and theologian Søren Kierkegaard (1813–1855) is well known. Kierkegaard's great opponent, his principal game, is Hegel. From Kierkegaard's point of view, Hegel may well be described as a dangerous bureaucrat of the spirit. Few students of Kierkegaard have raised questions about his political views. Nevertheless, there is evidence that tells us a little—and that little is ironic and eloquent, as is the rule with him. His reluctance to accept Hegel's philosophy is matched by his reluctance to see the rise of the democratic, parliamentary procedure as progress.

> All praise to the well-ordered state! How can anybody be so busy wanting to reform the state and to get the government changed! Of all forms of government the monarchical is the best, more than any other it favors and protects the private gentleman's quiet conceits and innocent pranks. Only democracy, the most tyrannical form of government, obliges everyone to take a positive part, as the societies and general assemblies of our time often enough remind one. Is this tyranny, that one man wants to rule and so leave the rest of us free? No, but it is tyranny that all want to rule, and in addition to that would oblige everybody to take part in the government, even the man who most insistently declines to have a share in governing.[14]

Readers today might characterize Kierkegaard as a reactionary on the basis of this passage. But certainly that would be to misunderstand. One has to read hundreds of pages before arriving at these lines, and it is easy to realize in the course of those many pages that his interest in political issues of his day was minimal. A church historian might place Kierkegaard's "politics" in the Lutheran tradition's extraordinary emphasis on separation of church and state. This too, however, no matter how interesting to discuss, would lead us away from what is the heart of Kierkegaard's thought and life: his disdain for mechanisms of whatever kind that might destroy the privacy he seemed to consider sacred, or at least, central to religious life. It surely never occurred to him to consider matters of administration very weighty; they did not deserve a single chapter in his writings. If anything, such matters were trifles that distracted from necessary reflection. Kierkegaard is part of the movement

---

13. Jacoby, *The Bureaucratization of the World*, 85.
14. Kierkegaard, *Concluding Unscientific Postscript*, 547–48.

in modern history that we have characterized by its concern for the inner life, and this movement at times has tended to be expressed in contrast to political reasonings and realities. (Our own necessity, as participants of the world we are alive in, to express our moral concern *through* political reasonings and realities should not cut us off from looking thoughtfully at other channels other human beings possess for being moral and for aiding one another. I include many people who are also on this earth at the present moment.)

As to the influence of Kierkegaard's thought—an influence that developed very slowly but surely—it can be understood especially well if we recognize that powerful expressions for human inner life were needed, not only vis-à-vis an "objective" philosophy (Hegel's), but vis-à-vis a world that rendered personal decisions more and more difficult.

Kierkegaard's stress on the individual and his fulmination against the crowd as "the untruth" shows a special irony, for it is actually easy to see that it is not in harmony with the New Testament. There Jesus Christ is portrayed as moved with compassion for the crowd, which seems to him like "sheep without a shepherd."[15] It is difficult to reconcile this with Kierkegaard's Christian existentialism. This ironic feature adds to the suggestion that the modern world brings in a new element with its concern for the individual. I believe it was the theologian Paul Tillich (1886–1965) who introduced the term "cosmic loneliness" to describe a fundamental experience of people in the modern era. Like Kierkegaard's disdain for the crowd, this would be impossible to translate back into biblical vocabulary. Tillich's phrase adds a tone of the space age, but nevertheless is akin to what Kierkegaard said and something that all modern people would recognize. The individual of course existed before. However, the individual now has taken on a significance *that earlier ages did not have the need to single out for religious attention.*

The list of discoverers of the individual is not a roll call of "lone birds" or singular exceptions. Most of the great Romantics were quite conscious of the importance of religion, and their awareness of religious issues had everything to do with their suspicion of the rational machinations of the state. A great example, and at the same time one of Kierkegaard's great heroes, was the German Johann Georg Hamann (1730–1788). Some of Hamann's wonderfully ironic pages—no easy going for hasty readers—might be rendered as follows: nowadays people

---

15. Mark 6:34.

talk about God as if He were merely an idea, while they talk about human reason as if we absolutely knew that it exists. Hamann is no doubt one of the most curious proponents Christianity ever had, and perhaps also a most typical specimen of modern *homo religiosus*. He was a customs official in the Prussia of Frederick II; he knew bureaucracy from within. But his involvement with the state did not prevent him from speaking against the fashions and certainties of his day. One of his publications is an attack on Frederick, and on the state and its tax system.[16] It is true, the bureaucratic forms were not as fiendish in Hamann's time as they would become later on. But what makes his ire on the subject so arresting is its prophetic quality; he saw that those bureaucratic methods were the external trappings of a great evil. He writes no mere political polemic, but passes judgment on the spirit of the age, which sought its justification in the state and had become unmindful of Christianity. Hamann wrote almost as if in anticipation of Kierkegaard. He discerned that the enlightened officials of his day were ever so *aware* of their enlightenment—to the detriment of any worthwhile understanding of religious matters, and hence of anything of importance to human beings. According to the consensus of the age, Hamann wrote, Christianity was at most "a *spiritual* something" (*ein geistiges Etwas*) or else "a material *nothing*" (*ein materielles Nichts*). These two interpretations, in his view, amounted to the same thing and only showed one and the same evil blindness. He spurned the notion of timeless laws of certainty that was so dear to the rationalism of his day; he referred to it scornfully as "the mechanism of common sense" (*Mechanismus des Sensus communis*).[17] With all his ironic skill he argued that by itself this mere mechanism was incapable of yielding any historical understanding. The essence of Christianity was the historical reality that absolutely escaped the ruling philosophy, the rationality of the leaders and "the public"—that same entity Kierkegaard would refer to as "the crowd."

Kierkegaard deserves to be credited with first seizing directly on our problem in the way his genius articulated the importance of the individual. Certainly, theological individualism never spoke in a more persuasive voice. And whatever was "official," and hence nonindividual, never met with greater resistance; the official church, the official state, the official school system, the official philosophy—all had to pay for their

---

16. Hamann, *Hierophantische Briefe*, presented by Schoonhoven in *Johann Georg Hamanns Hauptschriften erklärt*.

17. Ibid., 54.

officialdom under the onslaught of his attack. Moreover, I am certain that at one time or another almost every modern reader, whether consciously "religious" or not, takes a profound delight in those attacks. We take joy in them not necessarily because we have a precise grasp of all the arguments but rather because we intuit that something of the utmost value is defended. We sense that with the value of the individual, our entire world is at stake.

Recent Times

The rational mechanism that forces itself upon us has shown a face that neither Hamann nor Kierkegaard nor anyone in the prelude to our modernity could have imagined. Racial categorizing, deportations, occupations, concentration camps, saturation bombings, are all applications of reason that did not just seem to be, but *were designed* to break the spirit.[18] Did this relentless intensification of the rationalizing of the world blot out the cultivation of any inner life? Too many instances appear to indicate its success. Many individual stories may seem to prove that the world rationalization is no longer accompanied or even opposed by any serious inner concern. But can we truly believe this? Other accounts and stories also come to us. Often they are full of holes, or cluttered with baggage that sullies the "purity" we might wish for. But we have to bring to mind again that no religious tradition we look at is consistent or pleasant in all respects. Such are not characteristic features of any religious type. There is no reason to expect them upon entering into our own modern religious "type."

A Dutch Jew, Friedrich Weinreb, enjoyed the respect of many because of his Hasidic heritage. The Germans occupied Holland in 1940, and not too long thereafter the registration of Jews began, and then it was only natural that more and more distressed people sought Weinreb's counsel. When the Dutch department of labor, uninterrupted in its ordinary routine, but now in the service of the occupation forces, began to call up men (presumably for service to the occupiers), one of Weinreb's

---

18. The German anti-Nazi theologian Dietrich Bonhoeffer (1906–1945), who paid with his life for his resistance, saw Christianity as the way to freedom from all submission to demonic forces, and one might say, the way to freedom in the modern world. Through his writings his influence continued. Bonhoeffer's theology may be rediscovered time and again. Unfortunately, as a historical force, the influence of Bonhoeffer has remained limited or at least difficult to measure.

personal friends was among the conscripts. Then a strange series of events began. Weinreb had been born in Austria, knew German very well, and had a good sense of the workings of German bureaucracy. This background made him the right one to play the unusual role into which he was cast, step by step.

Weinreb was a trained economist, and thoroughly aware of the need Germany had for credit abroad. For the sake of his friend, he began by pretending that he was involved in a program to send Jews to South America in exchange for foreign currency. He wrote a letter implying this to the labor department and his friend's case was granted a delay. Thus a mere ruse succeeded, and certainly this initial step did not feel to anyone involved as if it amounted to an act of heroism, for at this early moment in the war the most dreadful operations of a modern bureaucracy were not yet known. One thinks of the little ways in which college professors must occasionally deceive the administration and its fondness for forms in order to perform their function as educators effectively and morally. All bureaucracies are readily deceived because they do not have imagination. For the citizens of Holland this simple fact was uncomfortable to face; there was no precedent in a decent, orderly state for the absolute necessity to make the discovery.

When Weinreb made that discovery and perpetrated his little deceit, the game continued as if by its own momentum. Inevitably, when Weinreb wrote more of the same sort of letters, some suspicion arose. In order to be as convincing as possible, he had paper with letterheads printed showing the name of a fictitious general in Berlin who supposedly was behind the transactions. Bureaucracy exists by virtue of an unquestioned hierarchy, and German bureaucracy in time of war of course knew that a general, an authority immediately related to the activity of the war, was close to the top. With a German typewriter purchased on the black market, Weinreb wrote a letter to himself, signing with the made-up name of the fictitious general. And this bureaucratic sham was effective for quite a while. Many people received delays in their forced labor, and a number of lives were saved.

The point that occurs to Weinreb according to the account he later wrote of these events is that so many people would rather have a piece of paper in their possession than take real action to save themselves from the danger surrounding them.[19] At one time, the growth of state adminis-

---

19. Friedrich Weinreb wrote his own recollections of the events in *Collaboratie en verzet 1940-1945*. The historian of the destruction of Dutch Jewry, Jacob Presser, wrote

trations was controversial, and people like Wilhelm von Humboldt raised their voices against it. Now, in astoundingly many instances, people had come to take the bureaucratic distortion of the world for real. A mere piece of paper felt like a warranty of life. This ludicrous displacement was no comedy of errors. Many of Weinreb's happy recipients of guarantees met their end in German death camps. Was Weinreb himself to be blamed for such things? After the liberation of the Netherlands, questions like this one eventually arose—and predictably, in a well-organized country with its established prewar traditions and reputation, guilt was discovered and some penalty meted out. This in itself rubs in the obstinacy with which bureaucracy makes itself felt. For our subject—religion in modern existence—endeavors to sort out the details of the case are not useful. But even if what Friedrich Weinreb did was no more than a pathetic gesture against a crushing power, it signifies a counteractivity in the same tradition as many a martyr.

The bureaucracy of the Third Reich had its secret police organization. Each modern nation today has its secret police. Two centuries ago this state of affairs—no matter how "reasonable" now—would have been impossible to explain to anyone. In modern times few people have not been exposed to the uncanniness of the rational order imposed by states. With a phase that began early in the nineteenth century, the passport was introduced as a document necessary for travel. Visas, special permits to visit certain countries, have become a general feature of life. For years American passports were adorned with lists of countries the bearer should not enter. The presumption of a *rationality* making these rules amused or irritated many people. The *source* of such reactions by its very nature escapes the realm of the rationality of the state that made up the rules. And if one tries to express what the source of amusement or irritation really is, it always has to do with the nature and purpose of human existence. Attempts to explain the amusement or distaste for such rules certainly do not deny the rational. Nevertheless, they seldom go very far in articulating themselves without touching religious certainties.

---

a preface to Weinreb's work. The person of Weinreb remained enigmatic, and Presser, though praising Weinreb, pointed that out in his own work *Ondergang: Vervolging en verdelging van het Nederlandse Jodendom 1940–1945*, 1:101–10. Weinreb was arrested after the war and found guilty of various deeds that were more self-serving than his account would make them appear. For a critical view of Weinreb, see Herzberg, *Kroniek der Jodenvervolging 1940–1945*, 261–80.

The mere fact of resistance against the pressure of a rationally organized system to force human existence in one direction or another is that characteristic feature that makes us "modern" religiously. Fundamentally, the mere occurrence of such resistance is a religious feature.

The struggle against the apartheid state in South Africa saw heroic figures, and martyrs. Among them, Nelson Mandela and Bishop Desmond Tutu will be remembered for a very long time. The fact that much of South Africa is "soaked" in Christianity may have something to do with the particulars of their martyrdoms—but not everything. I am certain one could identify typical modern religious individuals anywhere in the world. Whether the individual thinks of himself or herself as "religious" is beside the point. Our tradition constantly demonstrates its coherency as a spiritual reaction to the arrogance of a rationalized order.

The recognition of this modern refusal to bow down before the "reason of state" enables us to place diverse figures together, as I have done by speaking in one breath of Calvin and Descartes, Newton, and Kierkegaard. In each, a distinct concern for the preservation of the inner life is manifest in an original way and, often, in contrast to accepted rationality. Descartes, the great hero of reason, whose name is forever linked to the beginning of modern history, is made significant as a thinker because he was not a mere rationalist. The writer who early in the nineteenth century attempted perfect rationalism, the inventor of "positivism," Auguste Comte, might have become uninteresting as a thinker if he had not also conceived of his "cult of humanity" as a veneration and practice of the best, the most loving human attributes. Not agreement on basic details of philosophy, but the fundamental and ever new obsession with particularity, the inner being of man, makes all of us members of the modern age and participants in this "cult." Despite some appearances to the contrary, modernity is not a machine stamping out endless copies. The inner life is never a duplicate; it is original in every case. And that is the point: even when the rational side becomes enormous in its uniformity, it is not capable of wiping out the other side. That other side is by nature unpredictable. Somehow it can even become untouchable—mysteriously, even if killed.

One of the closest things we have to a total revelation of our type, modern religious man, might be the unsystematic, often puzzling and rambling assemblage of Hasidic stories that have been sifted, mishandled, disdained, and glorified ever since Martin Buber and others began the quest for their recovery. They do not come to us from what we regard as the bastion of modernity—Western Europe—but from the *shtetl* world farther east in Europe, a long way away from social and intellectual centers of Cartesianism, let alone Calvinism. The beginnings of the Hasidic movement under the Ba'al Shem Tov (the Master of the Good Name) take us back to the eighteenth century, the century of the first great bureaucratic attempts as well as of many pietistic exercises. "Cleaving to God, the continual practice of the presence of God, in some circles even ecstatic communion, were among the ideals cultivated by Hasidism."[20] The unpredictability of the experience of God's presence and also the involvement in very ordinary, lowly, and traditional activities of work, study, and amusement are elements often found in Hasidic tales. One story which compares Hasidism to flashes of lightning speaks to the unpredictability of God, the concern of God for man, the danger of the world, the presence of religion in the world:

> The Riziner declared that Hasiduth demands not only nobility of spirit, but also nobility of dress and manners. He wished to emphasize not only the duties of man to God, but also the duties of man to man. He cited the following parable: "A man walked on a country road one moonless night. From time to time flashes of lightning illumined the path. Once when he looked towards the sky to observe how the flash split the heavens, he fell into a pit. He climbed out with difficulty, and henceforward resolved to avail himself of the light from the flashes in order to see the world clearly.
>
> "Hasidism," added the Riziner, "is a flash of lightning in a dark universe. Avail yourself of it in order to walk through this world without disaster."[21]

The point that trying to discern how the lightning split the sky served no purpose is quite comical. Perhaps—for us, anyway—this teaching hits its mark more directly than Calvin's perorations against vain philosophical analysis. What comes across in many Hasidic stories with the greatest immediacy is that what matters religiously illuminates our existence in the here and now, where we walk.

I am not suggesting a genetic connection between the Hasidic world and the devout and less devout concerns for the inner life in Western Europe and in America. However, there is a structural parallel. Jews, whether mystically inclined or not, had centuries of experience trying

20. Werblowsky, "Judaism, or the Religion of Israel," 45.
21. Newman, *Hasidic Anthology*, 54.

to preserve the inward life in spite of officialdoms in charge of the world they lived in. It is no wonder that translations and retellings of Hasidic stories gained an eager audience where people came to feel the rigor of official rule.

A Religious Symbolism of Modern Man

We have been speaking alternately about the opposition of modern man's reason and his inner concern and about their complementarity. Which of the two relationships is more significant? The question comes to us naturally, because we are so familiar in our thought with political contrasts and alliances. But for knowing our subject, the character of modern religious man, does it really make a difference whether those two parts are against each other or side by side? Perhaps it would matter if for the sake of a description of this being we had to make a preliminary choice between sociology and psychology. In sociology we might think of opposing forces, in psychology of complementary halves. But we do not need to make such a choice in our discussion. For basically, religiously, in modern man, as in all religious types, what is central to the type functions before any epistemological decision is made. And in the case of our modern type, this means that reason and inner concern are in league before the intellect can stand back and sort out their relationship. The two are thrown into the arena of modernity together, in complementarity and combat simultaneously. The lightning splits the sky; you had better watch your step, making use of the only illumination you have. The immediacy of your inner life has a special priority. This insight is not exactly a production of the rational order governing us; rather, it is the new, altogether novel "enlightenment" that comes about unpredictably, now here, then there, not always, but often, under hardship, and never in the absence of the universal and penetrating force of rational, mechanical governing orders.

The modern relationship between reason and inner concern should be understood as a religious symbolism. As a rule we can begin to understand a religious myth or symbol by pinpointing the principal elements that occur together in it. Those elements are not normally thought of or felt as being the same: heaven and earth, north and south, male and female, light and darkness, suffering and salvation, and so on. The force of a religion shows itself in a human tradition by the self-evidence with which two crucial opposing and complementary sides occur together on various levels.

The force and persistence of the relationship between the two sides of modern man asks for comparison to the link between political power and religion in the ancient city, the togetherness of divine power and grace in the biblical texts, and each of the symbolic constellations we have looked at in previous essays. Like the other symbolisms, this modern symbolism is absolute in its authority and universal in its claim. It sets the scene for any serious human experience in the conflicts and tragedies of the world.

In this respect it is interesting to think once more about Antigone.[22]

King Creon was not exactly a modern bureaucrat, and Antigone was not a slave in a concentration camp or a victim of a modern secret police force. But the total claim of *our* symbolism makes it easy to feel close to this story of the ancient Greeks. And nevertheless, as much as we are stirred by Antigone, human beings remain historical beings, and there is a difference between the spiritual experience of Antigone and our own. Indeed, if Antigone could see us, perhaps she would not "recognize" us at all. Antigone stood against brute royal reason; but *that* reason fit clearly into a religious tradition. Antigone was an exception, but the powers she invoked to justify herself were powers that also fit into the recognized tradition. Both Antigone and Creon were conscious of their tradition; her drama builds step by step to a conclusion that all the participants might somehow have expected. The recognition of religious justifications seems significantly less evident among ourselves. Furthermore, the oppressed in modern times do not stand out as exceptional. Differences such as these make for the difference between Antigone's exaltation and a modern counterpart.

Survivors of concentration camps have occasionally spoken of moments of bliss they experienced during the period of their ordeal. Such experiences hardly lend themselves to public discussion and scrutiny. But where our present topic is concerned, we may say that what constitutes a modern difference is the *utter surprise* with which such bliss struck people; it did not require a conscious knowledge of any religious institution or instruction.

---

22. See essay 6.

Immediacy of Religion

I am not overly absorbed with whether everyone accepts the proposal that the concern for inner life vis-à-vis the rational state is a religious phenomenon, or sees the contrast between the two as the typical feature of modernity, or goes so far as to call this togetherness-in-opposition a religious symbolism. Although this book has been an effort to recover our critical sense in matters concerning religion, I care more for the honesty in our mutual approach to the problem of ourselves than for the technical accuracy of religiohistorical vocabulary; it seems to me that many of the great issues that have occupied us in recent times are immediately related to the necessity for honesty. Knowing I cannot prove my case, then, I do nevertheless want to conclude with some illustrations that to me seem eloquent.

In 1963 Hannah Arendt published *Eichmann in Jerusalem*, a work that aroused a great deal of controversy.[23] Arendt reflected on the case of Adolf Eichmann (1906–1962), who was one of the principal managers of the massive genocide of Jews during the Second World War. After the war Eichmann fled to Argentina. Israeli agents captured him there in 1960. An Israeli court convicted him, and he was executed by hanging.

The ordinariness of the bureaucratic life that brought so much suffering and death to so many formed part of the story Arendt told. An issue that especially preoccupied her was lack of resistance on the side of the Jewish victims of German persecution. And one of the responses to Arendt's assessments came from Gershom Scholem, the great scholar of Jewish mysticism. Considering the subject under review, one hesitates to speak of a controversy between him and Arendt, or say that Scholem's words prevail; all I can say is that they moved me, and I believe they are related closely to fundamental issues we are discussing in the present essay.

The history of Friedrich Weinreb cast a searchlight on the strange fact that sometimes we would rather cling to the security of a piece of paper than to our lives. The line between sheer rational orderliness and inner concern cuts right through us, modern people. Indeed, when critical events are unleashed on us, the opposition between a rational forceful order and a real concern for life is dramatic and mystifying, and tears

---

23. Arendt, *Eichmann in Jerusalem*, which was an elaboration of reports published in *The New Yorker* in 1961.

each of us apart. But none of this self-description hits the mark as well as we would like. Why was there not greater resistance?

I believe that Gershom Scholem did answer with more accuracy than anyone else. For he understood that the weakness in Hannah Arendt's observations was her blindness for religious life, and he wrote: *Der Heroismus der Juden hat nicht immer im Schieszen bestanden, und nicht immer haben wir uns dessen geschämt.* ("The heroism of the Jews has not always consisted in shooting, and we have not always been ashamed of that.")[24]

What this means for us is obviously not that the concern for inner life is necessarily pacifism, but that it exists on another plane than the brutality of the state, of any state, any mechanism of reason by itself. And as it is unpredictable—a quality among the typical features of religious symbols, since their re-presentation always amounts to a new interpretation—one cannot say where and how the pattern will reveal itself next.

Philosophers often have difficulty being at peace with such unpredictability and creativeness.[25] The unanticipated, novel expressions in art, or even the very ordinary experience of unexpected facial expressions before us, are the sort of things philosophy has a hard time being just to. To the extent all of us want to associate the detection of a pattern with the power to say how it will reoccur, we are all philosophers. We rely on intelligence, trusting that it operates in accordance with rules that themselves run in patterns, and we like the logic of clear definitions. We have of course been offered philosophies "of life" and "existential" philosophies which tried to address issues that were not easy to pin down, and often questions of religion figure prominently in them. But invariably, the facts of religion seem to outrun the observations these philosophies can offer.

---

24. Scholem, "Brief an Hannah Arendt," excerpted in Krummacher, *Die Kontroverse*, 210.

25. One philosopher who did say things most interesting to the historian of religions was Ludwig Wittgenstein. For example: "To convince someone of what is true, it is not enough to state it; we must find the road from error to truth" (*Remarks on Frazer's Golden Bough*, 1e). This statement applies to the task of the historian of religions as well as it does to the philosopher. And so does what Wittgenstein wrote immediately after: "I must plunge again and again in the water of doubt." Perhaps one of the best observations made by a philosopher on the subject of symbolism follows on p. 3e: "A religious symbol does not rest on any *opinion*. And error begins only with opinion." (*Einem religiosen Symbol liegt keine Meinung zum Grunde. Und nur der Meinung entspricht der Irrtum.*)

The Lithuanian-born French philosopher Emmanuel Lévinas has said things that do appear to come very close to what may constitute religion. Lévinas has made special efforts to elucidate what makes up human reality, and does not focus on "religion" as if it were an isolated province of our minds or sensitivities. His philosophical endeavor may somewhat resemble our religiohistorical attempt to describe religious structures as basic to human existence. Lévinas speaks of the "longing for the invisible." It is an important conception in his thought and provides the title of the opening section of his work *Totality and the Infinite*.[26] I know of no more accurate general expression for summing up the variety of currents that carry modern man's concern for the inner life. And certainly Lévinas means by this formula the desire of a metaphysical nature; it reaches out to something altogether different.

For a passing moment, we might recall Rudolf Otto's wordings "the altogether other" and "the Holy," but Lévinas does not refer to Otto. Unlike Otto's *principle* of *das ganz Andere*, *l'autre*, "the other," in Lévinas has a ring that is like a prophetic cry in the rational world of modernity.[27] It was Otto's intention to complete a philosophy that would take the religious dimension fully into account. In Lévinas there is no trace of this apologetic tendency. "L'autre" is not an idea at all, least of all an idea that needs to be supported in a "secular" world. It is more like a continuous reminder that we cannot ever complete a system of thought that will capture all the world of human reality. The "metaphysical desire" Lévinas writes about as fundamentally human can never be satisfied. In his words:

> We speak too lightly about satisfied desires or about sexual or even moral or religious needs. In that manner even love itself comes to be considered as the satisfaction of a sublime hunger. That way of speaking is possible only because most of our desires are not pure; not even love. The desires we can satisfy do not resemble the metaphysical desire except in the disappointments of their fulfillment, or in their exasperations and in that desire which *constitutes* lust. The metaphysical desire has another intention; that it longs for what is beyond everything that can completely satisfy it. It is like goodness; the desired does not bring a fulfillment, but a deepening.[28]

---

26. Lévinas, *Totalité et Infini*.
27. See also Lévinas, *Humanisme de l'autre homme*.
28. Lévinas, *Totalité et Infini*, 5 (my trans.).

At the conclusion of the introductory section, titled "The Desire for the Invisible," in *Totality and the Infinite* Lévinas writes:

> It seems foolish to reach out for the invisible when the acid experience of what is human in the twentieth century teaches that *needs* are the ground of our thoughts; needs explain society and history; hunger and fear get the better of all human resistance and all freedom. There is no denying this human misery—this dominance things and evildoers have over man. But *knowing* that this is how it is means being human. Freedom consists in knowing that freedom is in danger. Yet to know or to be aware means to have time to avoid and prevent the moment of inhumanity. The ceaseless delay of the hour of treason—this telling difference between humans and in-humans—implies the unselfish presence of Goodness, the desire for the absolutely Other or for the noble, the dimension of metaphysics.[29]

The strength of this passage cannot fail to impress us. It speaks to us so deeply that we hesitate to point out that exactly here we must watch our limits, and remember something about tradition. For indeed, at this point, something that is not intended by the author will also strike us: Lévinas' portrayal of what it is to be human describes the characteristic of modern religious man, and his words could *only* be spoken in *our* world. Lévinas writes of those inner experiences that take their form in reaction to phenomena of the modern world.

But Lévinas' words do not present the reality of all people at all times nor even their imaginable reality. Antigone, a monk in the desert, a Hindu ascetic in the forest, King David, or any Hittite king, a Buddhist, any premodern Christian—none could have understood this fascinating analysis. The thirst for the infinite, the desire that is unfulfillable, describes *us*. The totality in which modern man is caught is not a totality of which Plato or Aristotle might have spoken. The elements that mold us are phenomena of modern history. Today's explanations of human beings in terms of needs are part of modern totalitarianism. They are the obsessive drives of political regimes, and the forces that invade our own minds. Our resistance to them—no matter what form it takes, political, military, subversive, or peaceful, perfectly spiritual, but always welling up from an inner concern—is an absolute necessity.

While I am writing these words, commemorations are held for the victims of Auschwitz-Birkenau—close to the last time the few remaining

---

29. Ibid. (my trans.).

survivors will attend. The massive atrocities of our era have inevitably marked our common perspective. Since the days of Descartes we have collectively changed in our accumulating remembrance of cruelty. We might keep in mind that the philosophy of Lévinas is presented to us by a Jew who lived through the Nazi period. Lévinas was one of those who survived though the major portion of their family were murdered. Most certainly in his case "metaphysics" was not a luxury, to be indulged in one's spare time. What Lévinas gives us is a strong, philosophical reflection of the entire period of modern history, from figures such as John Calvin to the twenty-first century.

John Calvin, already in his day, felt the dominance that an evil, organized world had assumed over men, and clearly saw that this was a *religious* problem. His inveighing against the worthlessness of philosophical statements about God was a decisively modern act. *Calvin spent a great deal of time preparing people for persecution and death,* for the Protestants were repressed almost everywhere, fanatically and officially.

In the midst of this hard time of suffering, in April of 1552, five of Calvin's fellow pastors were caught in Lyons, in France, and condemned to the stake, for their faith and their rebellion. (As in all cases, until this very day, the two were the same—the word chosen depending on one's point of view.) Awaiting their execution (which took place in May of 1553), they received a letter from Calvin. His message provides no ordinary easing of suffering. It may be seen, however, as evidence of the spirit in the face of the brute and rational power of a state.

> My dear brothers,
>
> We have at last heard why the herald of Berne did not return that way. It was because he did not receive the kind of reply that we had so much desired. For the king has refused point-blank all the requests made by the Messieurs of Berne . . . This means that nothing more is to be looked for from that quarter.
>
> Indeed, wherever we look here below, God has blocked our path. But there is this consolation, that we can never be frustrated in the hope we have in Him and in His holy promises. You have already rested on this foundation, even at those times when it seemed likely that you would be helped by men—as we thought too. Yet, whatever the prospect has been that you would escape by human means, your eyes have never been so dazzled as to divert either your affection or your trust in one direction or another.

... But since it seems that it is God's will to make use of your blood to attest His truth, you can do no better than to prepare yourselves for this, beseeching Him so to subdue you to His good pleasure that nothing will hinder you from following wherever He calls you. For you know, my brothers, that we must be mortified in order to be offered to Him as a sacrifice.

It cannot otherwise be than that you should undergo fierce conflicts in order that what was said to Peter might be accomplished in you, that they shall carry you whither you would not. But you know in what strength you can fight—a strength on which no one has ever relied and found himself daunted, far less confounded.

And so, my brothers, take heart that you will be strengthened according to your need by the Spirit of our Lord Jesus so that you will never faint under the load of temptations, however heavy it be, any more than He did who won over it the victory so glorious that it is to us an unfailing pledge of our own triumph in the midst of our miseries.

Since it pleases Him to use you even to the extent of death in maintaining His cause, He will lend you a strong hand so that you can fight well, and He will not let one drop of your blood be in vain. And though the fruit may not appear all at once, in time it will surely show itself more abundantly than we can express. But as He has accorded you the privilege that your bonds have been renowned and that they have been noised everywhere abroad, it must happen that in spite of Satan your death should resound far more powerfully so that the name of our good God be magnified thereby.

... I shall not offer you sympathy nor offer you any further lengthy exhortations, knowing that the heavenly Father makes His own consolations real and precious to you, and that you take good care to meditate on what He sets before you in His Word. He has already made so clear to us the effect of His indwelling strength in you that we are well assured He will perfect you to the end.

Leaving this world is not for us an affair of chance. You know this, not only because of the certainty you have that there is a heavenly life, but also because you are assured of the gratuitous adoption of our God and you go as to your inheritance. That God should have ordained you to be His Son's martyrs is a work of superabundant favour.[30]

---

30. Text in Schmidt, *Calvin*, 110–13.

Does this letter seem cold and austere to us?[31] The situation of Calvin's friends can rightly be compared to that of any person in the modern world whose fate has been reduced to nothing by a state, and who has the end in sight; whose death is imminent because of a law that prevails, while he knows that it is *not* the law ...

Both Calvin and Lévinas fully accept the reality of the world's "reason" (the world that leads us into "the hour of treason" [Lévinas], or where "nothing more is to be looked for" [Calvin]). But each also stresses the certainty of its opposite. It seems to me that the certainty of God's favor of which Calvin speaks is a parallel to Lévinas' assurance of "the absolutely Other ... the dimension of metaphysics."

No experience, even the worst, denies the need for the clarity of philosophical analysis. Yet it is the immediacy of religious language that always stands out. The language of the historian of religions, like that of the philosopher, cannot have the last word.

> A Hasid narrated this: Once, Rabbi Jehuda Zwi addressed us at his table: "Today the Messiah, the son of Joseph is being born in Hungary and he will be one of the hidden Zaddikim. And when God allows me to live, I'll go there and see him." Eighteen years later the Rabbi traveled to the city of Pest in the company of myself and other Hasidim. We stayed in Pest for several weeks, without any one of us, pupils, knowing why he had come here. One day a young man with a short coat appeared in the inn, his face radiant like an angel's. Without asking permission, he went straight to the Rabbi's room and shut the door behind him. I stood not too far from the door, because I remembered those earlier words about the Messiah, and I waited for him, to greet him when he would leave and to ask him for his blessing. When after many hours he came out, the Rabbi accompanied him to the front door, and when I ran into the street, he had disappeared. But even now, after so many years, I still feel in myself the urge to live which I received then while he passed by.[32]

---

31. People familiar with martyrdom can recognize Calvin's language, whether they share his tradition or not. During the Second World War, some young Dutch resistance workers spent the night before their execution singing psalms and hymns and assuring each other with words that resembled Calvin's. A pastor who was caught for the "crime" of giving shelter to Jews explained to the Gestapo officer who questioned him, "I did what any Christian is supposed to do: I helped those who were persecuted; if you were persecuted, I would help you." Inevitably, his "crime" too led to his death.

32. Buber, *Schriften zum Chasidismus*, 539 (my trans.).

Bibliography

Adams, Charles J. "Söderblom, Nathan." In *The Encyclopedia of Religion*, edited by Lindsay Jones, 12:8505–6. 2nd ed. 15 vols. Detroit: Macmillan Reference, 2005.
Adams, James Luther. *The Prophethood of All Believers*. Boston: Beacon, 1986.
Ahlstrom, Sydney E. *A Religious History of the American People*. New Haven: Yale University Press, 1972.
Albanese, Catherine L. *America: Religions and Religion*. Wadsworth Series in Religious Studies. Belmont, CA: Wadsworth, 1981.
———. *Sons of the Fathers: The Civil Religion of the American Revolution*. Philadelphia: Temple University Press, 1976.
Arberry, A. J., trans. *The Holy Koran: An Introduction with Selections*. London: Allen & Unwin, 1953.
Arendt, Hannah. *Eichmann in Jerusalem: A Report on the Banality of Evil*. Rev. and enl. ed. New York: Viking, 1964.
———. *The Human Condition*. New York: Doubleday, 1959.
———. *The Origins of Totalitarianism*. New York: Doubleday, 1973.
Aristotle. *Metaphysics: Books X–XIV*. Translated by Hugh Tredennick. Loeb Classical Library. Cambridge: Harvard University Press, 1977.
———. *Politics*. Translated by Benjamin Jowett. In *Introduction to Aristotle*. Edited by Richard McKeon. New York: Modern Library, 1947.
Armstrong, Karen. "What Is Fundamentalism?" In *Promise and Peril: The Paradox of Religion as Resource and Threat*, edited by Anna Lännström, 11–21. Boston University Studies in Philosophy and Religion 24. Notre Dame: University of Notre Dame Press, 2003.
Arndt, Paul. *Mythologie, Religion und Magie im Sikagebiet*. Ende-Flores: Arnoldusdruckerei, 1932.
Augustine. *The City of God*. Vol. 1. Translated by Marcus Dods. New York: Modern Library, 1948.
———. *Of True Religion*. Translated by J. H. S. Burleigh. Chicago: Regnery, 1959.
———. *Select Letters*. Translated by James Houston Baxter. Loeb Classical Library 239. Cambridge: Harvard University Press, 1965.
Baal, Jan van. *Dema: Description and Analysis of Marind-anim Culture (South New Guinea)*. Koninklijk Instituut voor Taal-, Land- en Volkenkunde Translation Series 9. The Hague: Nijhoff, 1966.
Bakhuizen van den Brink, J. N., and J. Lindeboom. *Handboek der Kerkgeschiedenis*. Vol. 1. The Hague: Daamen, 1946.
Bareau, André et al. *Die Religionen Indiens*. Vol. 3. Die Religionen der Menschheit 13. Stuttgart: Kohlhammer, 1964.

Basham, A. L. *The Wonder That Was India*. 3rd rev. ed. London: Picador, 2004.
Basil. *Saint Basil, Πρὸς τοὺς νέους, in The Letters*. Vol. 4, *Address to Young Men on Reading Greek Literature*. Translated by Roy Joseph Deferrari and Martin R. P. McGuire. Loeb Classical Library. Cambridge: Harvard University Press, 1961.
Bayet, Jean. *Histoire politique et psychologique de la religion romaine*. Bibliothèque historique. Paris: Payot, 1957.
Bellah, Robert N. *The Broken Covenant: American Civil Religion in a Time of Trial*. The Weil Lectures 1971. New York: Seabury, 1975.
Benthall, Jonathan, and Jérôme Bellion-Jourdan. *The Charitable Crescent: Politics of Aid in the Muslim World*. London: Tauris, 2003.
Berger, Peter. *The Homeless Mind: Modernization and Consciousness*. New York: Vintage, 1974.
Bett, Henry. *Nicholas of Cusa. Great Medieval Churchman*. London: Methuen, 1932.
Bettelheim, Bruno. *The Informed Heart: Autonomy in a Mass Age*. New York: Free Press, 1960.
Bloch, Jules. *Les inscriptions d'Aśoka*. Collection Émile Senart, 8 Paris: Les Belles Lettres, 1950.
Bolle, Kees W., trans. *The Bhagavadgita: A New Translation*. Hermeneutics, Studies in the History of Religions 9. Berkeley: University of California Press, 1979.
———. *The Enticement of Religion*. Notre Dame, IN: University of Notre Dame Press, 2002.
———. *The Freedom of Man in Myth*. Nashville: Vanderbilt University Press, 1993.
———. *The Persistence of Religion: An Essay on Tantrism and Sri Aurobindo's Philosophy*. Studies in the History of Religions 8. Leiden: Brill, 1965.
———. "Remarks on Bhakti." *Brahmavidya: The Adyar Library Bulletin* 24 (1960) 111–24.
Boullata, Issa J. *Trends and Issues in Contemporary Arab Thought*. SUNY Series in Middle Eastern Studies. Albany: State University of New York Press, 1990.
Brinton, Crane. *The Shaping of Modern Thought*. Englewood Cliffs, NJ: Prentice Hall, 1950.
Brough, John. "Soma and *Amanita Muscaria*." *Bulletin of the School of Oriental and African Studies* 34 (1971) 331–62.
Brown, Truesdell S. "Euhemerus and the Historians." *Harvard Theological Review* 39 (1946) 259–74.
Bruno, Giordano. *Expulsion of the Triumphant Beast*. Translated and edited by Arthur D. Imerti. Lincoln: University of Nebraska Press, 2004.
———. *Spaccio della bestia trionfante*. 1584. Reprint, Bibliotheca rara 26. Milan: Daelli, 1863.
Bryson, Lyman, et al. eds. *Freedom and Authority in Our Time: Twelfth Symposium of the Conference on Science, Philosophy and Religion*. New York: Harper, 1953.
Buber, Martin. *Werke III, Schriften zum Chasidismus*. Munich: Kösel, 1963.
Burkert, Walter. *Homo Necans: The Anthropology of Ancient Greek Sacrificial Ritual and Myth*. Translated by Peter Bing. Berkeley: University of California Press, 1983.
Burrow, J. W., ed. and trans. *The Limits of State Action* (translation of Wilhelm von Humboldt, *Ideen zu einem Versuch die Grenzen der Wirksamkeit des Staates zu bestimmen*). Cambridge Studies in the History and Theory of Politics. Cambridge: Cambridge University Press, 1969.

Calvin, John. *Institutes of the Christian Religion*, Book 1. Translated by John Allen. Philadelphia: Presbyterian Board, n.d.
Carter, Stephen L. *The Culture of Disbelief: How American Law and Politics Trivializes Religious Devotion*. New York: Anchor, 1994.
Chantepie de la Saussaye, P. D. *Textbuch zur Religionsgeschichte*. 4th ed. Edited by A. Lehmann and A. Bertholet. Tübingen: Mohr/Siebeck, 1925.
Coedès, Georges. *The Indianized States of Southeast Asia*. Translated by Susan Brown Cowing. Honolulu: East-West Center, 1968.
Comte, Auguste. *Introduction to Positive Philosophy*. Translated and edited by Frederick Ferré. Indianapolis: Bobbs-Merrill, 1970.
Conlon, Frank F. *A Caste in a Changing World: The Chitrapur Saraswat Brahmans 1700–1935*. Berkeley: University of California Press, 1977.
Conze, Edward. *Further Buddhist Studies*. Oxford: Cassirer, 1975.
Cook, Michael. *Muhammad*. Past Masters Series. New York: Oxford University Press, 1983.
Coomaraswamy, Ananda K. "The Christian and Oriental, or True Philosophy of Art." In *Christian and Oriental Philosophy of Art*. New York: Harper, 1956.
———. *Hinduism and Buddhism*. New York: Philosophical Library, 1943.
———. *Spiritual Authority and Temporal Power in the Indian Theory of Government*. 1942. Reprinted, New York: Kraus Reprint, 1967.
Council of Societies for the Study of Religion Bulletin 32/2 (2003).
Covell, Ralph R. "The Christian Gospel and World Religions: How Much Have American Evangelicals Changed?" *International Bulletin of Missionary Research* 15 (1991) 12–17.
Dantinne, Jean. *La splendeur de l'Inébranlable (Aksobhyavyuha)*. Vol. 1. Publications de l'Institut orientaliste de Louvain 29. Louvain-la-Neuve: Université Catholique de Louvain, Institut Orientaliste, 1983.
Davids, T. W. Rhys, trans. *The Questions of King Milinda*. 2 vols. New York: Dover, 1963.
Dawood, N. J., trans. *The Koran*. Harmondsworth, UK: Penguin, 1956.
De Bary, William Theodore, ed. *Sources of Indian Tradition*. Vol 1. 2nd ed. New York: Columbia University Press, 1988.
Derchain, Philippe. "La religion égyptienne." In *Histoire des religions*, edited by Henri-Charles Puech, 3:63–140. 3 vols. Encyclopédie de la Pléiade 29. Paris: Gallimard, 1970.
Devaraja, N. K. "Is the Meeting of Religions Possible?" *Journal of Dharma* 1 (1975) 30–39.
Diels, Hermann, ed. *Die Fragmente der Vorsokratiker*. 5th ed. Berlin: Weidmann, 1934.
Diodorus. *Diodorus of Sicily*. Vol. 3. Translated by C. H. Oldfather. Loeb Classical Library 340. Cambridge: Harvard University Press, 1952.
Dörrie, Heinrich. *Der Königskult des Antiochos von Kommagene im Lichte neuer Inschriften-Funde*. Abhandlungen der Akademie der Wissenschaften in Göttingen, Philologisch-Historische Klasse. Göttingen: Vandenhoeck & Ruprecht, 1964.
Duméry, Henry. *Phenomenology and Religion: Structures of the Christian Institution*. Translated by Paul Barrett, OFM Cap. Hermeneutics, Studies in the History of Religions 5. Berkeley: University of California Press, 1975.
Dumézil, Georges. "Ideological Innovations." In *Archaic Roman Religion*, translated by Philip Krapp, 2:497–525. Chicago: University of Chicago Press, 1970.

Dumont, Louis. *Une sous-caste de l'Inde du Sud: Organisation sociale et religion des Pramali Kalar*. Ecole pratique des hautes etudes. Paris-LaHaye: Mouton, 1957.

Düx, Johann M. *Der Deutsche Cardinal Nicolaus von Cues und die Kirche seiner Zeit*. Regensburg: Manz, 1847.

Ebersole, Gary L. *Ritual Poetry and the Politics of Death in Early Japan*. Princeton: Princeton University Press, 1989.

Eggeling, Julius, trans. *The Sathapatha-Brahmana according to the Text of the Madhyandina School*. Pt. 4. 1897. Reprinted, Delhi: Motilal Banarsidass, 1972.

Eliade, Mircea, ed. *The Encyclopedia of Religion*. 16 vols. New York: MacMillan, 1987.

———. *The History of Religious Ideas*. Translated by Willard R. Trask. Chicago: University of Chicago Press, 1978.

———. "Methodological Remarks on the Study of Symbolism." In *The History of Religions: Essays in Methodology*, edited by Mircea Eliade and Joseph M. Kitagawa, 86–107. Chicago: University of Chicago Press, 1959.

———. *Myth and Reality*. Translated by Willard R. Trask. New York: Harper & Row, 1963.

———. "The Quest for the 'Origins' of Religion." In *The Quest: History and Meaning in Religion*, 37–53. Chicago: University of Chicago Press, 1969.

———. *The Sacred and the Profane: The Nature of Religion*. Translated by Willard R. Trask. New York: Harcourt, Brace, 1959.

Elton, Oliver. *The Nine Books of the Danish History of Saxo Grammaticus*. London: Norrœna Society, 1905.

Esposito, John L. *Islam: The Straight Path*. 3rd ed. New York: Oxford University Press, 1988.

———, ed. *Islam in Asia: Religion, Politics, and Society*. New York: Oxford University Press, 1987.

———. *The Islamic Threat: Myth or Reality?* 3rd ed. New York: Oxford University Press, 1999.

———. *Unholy War: Terror in the Name of Islam*. Oxford: Oxford University Press, 2002.

Fairman, H. W. "The Kingship Rituals of Egypt." In *Myth, Ritual, and Kingship*, edited by S. H. Hooke, 74–104. Oxford: Clarendon, 1958.

Fontenrose, Joseph Eddy. *The Ritual Theory of Myth*. University of California Publications. Folklore Studies 18. Berkeley: University of California Press, 1971.

Foy, Whitfield, ed. *The Religious Quest: A Reader*. 1978. Reprinted, London: Routledge, 1988.

Fromm, Erich. *Escape from Freedom*. New York: Holt, Rinehart and Winston, 1941.

———. *Man for Himself: An Enquiry into the Psychology of Ethics*. New York: Holt, Reinhart and Winston, 1964.

Ghazālī, Abu Hamid Muhammad al-. *On the Duties of Brotherhood*. Translated by Muhtar Holland. Woodstock, NY: Overlook, 1976.

Glassé, Cyril. *The Concise Encyclopedia of Islam*. San Francisco: Harper & Row, 1989.

Gokhale, Balkrishna G. "Early Buddhist Kingship." *Journal of Asian Studies* 26 (1966) 15–22.

Gonda, J. *Die Religionen Indiens*. Vol. 1, *Veda und älterer Hinduismus*. Religionen der Menschheit 11. Stuttgart: Kohlhammer, 1960.

Goodall, Jane. *The Chimpanzees of Gombe*. Cambridge: Belknap, 1986.

Hamann, Johann Georg. *Hierophantische Briefe*. Presented by E. Jansen Schoonhoven in *Johann Georg Hamanns Hauptschriften erklärt*. Vol. 5. Edited by Fritz Blanke et al., 49–71. Berlin: Gütersloher/Mohn, 1962.

Harman, William P. *The Sacred Marriage of a Hindu Goddess*. Religion in Asia and Africa Series. Bloomington: Indiana University Press, 1989.

Harrelson, Walter. "The Myth and Ritual School." In *The Encyclopedia of Religion*, edited by Lindsay Jones, 9:6380–82. 2nd ed. 15 vols. Detroit: Macmillan Reference, 2005.

Hatch, Nathan O. *The Democratization of American Christianity*. New Haven: Yale University Press, 1989.

Heesterman, J. C. *The Ancient Indian Royal Consecration: The Rajasuya according to the Yajus Texts and Annotated*. Disputationes Rheno-Trajectinae 2. The Hague: Mouton, 1957.

Heppe, Heinrich. *Die Dogmatik der evangelisch, reformierten Kirche*. Neukirchen-Vluyn: Moers, 1935.

Herzberg, Abel J. *Kroniek der Jodenvervolging 1940–1945*. 3rd ed. Amsterdam: Meulenhoff, 1978.

Hodgson, Marshall G. S. "The Shar'î Islamic Vision, c. 750–945." In *The Venture of Islam: Conscience and History in a World Civilization*, 1:315–58. 3 vols. Chicago: University of Chicago Press, 1974.

———. *The Venture of Islam: Conscience and History in a World Civilization*. 3 vols. Chicago: University of Chicago Press, 1974.

———. "The World before Islam." In *The Venture of Islam: Conscience and History in a World Civilization*, 1:103–45. 3 vols. Chicago: University of Chicago Press, 1974.

Hodgson, Peter C., ed. *Lectures on the Philosophy of Religion*, by G. W. F. Hegel. Translated by Robert F. Brown. Berkeley: University of California Press, 1988.

Holt, John Clifford. *Buddha and the Crown: Avalokitesvara in the Buddhist Traditions of Sri Lanka*. New York: Oxford University Press, 1991.

Hooke, S. H., ed. *Myth, Ritual, and Kingship*. Oxford: Clarendon, 1958.

Hopkins, Jeffrey, and Lati Rimpoche, trans. and eds. *The Precious Garland and The Song of the Four Mindfulnesses*. The Wisdom of Tibet Series 2. New York: Harper & Row, 1975.

Hornung, Erik. *Conceptions of God in Ancient Egypt: The One and the Many*. London: Routledge & Kegan Paul, 1982.

Hourani, Albert. *A History of the Arab Peoples*. Cambridge: Harvard University Press, 1991.

Houwink ten Cate, Philo H. J. "The Sun God of Heaven, the Assembly of the Gods, and the Hittite King." In *Effigies Dei: Essays on the History of Religions*, edited by Dirk van der Plas, 13–34. Studies in the History of Religion 51. Leiden: Brill, 1987.

Hume, David. *The Natural History of Religion*. 1757. Reprinted, edited by H. E. Root. Library of Modern Religious Thought. London: A. & C. Black, 1956.

Huntington, Samuel P. *The Clash of Civilizations and the Remaking of World Order*. New York: Simon & Schuster, 1996.

Ibn Khaldūn. *The Muqaddimah: An Introduction to History*. Translated by Franz Rosenthal. 3 vols. 2nd ed, with corrections and an augmented bibliography. Bollingen Series 43. Princeton: Princeton University Press, 1967.

Jacoby, Felix. *Die Fragmente der griechischen Historiker*. Pt. 1, *Genealogie und Mythographie*. Berlin: Weidmanusche, 1923.

Jacoby, Henry. *The Bureaucratization of the World*. Berkeley: University of California Press, 1973.
Jaspers, Karl. *Nikolaus Cusanus*. Munich: Piper, 1964.
Juergensmeyer, Mark. *The New Cold War? Religious Nationalism Confronts the Secular State*. Comparative Studies in Religion and Society 5. Berkeley: University of California Press, 1993.
Keith, Arthur Berriedale. *Rigveda Brahmanas: The Aitareya and Kasitaki Brahmanas of the Rigveda*. Cambridge: Harvard University Press, 1920.
Kern, Fritz. *Aśoka: Kaiser und Missionar*. Bern: Francke, 1956.
Ketelaar, James Edward. *Of Heretics and Martyrs in Meiji Japan: Buddhism and Its Persecution*. Princeton: Princeton University Press, 1990.
Kierkegaard, Søren. *Kierkegaard's Concluding Unscientific Postscript*. Translated by David F. Swenson. Princeton: Princeton University Press, 1944.
King, Noel Q. *African Cosmos: An Introduction to Religion in Africa*. The Religious Life of Man Series. Belmont, CA: Wadsworth, 1986.
Kirfel, Willibald. *Die Kosmographie der Inder*. Darmstadt: Wissenschaftliche Buchgesellschaft, 1967.
Kramers, J. H. "De Islam." In *De godsdiensten der wereld*, edited by G. van der Leeuw, 2:351–409. 2 vols. Amsterdam: Meulenhoff, 1941.
Krick, Hertha. *Das Ritual der Feuergründung (Agnyadheya)*. Veröffentlichungen der Kommission für Sprachen und Kulturen Südasiens 16. Sitzungsberichte (Österreichische Akademie der Wissenschaften. Philosophisch-Historische Klasse 399. Vienna: Österreichischen Akademie der Wissenschaften, 1982.
Kristensen, W. Brede. *Het leven uit de dood*. Haarlem: Bohn, 1926.
Kritzeck, James, ed. *Anthology of Islamic Literature from the Rise of Islam to Modern Times*. New York: Holt, Rinehart and Winston, 1964.
Krummacher, F. A., ed. *Die Kontroverse: Hannah Arendt, Eichmann und die Juden*. Munich: Nymphenburger, 1964.
Lamotte, Etienne. *Le Bouddhisme Indien*. Bibliothèque du Muséon 43. Louvain-la-Neuve: Université Catholique de Louvain, Institut Orientaliste, 1958.
Larson, Gerald James. "Nuclearization in the South Asian Region: Interactions between Pakistan and India." In *Promise and Peril: The Paradox of Religion as Resource and Threat*, edited by Anna Lännström. 37–58. Boston University Studies in Philosophy and Religion 24. Notre Dame, IN: University of Notre Dame Press, 2003.
Lazare, Bernard. *L'antisémitisme, son histoire et ses causes*. 1894. Reprint, Paris: Editions de la Différence, n.d.
Leeuw, Gerardus van der. "Phänomenologie der Religion." In *Die Religion in Geschichte und Gegenwart*, 1171–72. 2nd ed. Tübingen: Mohr/Siebeck, 1965.
Lehmann, Edvard. "Erscheinungswelt der Religion." In *Die Religion in Geschichte und Gegenwart*. 2nd ed. Tübingen: Mohr/Siebeck, 1965.
Lehmann, Edvard, and Hans Haas. *Textbuch zur Religionsgeschichte*. Leipzig: Diechert, 1922.
Leonard, Karen Isaksen. *Social History of an Indian Caste: The Kayasths of Hyderabad*. Berkeley: University of California Press, 1978.
Lévinas, Emmanuel. *Humanisme de l'autre homme*. Essais 6. Paris: Fata Morgana, 1972.
———. *Totalité et Infini: Essai sur l'extériorité*. Phaenomenologica 8. The Hague: Nijhoff, 1971.

Lewis, Bernard. *The Political Language of Islam*. Chicago: University of Chicago Press, 1988.
Library of Congress. *The Church and State under Communism: a special study*. Prepared by the Law Library, Library of Congress. Washington DC: U.S. Government Printing Office, 1964.
Lincoln, Bruce. *Holy Terrors: Thinking about Religion after September 11*. Chicago: University of Chicago Press, 2003.
———. *Theorizing Myth: Narrative, Ideology, and Scholarship*. Chicago: University of Chicago Press, 1999.
Mair, Victor H., trans. *Tao Te Ching*. New York: Bantam, 1990.
Mandelstam, Osip. *Selected Essays*. The Dan Danciger Publication Series. Translated by Sydney Monas. Austin: University of Texas Press, 1977.
Manuel, Frank E. *The Eighteenth Century Confronts the Gods*. New York: Atheneum, 1967.
Marsden, George M. *Fundamentalism and American Culture: The Shaping of Twentieth-Century Evangelicalism, 1870–1925*. New York: Oxford University Press, 1980.
Marty, Martin E., and R. Scott Appleby, eds. *Fundamentalisms Observed*. The Fundamentalism Project 1. Chicago: University of Chicago Press, 1991.
Masson-Oursel, Paul, et al. *Ancient India and Indian Civilization*. Translated by M. R. Dobie. The History of Civilization. New York: Barnes & Noble, 1967.
McLoughlin, William G. *Isaac Backus and the American Pietistic Tradition*. The Library of American Biography. Boston: Little, Brown, 1967.
McNeill, William H., and Marilyn Robinson Waldman. *The Islamic World*. Readings in World History 6. New York: Oxford University Press, 1973.
Mead, Sidney E. *The Nation with the Soul of a Church*. Harper Forum Books. New York: Harper & Row, 1975.
———. *The Old Religion in the Brave New World: Reflections on the Relation between Christendom and the Republic*. Jefferson Memorial Lectures. Berkeley: University of California Press, 1977.
Momigliano, Arnaldo. "Sibylline Oracles." In *The Encyclopedia of Religion*, edited by Mircea Eliade, 13:305–7. 2nd ed. New York: Macmillan, 1987.
Monier-Williams, Monier. *A Sanskrit-English Dictionary*. Oxford: Clarendon, 1899.
Mumford, Lewis. *The City in History*. A Harvest HBJ Book. New York: Harcourt, 1961.
Nanamoli and Bodhi, trans. *The Middle Length Discourses of the Buddha: A Translation of the Majjhima Nikaya*. 2nd ed. Teachings of the Buddha. Boston: Wisdom, 2001.
Nance, John. *The Gentle Tasaday: A Stone Age People in the Philippine Rain Forest*. New York: Harcourt Brace Jovanovich, 1975.
Newman, Louis I. *Hasidic Anthology*. New York: Schocken, 1963.
Nicholas of Cusa, Cardinal. *Das Werk des Nikolaus Cusanus: Eine Bibliophile Einführung*. Edited by Gerd Heinz-Mohr and Willehad Paul Eckert. Cologne: Wienand, 1963.
———. *Nicolas de Cusa Opera omnia*. 2 vols. Edited by Paul Wilpert. 1488; reprint, Berlin: de Gruyter, 1967.
———. *Nicolas de Cusa Opera omnia*. Edited by Ernst Hoffmann and Raymond Klibansky. Leipzig: Meiner, 1932, continued in Hamburg, 1949–1951.
———. *Nikolaus von Kues: Philosophisch-theologische Schriften*. 3 vols. Edited by Leo Gabriel and translated by Dietlind and Wilhelm Dupré. Vienna: Herder, 1964–67.
———. *De pace fidei*. N.p., n.d.

Niebuhr, H. Richard. *The Social Sources of Denominationalism*. 1929. Reprinted, A Meridian Book. New York: New American Library, 1975.

Nikam, N. A., and Richard McKeon, trans. and eds. *The Edicts of Aśoka*. Chicago: University of Chicago Press, 1958.

Nilsson, Martin P. *Geschichte der griechischen Religion*. Vol. 1, *Die Religion Griechenlands bis auf die griechische Weltherrschaft*. 2nd ed. Handbuch der Altertumswissenschaft 5,2,1. Munich: Beck, 1955.

———. *Geschichte der griechischen Religion*. Vol. 2, *Die hellenistische und römische Zeit*. 2nd ed. Handbuch der Altertumswissenschaft 5,2,2. Munich: Beck, 1961.

North, Patricia A. "Mysticism and Prophetism in Hildegard von Bingen and in Ramanuja: An Essay in History and Hermeneutics." PhD diss., University of California at Los Angeles, 1977.

Obeyesekere, Gananath. "Avalokiteśvara's Aliases and Guises." *History of Religions* 32 (1993) 368–73.

Olrik, J., and H. Raeder. *Saxonis Gesta Danorum*. Vol. 1. Copenhagen: Levin & Munksgaard, 1931.

Ortega y Gasset, José. *An Interpretation of Universal History*. Translated by Mildred Adams. New York: Norton, 1975.

———. *Revolt of the Masses*. New York: Norton, 1960.

Orzech, Charles D. *Politics and Transcendent Wisdom: The Scripture for Humane Kings in the Creation of Chinese Buddhism*. Hermeneutics, Studies in the History of Religions. University Park: Pennsylvania State University Press, 1998.

Otten, Heinrich. "The Religion of the Hittites." In *Religions of the Past*, edited by C. Jouco Bleeker and George Widengren, 318–22. Historia Religionum 1. Leiden: Brill, 1969.

Otto, Eberhard. *Gott und Mensch nach den ägyptischen Tempelinschriften der griechisch-römischen Zeit*. Abhandlungen der Heidelberger Akademie der Wissenschaften / Philosophisch-historische Klasse 1964/1. Heidelberg: Winter, 1964.

———. "Die Religion der alten Ägypter." In *Handbuch der Orientalistik, Religionsgeschichte des alten Orients*, edited by Bertold Spuler. Leiden: Brill, 1964.

Pannenberg, Wolfhart. *Anthropology in Theological Perspective*. Translated by Matthew J. O'Connell. Philadelphia: Westminster, 1985.

Péguy, Charles. *Notre jeunesse*. Éditions de la Nouvelle revue française. Paris: Gallimard, 1933.

Pelikan, Jaroslav. *The Spirit of Eastern Christendom (600–1700)*. The Christian Tradition: A History of the Development of Doctrine 2. Chicago: University of Chicago Press, 1974.

Pettazzoni, Raffaele. *La Religione nella Grecia antica ad Alessandro*. Collezione di studi religiosi, etnologici e psicologici 21. Turin: Edizioni Scientifiche Einaudi, 1954.

———. "The Monstrous Figure of Time in Mithraism." In *Essays on the History of Religions*, 180–92. Translated by H. J. Rose. Studies in the History of Religions 1. Leiden: Brill, 1954.

Pohlmann, Robert von. *Geschichte der sozialen Frage und des Sozialismus in der antiken Welt*. Vol. 2. Munich: Beck, 1925.

Presser, J. *Ondergang: Vervolging en verdelging van het Nederlandse Jodendom 1940–1945*. 2 vols. 's Gravenhage: Staatsuitgeverij/ Nijhoff, 1965.

Przyluski, J. *La Légende de l'empereur Açoka*. Annales du Musée Guimet. Bibliothèque d'études 32. Paris: Geuthner, 1923.

Renou, Louis, and Jean Filliozat. *L'Inde Classique, Manuel des Études Indiennes.* Vol. 1. Bibliothèque scientifique. Paris: Payot, 1947.

———. *L'Inde Classique, Manuel des Études Indiennes.* Vol. 2. Bibliothèque de l'École Française d'Extrême-Orient. Paris: Imprimerie Nationale, 1953.

Rosenberg, Hans. *Bureaucracy, Aristocracy and Autocracy: The Prussian Experience 1660–1815.* Harvard Historical Monographs 34. Boston: Beacon, 1966.

Russell, Bertrand. *Why I am not a Christian and other essays on religion and related subjects.* New York: Simon & Schuster, 1957.

Sandeen, Ernest R. "Fundamentalism and American Identity." In *The Social Meanings of Religion: An Integrated Anthology,* edited by William M. Newman, 287–300. Chicago: Rand McNally, 1974.

Sanders, Thomas G. *Protestant Concepts of Church and State.* Studies of Church and State. New York: Holt, Rinehart and Winston, 1964.

Sansom, G. B. *Japan: A Short Cultural History.* Rev. ed. New York: Appleton-Century, 1943.

Sartre, Jean-Paul. *Réflexions sur la question juive.* Paris: Gallimard, 1954.

———. *Anti-Semite and Jew.* Translated by George J. Becker. New York: Schocken, 1965.

Schippers, Jacobus W. *De ontwikkeling der Euhemeristische godencritiek in de Christelijke Latijnse literatuur.* Groningen: Wolters, 1952.

Schmidt, Albert-Marie. *Calvin and the Calvinistic Tradition.* Translated by Ronald Wallace. Men of Wisdom 10. New York: Harper, 1960.

Schneider, Herbert Wallace. *Religion in 20th Century America.* Rev. ed. Atheneum Paperbacks 25. The Library of Congress Series in American Civilization. New York: Atheneum, 1964.

Scholem, Gershom. "Brief an Hannah Arendt." *Neue Zürcher Zeitung* (Oct. 19, 1963).

———. "Jews and Germans." *Commentary* 42 (November 1966) 31–38.

Seidenberg, Roderick. *Post-Historic Man: An Inquiry.* Beacon Paperback 47. Boston: Beacon, 1957.

Shulman, David Dean. *Tamil Temple Myths: Sacrifice and Divine Marriage in the South Indian Saiva Tradition.* Princeton: Princeton University Press, 1980.

Sigmund, Paul E. *Nicholas of Cusa and Medieval Political Thought.* Harvard Political Studies. Cambridge: Harvard University Press, 1963.

Skinner, B. F. *Beyond Freedom and Dignity.* New York: Bantam, 1972.

Smith, J. M. Powis, and Edgar J. Goodspeed, trans. *The Complete Bible.* Chicago: University of Chicago Press, 1948.

Smith, Wilfred Cantwell. *The Meaning and End of Religion.* New York: Macmillan, 1963.

Snellgrove, David. *Indo-Tibetan Buddhism: Indian Buddhists and Their Tibetan Successors.* 2 vols. Boston: Shambala, 1987.

Söderblom, Nathan. *Das Werden des Gottesglaubens: Untersuchungen über de Anfänge der Religion.* 2nd ed. Leipzig: Hinrichs, 1926.

———. *The Living God: Basal Forms of Personal Religion.* Beacon Paperbacks. Gifford Lectures 1931. Boston: Beacon, 1962.

Sophocles. *The Theban Plays.* Translated by E. F. Watling.1947. Penguin Classics. Reprinted, Harmondsworth, UK: Penguin, 1974.

Staal, Frits, ed. *Agni: The Vedic Ritual of the Fire Altar.* 2 vols and 2 cassettes. Berkeley: Asian Humanities Press, 1983.

Stern, Fritz, ed. *The Varieties of History: From Voltaire to the Present*. New York: Vintage, 1973.
Stevens, Wallace. "Recitation after Dinner." In *Opus Posthumous: Revised, Enlarged, and Corrected Edition*, edited by Milton J. Bates, 86–88. New York: Knopf, 1989.
Strong, John S. *The Legend of King Aśoka: A Study and Translation of the Aśokāvadāna*. Princeton Library of Asian Translations. Princeton: Princeton University Press, 1983.
Stryk, Lucien, and Takashi Ikemoto, comp. and trans. *Zen: Poems, Prayers, Sermons, Anecdotes, Interviews*. Garden City, NY: Doubleday, 1963.
Susemihl, Franz. *Geschichte der griechischen Literatur in der Alexandrinerzeit*. Vol. 1. Leipzig: Teubner, 1891.
Tarn, W. W. *Alexander the Great*. Boston: Beacon, 1964.
Tsunoda, Ryusaku, Wm. Theodore de Bary, and Donald Keene, eds. *Sources of Japanese Tradition*. Records of Civilization: Sources and Studies 54. Introduction to Oriental Civilizations 1. New York: Col-umbia University Press, 1960.
Tucci, Giuseppe. "The Ratnavali of Nagarjuna." *Journal of the Royal Asiatic Society* (1934) 307–25.
Turner, James. *Without God, Without Creed: The Origins of Unbelief in America*. New Studies in American Intellectual and Cultural History. Baltimore: Johns Hopkins University Press, 1985.
Turner, Victor. *The Forest of Symbols: Aspects of Ndembu Ritual*. Ithaca, NY: Cornell University Press, 1967.
Vallauri, Giovanna. *Evemero di Messene: testimonianze e frammenti con introduzione e commento*. Pubblicazione della Facultà di Lettere e Filosofia 8/3. Turin: University of Turin, 1956.
———. *Origine e diffusione dell'evemerismo nel pensiero classico*. Pubblicazione della Facultà di Lettere e Filosofia. Turin: University of Turin, 1960.
Vattimo, Gianni. *After Christianity*. Translated by Luca d'Isanto. Italian Academy Lectures. New York: Columbia University Press, 2002.
Vidal, Gore. "The Great Unmentionable: Monotheism and Its Discontents." *Nation* 255/2 (1992).
Vieyra, Maurice. "Les religions de l'Anatolie antique." In *Histoire des religions*, edited by Henri-Charles Puech, 1:258–306. 3 vols. Encyclopédie de la Pléiade. Paris: Gallimard, 1970.
Voll, John A. "Fundamentalism in the Sunni Arab World: Egypt and the Sudan." In *Fundamentalisms Observed*, edited by Martin E. Marty and R. Scott Appleby, 345–402. The Fundamentalism Project 1. Chicago: University of Chicago Press, 1991.
Vries, Jan de. *Perspectives in the History of Religions*. Translated by Kees W. Bolle. Berkeley: University of California Press, 1977.
Wach, Joachim. *Das Verstehen: Grundzüge einer Geschichte der hermeneutischen Theorie im 19. Jahrhundert*. Vol. 3, *Das Verstehen in der Historik von Ranke bis zum Positivismus*. Tübingen: Mohr/Siebeck, 1926. Reprinted, Hildesheim: Olms, 1966.
———. *Types of Religious Experience*. Chicago: University of Chicago Press, 1951.
Wasson, Robert Gordon. *Soma: Divine Mushroom of Immortality*. Ethno-mycological Studies 1. New York: Harcourt Brace Jovanovich, 1968.
Weber, Timothy P. "The Two-Edged Sword: The Fundamentalist Use of the Bible." In *The Bible in America: Essays in Cultural History*, edited by Nathan O. Hatch and Mark A. Noll, 101–20. New York: Oxford University Press, 1982.

Weinreb, Friedrich. *Collaboratie en verzet 1940–1945: een poging tot onmythologisering.* 3 vols. Meulenhoff editie, E 167–69. Amsterdam: Meulenhoff, 1969.
Werblowsky, R. J. Zwi. "Judaism, or the Religion of Israel." In *The Concise Encyclopaedia of Living Faiths,* edited by R. C. Zaehner, 23–50. New Horizon Books. London: Hutchinson, 1959.
Wilson, David Sloan. *Darwin's Cathedral: Evolution, Religion, and the Nature of Society.* Chicago: University of Chicago Press, 2002.
Wittgenstein, Ludwig. *Philosophical Investigations.* 2nd ed. New York: Macmillan, 1958.
———. *Remarks on Frazer's Golden Bough.* Edited by Rush Rhees. Translated by A. C. Miles. Retford, UK: Brynmill, 1983.
X, Malcolm and Alex Haley. *The Autobiography of Malcolm X.* New York: Grove Press, 1965.
Yates, Frances A. *Giordano Bruno and the Hermetic Tradition.* Chicago: University of Chicago Press, 1964.
Young, Jean I., trans. *The Prose Edda of Snorri Sturluson.* Berkeley: University of California Press, 1964.
Zaehner, R. C., ed. *The Concise Encyclopedia of Living Faiths.* New Horizon Books. London: Hutchinson, 1959.
Zeyde, M. H. van der. "De letterkunde in de Lage Landen." In *Nederland tussen de Natiën,* edited by Jan Steffen Bartstra and Willem Banning, 1213–38. 2 vols. Amsterdam: Ploegsma, 1946.

Name Index

Abraham, 164, 171–72
Abū Bakr, 183–84
Adam, 30, 49, 71
Adams, Charles J., 158, 221
Adams, James Luther, 66, 72, 221
Adang, 30
Aditi, 122
Adonis, 62
Ahlstrom, Sydney E., 5, 64–65, 67, 221
Ajātaśatru, 136, 143, 154
Akbar, 140
Albanese, Catherine L., 18, 221
Alexander the Great, 92–96, 103, 124
al-Hasan. See Hasan, al-
al-Husayn. See Husayn, al-
ʿAli, 184–86
Allah, 169, 172, 174, 177–78, 181, 183, 194
Antigone, 105–7, 110–13, 213, 217
Aphrodite, 92
Appleby, R. Scott, 64, 227
Aquinas, Thomas, 70, 97
Arafat, Yasir, 188
Arberry, A. J., 172, 221
Arendt, Hannah, 202, 214–15, 221
Aristotle, 10, 39–40, 55, 97, 217, 221
Arjuna, 117
Armstrong, Karen, 72, 221
Arndt, Paul, 30, 221
Aronowicz, Annette, xxi
Aśoka, 20, 124, 137–45, 148, 150, 154
Astarte, 60, 62
Athena, 92
Atyarāti Jānaṃtapi, 152

Augustine, Saint, 11, 15, 33, 43, 45, 50, 70, 75, 221

Baal, 61
Baal, Jan van, 89, 221
Baʾal Shem Tov, 211
Bacon, Francis, 198
Bakhuizen van den Brink, J. N., 180, 221
Bareau, André, 139, 221
Barrows, John Henry, 159
Basham, A. L., 143, 222
Basil, Saint, 11–12, 15–16, 222
Bathsheba, 101
Baxter, James Houston, 11
Bayet, Jean, 41, 222
Bellah, Robert N., 18, 222
Bellion-Jourdan, Jérôme, 176, 222
Benthall, Jonathan, 176, 222
Berger, Peter, 57–58, 222
Bett, Henry, 74, 222
Bettelheim, Bruno, 202, 222
Bimbisāra, 136, 143
bin Laden, Osama, 166
Bivens, Lynn, xxi
Bloch, Jules, 142–43, 222
Boden, Joseph, 156–57
Bodhi, 25, 222
Boehme, Jakob, 200
Bolle, Kees W., xiii–xviii, 5, 18, 80, 111, 117, 130, 222
Bonhoeffer, Dietrich, 207
Bottéro, Jean, xv
Boullata, Issa J., 166, 222
Braha, Tycho, 198
Bṛhaduktha, 152
Brinton, Crane, 197–98, 222

NAME INDEX

Brough, John, 118, 222
Brown, Truesdell S., xx, 41, 222
Bruno, Giordano, 196–97, 222
Bryson, Lyman, 202, 222
Buber, Martin, 210, 220, 222
Buddha, 7–8, 24–26, 34, 111, 124, 135–36, 139, 153
Burkert, Walter, 58, 222
Burrow, J. W., 203, 222
Bush, George W., 21

Calvin, John, 32, 61, 74, 151, 182, 197, 199–201, 210–11, 218, 220, 223
Carrasco, David, x
Carter, Stephen L., 58, 223
Chantepie de la Saussaye, P. D., 18, 155, 223
Charivarius. *See* Gerard Nolst Trenité
Coedès, Georges, 154, 223
Comte, Auguste, 68–70, 210, 223
Confucius, 125, 155
Conlon, Frank F., 14, 223
Constantine, 119, 137, 140, 145
Conze, Edward, 147, 223
Cook, Michael, 166, 223
Coomaraswamy, Ananda K., 126–32, 141, 194, 223
Copeland, Tim, x, xv, xxi
Copernicus, Nicolaus, 198
Covell, Ralph R., 65, 223
Creon, 105–13, 213
Cummings, Randal, xiii
Cusanus. *See* Nicholas of Cusa

Dante, 127, 131
Dantinne, Jean, 153–54, 223
Darius, 93
David, 101–2, 145, 151, 175, 217
Davids, T. W. Rhys, 151, 223
Dawood, N. J., 174, 176, 223
De Bary, William Theodore, 139–40, 144, 223, 230
Debussy, Claude, xiv
Denning-Bolle, Sara J., ix–xi, xiii–xiv, xxi
Derchain, Philippe, 95, 223
Descartes, René, 198–99, 210, 218

Devaraja, N. K., 15, 223
Diels, Hermann, 38, 223
Dijksterhuis, Eduard Jan, 199
Diodorus, 37, 40, 44, 223
Dionysius, 92
Dörrie, Heinrich, 42, 223
Duméry, Henry, 10, 12, 223
Dumézil, Georges, 41, 119,
Dumont, Louis, 14, 224
Durmukha Pāñcāla, 152
Düx, Johann M., 74, 224

Ebersole, Gary L., 160, 224
Eggeling, Julius, 129, 224
Eichmann, Adolf, 214
Eliade, Mircea, xiii–xvi, 18, 22, 27, 36, 41–42, 54, 59, 158, 194, 196, 224
Elton, Oliver, 46, 224
Epicurus, 200
Erasmus, Desiderius, 157
Ernst, Carl W., xx
Esposito, John L., 164, 166, 176, 183–84, 224
Eteocles, 105
Euhemerus, 36–45, 48–49, 51, 54–55
Eusebius, 37
Eve, 30, 49, 71
Ewang, 30

Fairman, H. W., 97–98, 224
Fāṭimah, 185
Faxian, 150
Feuerbach, Ludwig, 68
Filliozat, Jean, 118, 139, 229
Fontenelle, Bernard Le Bovier de, 51
Fontenrose, Joseph Eddy, 98, 224
Foy, Whitfield, 177, 224
Frankfort, Henri, 88
Frazer, James, 119, 123
Frederick II, 206
Freud, Sigmund, 5
Frigga, 46, 48
Fromm, Erich, 202, 224
Funkenstein, Amos, xxi

NAME INDEX 235

Gabriel, Leo, 73
Galileo, 198
Gandhi, Mohandas, 84
Ghazālī, Abu Hamid Muhammad al-, 177, 187, 224
Glassé, Cyril, 166, 224
Gokhale, Balkrishna G., 134, 136, 224
Gonda, J., 118, 121, 123, 131, 224
Goodall, Jane, 89, 224
Goodspeed, Edgar J., 42, 229
Gunkel, Hermann, 97

Haas, Hans, 226
Haemon, 113
Hamann, Johann Georg, 205–7, 225
Hamilton, Alexander, 175
Hanson, K. C., ix–x
Harman, William P., 128, 225
Harrelson, Walter, 97, 225
Hasan, al-, 185
Hatch, Nathan O., 66, 225
Hayes, John, x
Heesterman, J. C., 118–20, 122, 131, 225
Hegel, G. W. F., 12, 69, 170, 173, 204–5
Heppe, Heinrich, 201, 225
Herodotus, 51
Herzberg, Abel J., 209, 225
Hildegard von Bingen, 151
Hobbes, Thomas, 175
Hodgson, Marshall G. S., 166, 172, 180–82, 225
Hodgson, Peter C., 173, 225
Holt, John Clifford, 154, 225
Homer, 51
Hooke, S. H., 97, 225
Hopkins, Jeffrey, 149–50, 225
Hornung, Erik, 95, 225
Hourani, Albert, 166, 178, 183, 185, 225
Houwink ten Cate, Philo H. J., 90–91, 225
Howell, Peter, xxi
Humboldt, Wilhelm von, 203, 209, 222
Hume, David, 51–53, 175, 225

Huntington, Samuel P., 164, 225
Husayn, al-, 185
Hussein, Saddam, 188

Ibn Khaldūn, 13–14, 16, 225
Ieyasu, 154–56
Ignatius of Loyola, 200
Ikemoto, Takashi, 147, 230
Indra (Śakra), 152–53, 194
Iocasta, 105
Isaiah, 104
Ismene, 106–7, 111
Ithobel, 62–63

Jacoby, Felix, 37, 44, 225
Jacoby, Henry, 202–3, 226
Jānaṃtapi, Atyarāti, 152
Jaspers, Karl, 73, 76, 226
Jefferson, Thomas, 175
Jesus Christ, 71, 73, 75, 77, 82, 102, 125, 135, 165, 172, 179, 189, 205, 219
Juergensmeyer, Mark, 130, 226

Kaplan, Ellen, ix–x, xv, xxi
Keene, Donald, 230
Keith, Arthur Berriedale, 152, 226
Kern, Fritz, 140–41, 226
Ketelaar, James Edward, 156, 159–62, 226
Khadīja, 185
Khanna, Satti, xx
Kierkegaard, Søren, 204–7, 210, 226
King, Noel Q., xxi, 58, 226
Kirfel, Willibald, 151, 226
Kierkegaard, Søren, 204–7, 210, 226
Kitagawa, Joseph, xiii
Kooij, Karel R. van, x
Kramers, J. H., 183–84, 226
Krick, Hertha, 118, 123, 226
Kristensen, W. Brede, 194, 226
Kritzeck, James, 166, 226
Kronos, 37
Kṛṣṇa, 117
Krummacher, F. A., 202, 215, 226
Kuhn, Adalbert, 117

Lactantius, 44–45

NAME INDEX

Ladner, Gerhart, xx
Lamotte, Etienne, 136, 139, 143, 226
Lao Tzu, 85
Larson, Gerald James, 164, 226
Lazare, Bernard, 188–92, 226
Leahy, Sally, xxi
Lease, Gary, xxi
Leibniz, Gottfried Wilhelm, 199–200
Lehmann, Edvard, 18, 226
Leeuw, Gerardus van der, 18, 29, 125, 226
Leonard, Karen Isaksen, 14, 226
Lévinas, Emmanuel, 216–18, 220, 226
Lewis, Bernard, 166, 227
Lincoln, Abraham, 175
Lincoln, Bruce, 117, 166, 227
Lindeboom, J., 180, 221
Linnaeus, Carl, 128
Loewenberg, Peter, xxi
Long, Charles H., x, xiii
Long, Jerome, xxi
Louis, 119
Lucian, 42
Luther, Martin, 74, 165–66, 200

Maerlant, Jacob van, 49
Mair, Victor H., 85, 227
Mandela, Nelson, 210
Mandelstam, Osip, xxv, 17, 227
Manuel, Frank E., 51, 227
Marcus Aurelius, 140
Marduk, 169
Mars, 194
Marsden, George M., 5, 64, 227
Martel, Charles, 165
Martin, John Hilary, xxi
Marty, Martin E., 64, 227
Marx, Karl, 69, 170
Mary, 50, 179
Masson-Oursel, Paul, 139–41, 144, 227
McKeon, Richard, 139, 144, 228
McLoughlin, William G., 137, 227
McNeill, William H., 166, 227
Mead, Sidney E., 6, 18, 227
Mehmet, 165

Micah, 104
Milinda (Menander), 151
Mit-Othin, 46
Momigliano, Arnaldo, 43, 227
Monier-Williams, Monier, 157, 227
Morenz, Siegfried, 95
Moses, 125
Mowinckel, Sigmund, 97
Muʿāwiya, 186–87
Muhammad, 82, 125, 170–76, 178, 181–86
Müller, F. Max, xvi–xvii, 117
Mumford, Lewis, 88

Nāgārjuna, 33–34, 149–51
Nāgasena, 151
Nanamoli, 25, 227
Nance, John, 19, 227
Napolean, 65
Nathan, 61, 101–2, 145, 151, 175
Newman, Louis I., 211, 227
Newton, Isaac, 198–99, 210
Nicholas of Cusa (Cusanus), 41, 73–80
Niebuhr, H. Richard, 65, 228
Nietzsche, Friedrich W., 33, 57
Nikam, N. A., 139, 144, 228
Nilsson, Martin P., 43, 92, 106, 228
North, Patricia A., 151, 228

Obeyesekere, Gananath, 154, 228
Odin, 45–49, 194
Oedipus, 105, 107–8, 113
Olrik, J., 46, 228
Ortega y Gasset, José, 83, 202, 228
Orzech, Charles D., 135, 228
Osman, 165
Otten, Heinrich, 90, 228
Otto, Eberhard, 97–98, 228
Otto, Rudolf, 19–20, 27, 137, 216
Ouranos, 37, 44–45, 48

Pannenberg, Wolfhart, 30, 228
Paul, Saint, 78, 83, 140, 201
Péguy, Charles, 191, 228
Pelikan, Jaroslav, 179, 228
Pettazzoni, Raffaele, 24, 92–93, 228
Pilate, 102

NAME INDEX

Plato, 10, 31, 127, 181, 217
Pohlmann, Robert von, 42, 228
Polynice, 105–6, 109, 111
Presser, Jacob, 208–9, 228
Priam, 48
Przyluski, J., 142, 228
Puhvel, Jaan, xxiii

Qaddafi, Muammar al-, 188

Ranke, Leopold von, 47, 87
Reagan, Ronald, 21
Renou, Louis, 118, 139, 229
Raeder, H., 46, 228
Reid, Jennifer, x, xiii–xviii
Richards, John F., xx
Rimpoche, Lati, 149–50, 225
Rogger, Hans, xxi
Roland, 165
Rosenberg, Hans, 202, 229
Russell, Bertrand, 68, 229

Śakra. See Indra
Samuel, 101
Sandeen, Ernest R., 65, 229
Sanders, Thomas G., 137, 229
Śaṅkara, 15, 17
Sansom, G. B., 155, 229
Sāriputra, 153
Sartre, Jean-Paul, 188, 229
Saul, 101
Saxo Grammaticus, 44–48, 51
Schiller, Friedrich von, 203
Schippers, Jacobus W., 40, 43–44, 229
Schleiermacher, Friedrich, 170, 173, 229
Schmidt, Albert-Marie, 219, 229
Schneider, Herbert Wallace, 66–67, 229
Scholem, Gershom, 191, 214–15, 229
Seidenberg, Roderick, 202, 229
Shulman, David Dean, 129, 229
Sigmund, Paul E., 74, 229
Skinner, B. F., 202, 229
Smith, Adam, 170
Smith, J. M. Powis, 42, 229
Smith, Wilfred Cantwell, 6, 171, 229

Snellgrove, David, 154, 229
Söderblom, Nathan, 158–59, 229
Solomon, 60–62, 101
Sophocles, 105–14, 229
Spencer, Herbert, 53–55, 68, 70
Spinoza, Benedict, 157, 198
Staal, Frits, 117, 229
Stalin, Joseph, 166
Stern, Fritz, 87, 230
Stevens, Wallace, 195, 230
Strong, John S., 142, 230
Sturluson, Snorri, 45, 48, 54
Stryk, Lucien, 147, 230
Sumana (Susima), 143
Susemihl, Franz, 41, 230

Takasui, 147
Tarn, W. W., 94, 230
Thomas Aquinas. See Aquinas, Thomas
Thor, 48
Tillich, Paul, 27, 205
Tocqueville, Alexis de, 66
Trenité, Gerard Nolst (Charivarius), 126
Tróán. See Priam
Trór. See Thor
Tsunoda, Ryusaku, 155, 230
Tucci, Giuseppe, 149, 230
Turner, James, 58, 230
Turner, Victor, 121, 230
Tutu, Desmond, 210
Tylor, E. B., 53–55

ʿUmar, 184, 186
ʿUthman, 184–86

Vallauri, Giovanna, 42, 230
Vāsiṣṭha Sātyahavya, 152
Vattimo, Gianni, 30, 230
Vidal, Gore, 168, 230
Vieyra, Maurice, 90, 230
Voll, John A., 176, 230
Voltaire, 42
Vondel, Joost van den, 60–63, 71, 79
Vries, Jan de, xv, 11, 53, 230
Viṣṇu, 115, 127

NAME INDEX

Wach, Joachim, xiii–xvii, 27–28, 47, 143, 230
Wagar, W. Warren, xxiii
Waghorne, Joanne Punzo, xx
Waldman, Marilyn Robinson, 166, 227
Wasson, Robert Gordon, 117, 230
Weber, Timothy P., 65, 230
Weil, Simone, 31–34
Weinreb, Friedrich, 207–9, 214, 231
Werblowsky, R. J. Zwi, 211, 231
Wessels, Ben, xv, xvii
White, Lynn, xx
Wilhelm, 119
William of Orange, 96
Wilson, David Sloan, 63, 231
Wittgenstein, Ludwig, 33, 215, 231

X, Malcolm, 177, 231
Xenophanes, 38–40, 55
Xuanzang, 150

Yahweh, 103–5, 169, 194
Yama, 150
Yates, Frances A., 196, 231
Young, Jean I., 48, 231

Zaehner, R. C., 9, 231
Zaid, Rhona, xx
Zeus, 37, 40, 55, 92, 107
Zeyde, M. H. van der, 50, 231
Zwi, Jehudah, 220
Zwingli, Huldrych, 200

Subject Index

Abrahamic religions, 164
advaita, 16
Africa, 58, 157, 170, 177. *See also* North Africa
akitu festival, 27, 120
Aitareyabrāhmaṇa, 128, 151–53
Akṣobhyavyūha, 153
altars, 118
ancestor worship, 53
anointing, 101, 122, 129, 152
Antigone, 105–14, 213, 217
anti-Judaism, 167, 188, 190
antiritual, 5
anti-Semitism, 167, 188–89, 191
Arabs, 77, 167, 172, 176–79, 184, 188
Asia, 48, 135, 154, 156–57, 160–61, 166, 170, 177–78, 187
Asia Minor, 90
āśrama, 14
atheism, atheist, 42, 57, 87, 198
authority, xix, 4, 14, 60, 81–83, 96, 108, 111, 113, 125, 136, 143–44, 148, 162, 174–75, 179, 181, 185, 208, 213
avyakta/vyakta, 16

Babylon, Babylonian, 3, 90, 120. *See also* Mesopotamia
Bangladesh, 166
Baptist, 66
belief/s, 10, 39, 60, 68, 70, 91, 103, 129, 164, 197
Bhagavadgītā, xv, 117, 130
bhakti, 115
bhikku, 25
Bible, 21, 51, 67, 73, 95, 100, 158

brahman, 123
Brahmanism, xv, 115–34, 148, 151
Brahmanic texts, 116–17, 130, 151
brahmin, 15, 24–25, 115–16, 118, 121–23, 127–29, 131–32, 148, 152
Brahmotsava, 27
Buddhism, 7–8, 14, 24, 31–32, 114–15, 124, 132, 134–63, 165
  Mahāyāna Buddhism, 149, 151, 153
  Theravada Buddhism, 151
  Zen Buddhism, 146–47, 162

Calvinism, 211
Cambodia, 154
Caṇḍāśoka. *See* Aśoka
canon, 7
Cartesianism, 211
Chechnya, 166
China, Chinese, 85, 99, 150, 181
Christianity, xvii, 8–16, 21–24, 26–27, 30–32, 38, 41, 43, 50, 65, 68, 87, 90, 94, 137, 145, 148, 154–59, 161–68, 172–73, 178–83, 189–90, 192, 206–7, 210
chronos, 23, 26–27
Chthonic deities, 113
church and state, xix, 14, 84, 99, 102, 136–37, 146, 175, 204
Confucianism, 9, 29, 155, 181
Congregationalism, 66
Constantinople, 165
conversion, 5, 150, 156, 178–80
Copts, 26

Counter-Reformation, 200
creeds, 72, 102, 107, 178–79
Crusades, 165

Dakṣiṇās, 121
Dayaks, 28
dharma, 34, 116–17, 123, 137–39, 141, 144–45, 148, 152, 154
dharmaśāstra, 125, 145
dogma, 4–5, 91, 185

Easter, 27
Eastern Orthodox churches, 167
Egypt, Egyptians, xvii, 6, 9, 26, 31, 93, 95–100, 103, 114, 128, 185
enlightenment, 25, 85, 206, 212
Enlightenment, the, 51, 54–55, 63, 79, 83, 189, 198
Eucharist, 32, 74–75, 78
Euhemerism, 35–57, 69

faith, 7–10, 15, 65, 71, 76, 78, 116, 158, 171, 176–80, 182–83, 186, 190, 218
fides, 76–77
France, 4, 31, 141, 165, 190, 203, 218
fundamentalism, 64–73, 79, 80, 168, 176
funeral, 28, 96, 105, 148, 160

Germany, xvii, 20–21, 31, 47, 68, 156, 160–63, 189, 191–92, 203, 207–9, 214
Greek Orthodox Church, 11, 75
Greece, Greeks, xvii, 10, 12–14, 24, 36, 40–43, 93, 99, 105–6, 108, 111, 114, 138, 143, 151, 171, 181, 193, 213
guru, 184

Hadith, 175–76, 183
Hasidism, 207, 210–12, 220
hierophany, 27
Hinduism, xx, 4, 6, 14–16, 19, 23–24, 27, 31, 68, 114–16, 118–20, 124–28, 132, 134, 141, 148–49, 153–54, 161, 164–65, 178, 184, 187, 194–95, 217
History of Religions, ix, xiii, 17, 21–22, 34, 64, 72, 83–84, 126–27, 157–58
Hittites, 26, 90–92, 217
Holi festival, 27–28
Holiness churches, 66
Holland, x, xiv, xvii, 61, 96, 156, 207–8. *See also* Netherlands
holy war, 179, 184, 186
Hussites, 73–74, 76

Inca, 100, 128
Indians, xv, xvii, 4, 6, 9, 14–16, 20, 22, 33, 77, 81–82, 115, 116, 118–34, 137, 141, 166, 171, 178, 203
Indonesia, 30, 166, 178
inner life, xviii, 5–6, 91, 199–203, 205, 207, 210–12, 214
Interpretation, 18–34
Iran, 178–79, 182, 186–87
Iraq, 21, 88, 182, 185–88
Isaiah, book of, 103–4
Islam, x, xvii, xx, 8–9, 12, 14–15, 21, 26, 60, 67, 94, 115, 124, 148, 164–92, 194
Israel (ancient), xv, 8, 27, 61, 92, 94, 97, 99, 100–101, 103–5, 124, 134, 169, 171, 173, 175, 188
iṣṭis, 121
Italy, 21, 162

Jainism, 14, 139
Japan, Japanese, 21, 99, 100, 154–56, 159–63
Jātaka, 135
jāti, 14
Jerusalem, 105, 130, 190
jihad, 179, 184
Judaism, Jews, xvii, 8–9, 31–32, 58, 60, 62, 77, 94, 102, 115, 148, 164, 167–68, 171–73, 179, 182–83, 188–92, 207–8, 211, 214–15, 218, 220
Judeo-Christian, 167
Judeo-Christiano-Islam, 167

Judith, book of, 89

Ka'ba, 183
kairos, 24, 26–29
kāla, 26
Kaliyuga, 81
    Khalīfa (caliph), 184–87
Kings, books of, 95
kingship, 7, 42, 45, 87–103, 124, 129–31, 134–45, 147–50, 152–54
kṣatriya, 122–23, 132
Ku Klux Klan, 168

Lutheran, 197, 204

Macedonia, 96, 124
mahābhiṣeka, 152
Mahāyāna Buddhism. *See* Buddhism, Mahāyāna
Mahāyānasūtra, 153
mantra, 127, 130
Mazdeans, 182
Mennonite, 62–63
Mesopotamia, 28, 88, 93, 97, 169. *See also* Babylon, Babylonia
Micah, book of, 104–5
Mithraism, 23–24
mokṣa, 82
monophysites, 180
monotheism, 164–92
Mūlamādhyamikakārikā, 33
mysticism, mystics, xv-xvi, 74, 78–80, 197, 200–201, 203, 211–12, 214
myth, mythology, xv, 18, 20, 22, 30, 36–39, 41, 44–45, 47, 49, 51, 53–54, 57, 79–80, 82–83, 90, 93, 95, 99–100, 102–3, 107, 111–14, 117, 128, 151, 154, 171, 185–87, 193, 196, 212
Myth and Ritual School, 97–98

Nation of Islam, 177
Nazis, National Socialism, 20–21, 161–62, 207, 218
Netherlands, the, x, 50, 65, 158, 209. *See also* Holland

Norse, 20, 45, 48–49
nirvāṇa, 7, 34, 144–47
North Africa, 179

oracles, 127

pagans, paganism, 11–12, 20, 41, 43, 45, 50, 55, 60, 62, 76, 165, 178, 181, 183
Pali texts, 134
Puruṣasūkta, 127
Persians, 93
philosophia perennis, 127, 132
piety, pietism, 5–7, 11, 181–82, 200
Platonism, 32
polytheism, 52–53
prayer, 91–92, 101, 104, 130, 176, 184
primitivism, 24, 47, 70, 84, 118–19
prophets, prophecy, 8, 14, 49, 61, 72, 82, 101–2, 104, 106, 147, 154, 162, 170–76, 184, 187, 206, 216
Prose Edda, 48
Protestant Reformation. *See* Reformation
Protestantism, 5, 64–66, 70–71, 84, 173, 176, 182, 199–201, 218
pseudo-religion, 20–22
Puranic texts (Purāṇas), 81, 125

Qur'an, 171–72, 174–76, 178, 184, 192

Rājasūya, 117–33, 152–53
Rāshidūn, 183
Ratnāvalī, 149–50
Reformation, 9, 22, 74, 186, 200–201
Reformed, 63
religion
    essence of, 19, 84
    as institution, 10–13
Religion in Geschichte und Gegenwart, Die, 159
religious propaganda, 13–14, 124
Remonstrants, 62

SUBJECT INDEX

Renaissance, 38, 70, 73, 76, 196–97, 200–201
resurrection, 23, 27, 165
Ṛgveda, 127
rituals, ritualism, ritualists, xv, 4–6, 18, 23, 57, 83, 91, 93, 96–99, 117–25, 128–32, 152, 160, 184–85, 187. *See also* antiritual
Rock Edicts, 138–40, 144
Roman Catholicism, 4, 61–62, 63, 155, 197, 200
Rome, Romans, 9, 41, 43, 102, 181, 189–90
Russia, 3, 84, 160, 166

sacraments, 23, 28, 73, 75–79
sacred and profane, 59
sacrifice, 4, 6, 27, 45, 63, 75, 81, 103, 121
saddharma, 139, 155
salvation, 9, 71, 75, 78, 102, 125, 140–41, 174, 201, 212
samaya, 26–27
samayāḥ, 24
saṃsāra, 34
saṃskāra, 28
saṃyama, 16
sanctification, 55, 59–60
saṅgha, 135
Sanskrit, x, 22, 26, 116, 119, 122–23, 126, 129, 143, 156, 178
sapientia, 76–77
Śatapathabrāhmaṇa, 129
sattva, 16
satya, 16
scientia, 76
scripture, 7, 15–16, 125, 156, 172
secularism, secularity, secularization, xx, 14–15, 17, 19, 31, 34–84, 87, 95, 145, 157–58, 160, 170, 172, 176, 179, 216
Septuagint, 42
sharīʿa, 176–77
Shīʿa, 185
Shīʿites, 28, 185, 187
Shinto, 9, 29, 160

Sibylline Books, 42
skandhas, 8, 145
soma, 117–18, 121, 131
sophia, 76
Soviet Union, 84, 164, 166, 189
Spain, 31, 165, 177
Sufis, 184
Sun God, 90–92
Sunnī, 176, 183
Sweden, 48
Swedenborgianism, 84
symbol, symbolization, xvi, 8, 14, 18, 20, 22, 29–30, 35–36, 41, 57, 72, 80, 83, 96–97, 115, 121, 128, 147, 168, 178–79, 184, 193–94, 212–15
Syria, 90

Tantrism, tantric texts, xv, 6, 22, 81
Taoism, 32, 181
Tao Te Ching, 85
tapas, 16
Tasaday, 19
theocracy, 173, 187–92
Theravada Buddhism. *See* Buddhism, Theravada
Tibet, 32, 154
Tibetan Book of the Dead, 32
Torah, 171, 191–92
tradition, xix, 4, 6, 8, 10, 15–16, 19–22, 24, 26–36, 40, 45, 49–50, 53–56, 58–60, 79–84, 90, 92, 94, 99, 108, 116, 118, 124, 127, 130, 133, 144–46, 151–52, 158, 160, 164, 166–67, 175, 192, 194–95, 213
transcendence, 18, 31, 75, 77–78, 94–95, 103, 115, 141
tritheism, 179
trivarṇa, 122

umma, 172, 183, 186
utsava, 119

vaiśya, 122–23, 127
varṇa, 14, 115, 122
Vedism, 22, 115–17, 119, 125, 130, 132, 152–53

Viṣṇu, 127

Wisdom of Solomon, 42

yoga, 16, 31
yugas, 81

Zen Buddhism. *See* Buddhism, Zen
Zervanites, 24
Zoroastrianism, 179, 182

www.ingramcontent.com/pod-product-compliance
Lightning Source LLC
Chambersburg PA
CBHW030615230426
43661CB00053B/1997